THE NATURAL HOME

Simple, Pure Cleaning Solutions and Recipes for a Healthy House

THE NATURAL HOME

Simple, Pure Cleaning Solutions and Recipes for a Healthy House

ISABELLE LOUET AND SYLVIE FABRE

BLACK DOG
& LEVENTHAL
PUBLISHERS
NEW YORK

Black Dog & Leventhal Publishers
Hachette Book Group
1290 Avenue of the Americas
New York, NY 10104
www.hachettebookgroup.com
www.blackdogandleventhal.com

First edition: April 2018

Black Dog & Leventhal Publishers is an imprint of Hachette Books, a division of Hachette Book Group. The Black Dog & Leventhal Publishers name and logo are trademarks of Hachette Book Group, Inc.
The publisher is not responsible for websites (or their content) that are not owned by the publisher.

The Hachette Speakers Bureau provides a wide range of authors for speaking events. To find out more, go to www.HachetteSpeakersBureau.com or call (866) 376-6591.

Print book interior design by Sheila Hart

LCCN: 2017956624

ISBNs: 978-0-316-47826-7 (trade paperback), 978-0-316-47825-0 (ebook)

Printed in China

IM

10 9 8 7 6 5 4 3 2 1

CONTENTS

1

Easy and effective

NATURAL
HOUSEWORK

Making homemade products

MAKING HOUSEWORK EASY

. . . AND NATURAL

Baking soda, lemon, oil-based soaps, white vinegar—these all-natural and green products are more popular than ever, as many of us want to avoid introducing chemicals into our homes and pollutants into the environment.

These natural products are not only efficient and economical but they also clean, bleach, disinfect, and deodorize better than store-bought cleaning products. There is every reason to embrace and adopt natural cleaning in order to make your home shine while keeping it free of pollutants.

▶ Using them well

On their own or combined, baking soda, white vinegar, and so on, succeed in all tasks—from the most stubborn limescale deposits to the dullest of windows—given their many cleaning powers. However, to obtain good results, you should take the time to discover their properties and learn to use them correctly. In no way should lemon concentrate be used instead of real lemon or salt not left long enough when cleaning a rug. Like a cook, learn to adapt a recipe to your needs. Adjust the dosage to obtain the right quantity, the right texture. Home remedies are not an exact science; they are the result of much trial and error.

▶ It's up to you to decide

These products do not have the same consistency, or the same properties, nor do they belong to the same families, yet they have the same benefits and cleaning powers. They all remove grease and limescale, add shine, and so on. So there is no need to adopt all of them; choose the one that you prefer—the easiest to use, the one with the best scent, the most odorless, or, more simply, the one already stored in your cupboard. The benefit of this is that you can change products as you please.

▶ Vigilance is key

Whatever the object to be cleaned—fabric, wood floors, marble mantelpiece—be cautious; always carry out a test on a small area to make sure that it can withstand treatment. When in doubt, stop and ask an expert for advice.

In addition, be careful: Although it is true that these natural products make miracles in our homes, they are not all harmless, as is the case with turpentine and soda crystals. They need to be handled with care and kept away from children; mixing them up must be avoided.

Safety first and foremost

*TO AVOID ANY ACCIDENTS, WHETHER USING NATURAL PRODUCTS OR NOT,
FOLLOW THE SAFETY INSTRUCTIONS.*

▶ Store the products in their original packaging to avoid any confusion. Baking soda can be mistaken for confectioners' sugar or salt.

▶ If you make your own washing detergent or any other cleaning product, never store them in water bottles, soda pop bottles, or containers with food or candy labels. If these products are ingested by mistake, there could be serious consequences.

▶ Carefully and legibly label any products you make yourself. List their ingredients. If someone other than you uses them, they must know what they are handling.

▶ Don't try to save time by mixing products. You would achieve disappointing results, and, above all, dangerous chemical reactions (such as toxic fumes) could be emitted.

▶ Whether dangerous or not, always store household products out of the reach of children and pets.

To avoid chemicals that pollute our homes and the planet, choose products that have been known to work for centuries. Here are the essentials to have in your cabinet to make your home sparkle and shine.

THE IDEAL CABINET

BLEACHING AGENTS

These are the kings of whiteness when it comes to looking after laundry, furniture, and materials. Bonus: Thanks to their disinfectant properties, they are your best allies for killing mold and germs.

▶ **Hydrogen peroxide**

Also called *peroxide*, this antiseptic can be found in pharmacies. It is made naturally with enzymes called *peroxidases*.

• **It is used** for removing stains, soap residue, and mold.

• **Instructions:** The dosage is mainly one part hydrogen peroxide to 20 parts water for stain removal; 30 parts water for laundry whitening; and 60 parts water for the bleaching of enamel, wood, and large surface areas.

▶ **Sodium percarbonate**

When it comes into contact with water, it releases "active oxygen" (hydrogen peroxide), which has powerful bleaching and disinfectant properties.

• **It is used** for bleaching and removing stains from fabrics; cleaning and disinfecting floors, terraces, enamel bathtubs, bathroom tiles; and getting rid of mold and soap residue.

• **Instructions:** Mix 1 to 3 tablespoons per quart (liter) of water.

❶ WARNING: To be used with caution. Use gloves and avoid all contact with skin and eyes.

❶ CONTRAINDICATION: Do not use on aluminum or waxed, painted, or varnished surfaces unless you want to strip them down. Sodium percarbonate is combustible and should be kept away from flammable products such as alcohol and essential oils.

CLEANING AGENTS

They have many virtues, but their specialty is getting rid of the most stubborn stains while protecting materials.

▶ **The potato**

With its 4,000 varieties, the potato is an absolute treasure trove:

• **It is used** for bleaching, cleaning, removing black stains, descaling, weeding, and adding shine to crystal, mirrors, and tiles.

- **Instructions:** While its cooking water is very effective, the potato is often used cut in two. Sometimes the starch is used.

▶ Marseille soap

This French product can be difficult to find at your local supermarket; however, it can often be found online. Prepared by hand, true Marseille soap is made from at least 72 percent vegetable oil (olive, palm, copra) and caustic soda. It is biodegradable and contains no perfume, color-

☞ Did you know?

Marseille soap is the only cleaning product that has had the honor of having its production method standardized by Louis XIV. In 1688, the Edict of Colbert introduced regulations regarding its production: cooking in large cauldrons, exclusively using pure vegetable oils, and forbidding the use of animal fats.

💡 TIP

Know how to choose your Marseille soap

The white soap—made from palm oil (extracted from the palm oil fruit), peanut oil, or copra oil—is particularly suitable for laundry and house cleaning, whereas the brown/green soap—made from olive and copra and/or palm oil—is more recommended for body care.

---

ing, or additive. The inscription "Extra pure, 72% oil" or the name of the soap factory should appear on the soap as a guarantee of its authenticity.

- **It is used** for demisting; cleaning tiles and laundry; protecting paintbrushes; removing stains, including white marks; and so on.
- **Instructions:** To dilute it more easily, grate it or make shavings.

▶ Black soap

- Also popular in France, black soap (savon noir) can also be difficult to find in many U.S. stores, so try searching for it online under the name Marius Fabre.

It has not been as popular as its cousin, Marseille soap, because of its dark color, thick consistency, and strong smell.

TIP

Know how to choose your black soap

The black soap used for the home is different from the one used for body care. In solid, soft, or liquid form, black soap is made of a fatty matter that can be olive oil, flaxseed oil, walnut oil, corn oil, or even glycerin. The one for the body, better known as Moroccan Beldi soap, has a thick, dark or black consistency and is made from lye and olive paste.

• **It is used** for bleaching enamel, demisting, removing grease and stains, washing laundry and floors, refreshing sealants and even leather, and cleaning silverware, brass, and copper.

• **Instructions:** In liquid form or as a paste, it is used pure or diluted, according to need. You don't need to rinse it most of the time.

DEODORIZING AGENTS

They have descaling, cleaning, and degreasing properties and have the added advantage of being brilliant at absorbing bad odors.

▸**Natural cork**

In addition to being famed for preserving wine and enabling it to age well, it is a very useful tool in the house.

• **It is used** for preserving fruit, deodorizing, and lessening white marks.
• **Instructions:** It is used like an eraser.

▸**Coffee**

While some fortune-tellers use coffee grounds to predict the future, previous generations discovered it had other virtues.
• **It is used** for removing grease, cleaning drains, deodorizing, gardening, cleaning tiles and carafes, polishing off scratches on a wooden piece of furniture, reviving

 *Did you know?*

Dry coffee grounds do not leave a smell.

an old parquet floor, removing ashes from the chimney, and even deterring ants.
• **Instructions:** Collect your coffee grounds (including the ones in pods), pour them into a plastic bottle, and store in a dark, dry place. Leave the bottle open so that they do not go moldy with condensation. They will keep for a few weeks without any problem.

TIP

Soft, smooth hands

The small grains of coffee grounds can be used for light exfoliation. Rub your hands with a generous helping of moist coffee grounds and rinse them with clean water to make them soft again.

▶ Milk

It is not only an important part of our diet, but also a useful tool for cleaning the house.
• **It is used** for softening leather, deodorizing, removing stains, making silverware shine, eradicating cockroaches, and stiffening sheer curtains and drapes.
• **Instructions:** Most of the time it is used directly to moisten a sponge.

DESCALING AGENTS

They are unrivaled in their ability to restore shine to chrome and enamel, while also eliminating limescale.

▶ Lemon

It is tiny but has maximum strength. It is a cleaning champion as well as a beauty secret and a flavor enhancer in the kitchen.
• **It is used** for bleaching enamel and linens, stripping down sealants, disinfecting, deodorizing, descaling, eradicating moths, adding sheen to metals, polishing copper, and even repelling ants.
• **Instructions:** It can be cut in half or juiced and squeezed onto a sponge, used pure or slightly diluted, depending on the recipe.

☞ Did you know?

Before squeezing it, roll your lemon two or three times with the palm of your hand on your worktop. This will soften it and its pulp will break more easily. If it's a bit dry, soak it in hot water for three minutes or place it in the microwave for fifteen seconds.

See Chapter 4 for more about cleaning with lemons.

▶ **Salt**

Used in feng shui for purifying the home, its small grains also give it impressive exfoliating properties.

• **It is used** for deodorizing; removing stains; descaling chrome; cleaning drains; removing grease from the oven, hot plates, or frying pan; refreshing the color of basketwork; slowing down the burning of candles; and repelling ants.

• **Instructions:** It is sprinkled or combined with another ingredient and is used dry or moistened.

STAIN-REMOVING AGENTS

These are the only ones that can save our precious belongings from grease, blood, and varnish stains because they respect the most fragile of materials.

▶ **Wood ash**

It is rich in minerals (calcium, magnesium, lye, silica). Previous generations used it

A strange mix

Often used together, white vinegar and baking soda create a chemical reaction when combined. The mixture becomes foamy and expands because of the release of carbon dioxide. It is not harmful but do open windows or dilute it to prevent any irritation (to the eyes and nose).

for housework, as well as for making soap and laundry detergent.

• **It is used** for removing grease, adding shine to silverware and copper, cleaning windows, and making laundry detergent.

• **Instructions:** To be effective, it needs to come from untreated dry wood. Before using it, sieve it until only a fine powder is left and you have got rid of any residue and fragments that could scratch or damage your possessions. It is used either as a paste (mixed with water) or in powder form.

▶ **Talcum powder**

There are two kinds of talcum powder on the market: a mineral type, primarily made of magnesium silicate, and a man-made type. Neither poses any danger to health, and it is a great ally for removing grease stains, making the house shine, and making sure your skin doesn't get too dry.

• **It is used** for removing grease and stains, easing the opening of windows, silencing creaks and cracks, eliminating mold on books, and restoring fur.

• **Instructions:** Use dry, as a paste, or lightly damp on a sponge.

◆

MULTISTAIN-REMOVING AGENTS

One of these products is enough to clean up the whole house, from floor to ceiling, as they are so efficient everywhere.

▸ **Baking soda**

This is the most famous and the most commonly used of natural products, which, importantly, also happens to be one of the cheapest. This fine, white powder is edible, biodegradable, nontoxic, odorless, antacid, anti-limescale, preservative-free, soluble in water, and a soft abrasive: Clearly it combines many advantages.

• **It is used** for cleaning, softening, descaling, deodorizing, bleaching laundry and sealants, removing grease from floor to

Still effective or not? TIP

Has the box of baking soda been lying around the cabinet forever? To find out if it's still good, pour a tablespoonful in a glass of water and add a few drops of lemon or vinegar. If it starts to fizz, then it still works. If nothing happens, then it has lost all its properties and it is time to get a new packet.

ceiling, making silverware shine, getting rid of mold, reviving colors, and so on.

• **Instructions:** Baking soda can be used in powder form, as a paste, or diluted.
See Chapter 3 for more about cleaning with baking soda.

ⓘ WARNING: Don't mistake it for lye.

▸ **Natural multipurpose clay cleaner**

Also called multipurpose natural clay cleaner or multipurpose cleaning clay, this product is primarily made of white clay and soap and comes in the form of a compact, dry, and gently abrasive paste.

• **It is used** for removing stains and grease; descaling; cleaning windows, ceramic and induction cooktops, metals (silverware, chrome, stainless steel, copper); polishing delicate surfaces; renovating tile sealants; reviving whites; and so on.

• **Instructions:** To use it, you just need to scrape some out of the container with a damp sponge and then rinse with clean water, before wiping off with a lint-free cloth.

▶ Toothpaste

Toothpaste is gently abrasive and excellent for maintaining the house.

To transform toothpaste into a cleaning product, choose the simplest type of toothpaste. Forget the ones with flavorings or that are rich in fluoride or other minerals. Alternatively make your own paste.

• **It is used** for removing stains; descaling; removing streaks on glasses; adding shine to silverware, chrome, gold, and copper; cleaning the enamel of the bathtub, sink, and toilets; eliminating mold; reviving the soleplate of an iron; cleaning the refrigerator's and freezer's sealants; removing scratches or traces of pencil on the wall; preventing condensation; filling holes; and renovating shoes.

• **Instructions:** It is used as a paste applied on a sponge.

▶ White vinegar

Colorless and nontoxic, it replaces all detergents, grease removers, and other chemical weed killers at home and in the garden. The only drawback is its smell, which is strong, persistent, and stings the eyes (without irritating them) but it evaporates rapidly, thankfully.

• **It is used** for cleansing, descaling, removing grease, peeling off deposits, cleaning drains, softening laundry, removing stains, and adding shine to mirrors, metals (copper, brass, and chrome), and porcelain.

• **Instructions:** Use pure, diluted in water (50/50), combined with salt or baking soda, cold or warm.

See Chapter 2 for more about cleaning with vinegar.

❶ WARNING:

• Don't use it with bleach, as this combination releases toxic fumes.

• Make sure you always open windows when you use it, especially if you heat it up. Its strong smell can cause coughing and eye irritation.

• White vinegar should never be used on marble surfaces.

Storing baking soda and white vinegar in the cabinet is a first step but using them on a daily basis is even better. To achieve this and to swap chemicals for natural products, you can make your own grease removers, cleaners, and other disinfectants in advance.

HOMEMADE PRODUCTS

THE PERFECT ALCHEMIST'S MANUAL

The advantage of some natural products is that they combine beautifully, but remember to follow the rules.

▸Vigilance is key

To avoid accidents, be it with natural products or not, respect safety rules:

• If you make your own laundry detergent or any other cleaning product, never store them in water or soda bottles or in food or candy boxes. They can be toxic if swallowed in large quantities. Choose household product bottles that are easily identifiable.

• Label homemade products carefully and legibly. List their components. If someone else uses them instead of you, they must know what they are using.

• Write the date it was made. Products' shelf life varies.

• Do not try to save time by mixing products. The result would be disappointing and, above all, could be dangerous; you might create a chemical reaction that produces toxic fumes.

• Dangerous or not, always store household products out of the reach of children as well as pets. The ideal thing is to keep them in a cupboard high up.

▸Careful with essential oils

Oils should always be handled with care. You should follow instructions (wearing gloves, avoiding contact with skin, using the right dosage); otherwise they can quickly become toxic and harmful. You should also avoid using them near people with allergies, children, and pets.

▸A little piece of advice

Like a cook, learn to adapt a recipe to your needs. Adjust the dosage to obtain the right quantity, the right texture. Home remedies are not an exact science; they are the result of much trial and error.

EVERYTHING FOR THE LAUNDRY

Homemade laundry detergent has numerous advantages: It is effective on laundry, is good for the washing machine, and is economical. The only disadvantage is that you have to make it. But once you've got into it, there's no going back.

▸ Fabric softener
You need:
- 3 quarts (3 liters) white vinegar
- ½ quart (½ liter) water
- 2 tablespoons baking soda
- 15 drops essential oil (lavender or tea tree)

Mix all the ingredients in a container until you obtain a smooth liquid. Pour into an old bottle previously rinsed and dried. Use a capful for a medium load.

▸ Laundry detergent for whites
For 2 quarts (2 liters) of laundry detergent, you need:
- 2 quarts (2 liters) water
- 6½ tablespoons Marseille soap shavings (for removing grease and cleaning)
- 3 tablespoons baking soda (for bright whites and colors)
- 1 tablespoon white vinegar (for preserving colors, softening linen, and descaling the washing machine)
- (Optional) 5 drops true lavender essential oil (to disinfect and perfume)

In a large pan, heat the water. When it is simmering, add the Marseille soap shavings, baking soda, and vinegar. Mix everything until it dissolves and leave to cool for at least 1 hour. Pour the solution into a bottle, then add 1 quart (1 liter) of lukewarm water and the (optional) essential oil. Shake well. The following day, have a look: If it is still thick, add 1 quart (1 liter) of water.

▸ Ivy leaf laundry detergent
Ivy leaves contain saponin (5 to 8 percent), surfactants with detergent and foaming properties.
You need:
- 30 to 50 common ivy leaves
- 1 quart (1 liter) water
- 1 tablespoon baking soda

Clean the leaves with clean water. Crumble them or cut them into pieces in a pan. Add the water and cover. Bring to a boil for about fifteen minutes. Add the percarbonate on medium heat and mix until completely dissolved. Remove from heat. Leave to stew overnight with the lid on. Filter through a sieve covered with a fine muslin by pressing the leaves hard to extract all the active components. Pour into a bottle carefully labeled with the name of the product. Use about a cupful per wash.

❶ **WARNING:** Ivy berries are toxic for humans, so we use only the leaves. However, their sap can cause skin irritation, so it is best to wear gloves during preparation.
- If you are pregnant, don't use them at any point during pregnancy.
- Do not swallow.
- If in doubt, seek advice from a specialist.

▸ **Marseille soap laundry detergent**
You need:
- 3 quarts (3 liters) water
- 5.5 ounces (156 grams) Marseille soap, grated or in shavings
- 1 coffee cup soda crystals
- 1 teaspoon lavender, sweet orange, or tea tree essential oil (careful with allergies)

Bring the water to a boil, and then add the soap, either grated or in shavings, and the soda crystals. Mix together on medium heat until everything is dissolved. Remove from heat and leave to cool. Add the essential oil to give a note of freshness.

If the preparation is too thick, dilute it with lukewarm water until it becomes smooth.

Pour about 1 cup (235 milliliters) into the detergent drawer at each wash, making sure to shake the bottle beforehand.

◆

EVERYTHING FOR THE DISHES

This is the household product we use the most. To avoid chemicals and bleaching agents, use these products:

▶ Marseille soap dish soap

For half quart (half liter) you need:

- 0.5 ounces (14 grams) Marseille soap
- ⅓ quart (⅓ liter) of water
- 1 teaspoon baking soda
- 1 tablespoon white vinegar
- 4 drops tea tree, lemon, or lavender essential oil

Grate the soap in a salad bowl. Bring the water to a boil, remove from heat, and then pour onto the soap. Mix until the shavings have dissolved completely. Allow to cool. Add the baking soda and then the white vinegar. Be careful, as a chemical reaction takes place and the liquid begins to foam profusely.

Add the drops of essential oil to perfume the solution. Pour into an old dish soap bottle previously rinsed and dried.

▶ Black soap dish soap

You need:

- ¾ quart (¾ liter) water
- 3 tablespoons black soap
- 2 teaspoons baking soda
- 3 tablespoons soda crystals
- 10 drops tea, lavender, or lemon essential oil

Bring the water to a boil. On medium heat, add the soap and mix until it is completely dissolved. Remove from heat and add

the baking soda, then the crystals. Watch out for a chemical reaction. Leave to cool before adding the drops of essential oil and pouring into an old dish soap bottle previously rinsed and dried.

❶ WARNING: This product does not foam and should be used in small quantities. Two teaspoons in a large bowl will do the trick.

▶ Dishwasher soap

You need:

- 3 lemons, ideally untreated
- 7 ounces (198 grams) coarse salt
- 3.5 fluid ounces (100 milliliters) white vinegar
- 7 fluid ounces (210 milliliters) water

Cut off the ends of the lemons, then slice them. Grind them very finely with the coarse salt in a blender. Pour the mixture in a saucepan and then add vinegar and water. Cook on medium heat, stirring regularly. Remove from heat and put back in the blender for 20 seconds. Leave to cool and pour in an old laundry detergent bottle previously rinsed and dried. Pour a large tablespoon into the dishwasher's detergent dispenser per wash.

EVERYTHING FOR SCOURING AND DESCALING

There is no need to spend a fortune: You will get rid of traces and stains with a few well-chosen and well-combined components.

▸ Scouring cream cleaner

You need:

- 8 tablespoons baking soda
- 2 tablespoons white vinegar
- 5 drops lemon or bergamot essential oil
- 5 drops orange essential oil

Pour the baking soda, then the vinegar, then the essential oils into a bottle.

🔴 **WARNING:** A chemical reaction will happen and the mixture will foam. Don't panic—that's normal. However, to avoid the strong smell of vinegar, prepare your mixture in a well-ventilated room, with the windows open.

▸ Toilet descaler

You need:

- 2 tablespoons liquid black soap
- 6 tablespoons baking soda
- 2 cups (475 milliliters) white vinegar
- 8 cups (2 liters) water
- 1 teaspoon essential oil of your choice

Mix all the ingredients in a bucket. Watch out for the chemical reaction between baking soda and vinegar; allow the mixture to drop down again, and then pour it into a spray bottle that you will label carefully.

Spray as required on the whole toilet; leave for a few minutes and then dry.

EVERYTHING FOR REMOVING GREASE

These are used for all surfaces and combine gentleness and efficiency.

▶ Multipurpose disinfectant

You need:

- 1 quart (1 liter) water
- 1 small cup (235 milliliters) white vinegar
- 2 tablespoons baking soda
- 1 tablespoon tea tree, lemon, or lavender essential oil, as you wish

Bring the water to a boil. Remove from heat and add the vinegar and then the baking soda. Watch out for the chemical reaction. Always work in a well-ventilated room. Allow the foam to drop down again, mix in the essential oil, and then pour into a previously rinsed and dried bottle. Label the bottle.

▶ Floor polish

You need:

- 3 tablespoons turpentine
- 5 tablespoons white vinegar
- 4 tablespoons olive oil

Mix all the ingredients together, then apply the mixture with a brush or cloth.

▶ Multipurpose cleaner

You need:

- 1 quart (1 liter) water
- 2 tablespoons liquid black soap
- 1 teaspoon baking soda
- 5 to 6 drops lavender, lemon, or mint essential oil

Mix all the ingredients together, and then pour the mixture into a spray for easy use.

▶ Tile and laminate floor cleaner

You need:

- 1.5 pounds (680 grams) liquid black soap for removing grease and cleaning

- 1 pound (450 grams) flaxseed oil for nourishing and adding shine
- 15 fluid ounces (440 milliliters) water
- 30 drops tea tree essential oil for its bactericide properties

Mix all the ingredients together, and then pour the mixture into a 2-quart can. Use a capful for every 2 quarts of water to get clean, disinfected, and shiny floors.

▸**Window-cleaning soap**

You need:

- 1.5 cups (350 milliliters) white vinegar
- 3.5 fluid ounces (100 milliliters) water
- 5 drops tea tree essential oil

Mix all the ingredients together into a spray bottle and it's ready to use.

EVERYTHING FOR CLEANSING

There is nothing better than citrus for perfuming your home delicately, while baking soda is the champion for absorbing smells and white vinegar is a first-class disinfectant.

▸**The "Fanta Lemon" deodorizer**

You need:

- 1 teaspoon baking soda
- 2 cups (475 milliliters) hot water
- 1 teaspoon lemon juice

Mix everything in a spray bottle. Shake before each use, then spray.

It is best to proceed methodically, as you don't clean the living room the same way that you clean the bedroom or kitchen. This is an effective solution for making the whole house shine in record time.

A DIFFERENT TYPE OF HOUSEWORK FOR EACH ROOM

IN THE LAUNDRY ROOM

Laundry is like a second skin, so we should not let it get grimy or dull, when it takes so little to restore its brightness.

The weekly clean

▶**Sparkling clean laundry**
Use the Natural Laundry Detergent recipe in Chapter 5 to make your laundry shine even brighter.

• **A blood, butter, or motor oil stain?** Remove it before you put it in the machine, or hot water will set it.

• **Has your child come back from soccer practice all covered in dirt?** Add a handful of soda crystals to your laundry to strengthen its cleaning properties.

• **To restore your sheets' original whiteness,** pour 10.5 fluid ounces (310 milliliters) of baking soda for a medium load of laundry in the detergent dispenser, at the last rinse.

• **What about the softener?** White vinegar is perfect for making laundry soft, but do add some citrus zest. Leave the zest of two citrus fruit (lemon or orange) to infuse with 3 cups (700 milliliters) of white vinegar overnight in a mason jar. Sieve into a bottle, making sure you remove the zest, and it's ready: 2 tablespoons into the detergent dispenser and your laundry will smell nice and fresh.

• **To get laundry that is always clean while maintaining your washing machine,** descale it regularly by pouring ½ quart of white vinegar into the drum, then running an empty hot wash.

TIP

Looking for lonely socks

If you don't have a mesh laundry bag, then slip your socks into a pillow case.

The pillow test
TIP

Fold your pillow in two and place a shoe encased in a plastic bag on top. If the pillow springs open, you can still use it for a while longer. If it remains folded, then it's time to change it.

The every-3-to-6-months clean

▸ **Everything for the bed**
• **A duvet needs to be cleaned regularly to avoid becoming a dust mite trap.** We like to cuddle in it to sleep but we sweat in it as well. Synthetic duvets are easily cleaned in the washing machine, whereas feather duvets require additional care. To limit the risk of seeing feathers get stuck together, add two tennis balls to the drum. Be careful: It's best to dry it in the local Laundromat. Large-capacity dryers ensure sufficient ventilation to limit the risk of feathers becoming stuck together and rotting as they dry.
• **Don't forget the pillows!** Synthetic ones should be washed every 3 months and feather ones once to twice a year. Latex contour or memory foam pillows

should not be washed, as they will lose their shape and become damaged. So to keep them in shape, rub them regularly with a dry brush and cover them with a pillowcase.

IN THE KITCHEN

The kitchen is the central hub of activity and the true heart of the home. It's here that the children do their homework, that we work, that we entertain friends...so it is the room that gets the most dirty.

The weekly clean

Don't let stains become ingrained. The more you wait, the harder it is to get rid of them. It is essential to take some steps to keep your kitchen always immaculate.

▸ **Gleaming tiles**
• **Make your tiles shine** by applying a paste made from 1 part water to 1 part baking soda. Leave for an hour, and then rinse with clean water.
• **Have you boiled potatoes for dinner?** Their cooking water is an excellent cleaner for tiles. Pour it very hot onto your

tiled floor, making sure not to burn yourself. Scrub with a heavy-duty scrub brush, wait 10 minutes for the starch to absorb the grease, rinse, and dry.

▶Sparkling chrome

• **To descale chrome-plated items,** scrub them with half a lemon. Leave for 10 minutes, rinse, and dry. Is the limescale still there? Sprinkle the lemon with salt.

• **To restore their shine,** use a cloth sprinkled with flour. Don't rinse or you will get a sticky paste.

• **A small rust stain?** Scrub it with an onion cut in half to make it disappear.

▶A clean worktop backboard

Whether it is stainless steel, glass, or tiles, there is nothing better than a good cleaning with a sponge dipped in black soap for removing grease splatters. Make circular movements from the outside to the inside to avoid spreading the grease. Once you have removed all the grease, rinse with vinegary water, and then dry with a microfiber cloth.

▶A sink that is always clean

• **If it's resin,** a wipe with a sponge soaked in soapy water (1 teaspoon of Marseille soap) or dish soap will be enough to remove the grease. Rinse with clean water and dry with a nonfluffy cloth. Still not clean enough? Scrub the sides and the bottom with half a lemon, leave for 3 minutes, rinse, and dry with a nonfluffy cloth. Are the stains still there? Use black soap. Mix a quarter-sized amount of black soap in a small bowl of lukewarm water. Rub gently. Leave, rinse, and dry with a soft dry cloth.

🛈 WARNING: Resin sinks and bathtubs hate abrasive products.

TIP

Removing rust from tiles

Cover the stain with lemon juice, and then sprinkle with table salt. Leave for an hour before scrubbing with a heavy-duty scrub brush and rinse.

TIP

To make enamel shine

Wipe the surfaces with a soft cloth dipped in turpentine. No need to rinse unless the smell bothers you.

• **If it's enamel,** it's time for baking soda. Cover a sponge with it and scrub to get rid of the black stains that are left on the inside and bottom of the sink when you wash pots and pans.

Scrub the insides with half a lemon to remove any yellow film from the enamel and restore its original whiteness. Leave for 5 minutes, rinse with clean water, and polish with a dry, nonfluffy cloth.

Multipurpose cleaner is once again a miracle tool for making the sink sparkling clean. Scrub, concentrating on any stubborn stains, leave for a few minutes, rinse, and dry as always with a soft cloth.

• **If it's stainless steel,** be careful not to scratch it. Scrub the insides with a cloth dipped in a mixture of vegetable oil and lemon juice.

Finish with a microfiber cloth to make it shine. To round off your cleaning and restore luster to your sink, make a ball with three paper towels and dip it in white vinegar mixed with a few drops of vegetable oil and scrub. Wipe off unsightly black stains with a sponge dipped in black soap, flaxseed oil, and glycerin.

▶ **A powerful oven**
As the insides accumulate dirt, bad smells mix in with nice cooking smells. Clean the insides when they are still lukewarm with a damp sponge dipped in black soap. Leave overnight before rinsing with clean water. Add a little baking soda for removing impurities, disinfecting, and getting rid of bad odors.

• **Do you need an express clean?** Mix the equivalent of a capful of liquid black soap with hot water, pour it all in a spray

☞ *Did you know?*

Your stainless steel sink will be as clean as new if you sprinkle it with a large tablespoon of flour. It will become glossy by polishing it with a soft cloth.

bottle...and spray. Leave for 30 minutes, and then rinse with a large quantity of water and a wet sponge. Finish off the cleaning by wiping with a sponge dipped in white vinegar to avoid a layer of grease forming on the insides.

▸A gleaming gas range

• **If the burners go out suddenly,** it is time to strip them down. Leave them to soak overnight in a bowl filled with vinegar before rinsing them with clean water and drying them meticulously.

• **Are there ingrained burn stains?** Lay down some papers towels around the burners and douse them in vinegar. Leave to soak overnight and in the morning you will be pleasantly surprised by how easily these stains come out.

• **To make the gas cooker shine,** add a few drops of white vinegar on a sponge dipped in soapy water and wipe.

▸A nice and smooth linoleum

New plastic or PVC floor coverings—imitation wood, concrete, stone, or tile—look great as long as they don't become stained or faded. The first thing to do to renovate this surface is to remove grease from it with water mixed with white vinegar and Marseille soap.

• To remove stubborn stains (burns, coffee, candles), baking soda is required. Sprinkle the stain and scrub with a damp sponge. Rinse and dry.

• To make it shine, whisk two egg yolks together, and then mix them with a quart of water. Apply this lotion evenly onto the flooring and leave it to dry without rinsing.

❶ WARNING: These floor coverings will not tolerate abrasive products, bleach, acetone, or even black soap, which is too potent and will become sticky.

▸Impeccable hot plates and cooktops

• What is the quickest solution for restoring smooth and sparkling hot plates? The multipurpose clay cleaner! Apply some with a damp sponge, scrub, rinse, and wipe with a clean cloth. What if you don't have any? Mix a teaspoon of white vinegar with two spoonfuls of dish soap. Soak a damp sponge with this and scrub. Rinse and dry with a soft cloth. If you are bothered by the smell of vinegar, use black soap. Place a dime-sized amount on a damp sponge. There is no need to rinse. Leave it to dry and polish with a soft cloth.

• When it comes to stubborn stains, the ideal thing is to cover them with black soap paste and leave for 5, 10, or 15 minutes, according to the size of the stain. Then carefully scrub with a special glass-ceramic scraper,* rinse with clean water, and finish off with a sponge dipped in white vinegar.

* Generally delivered with the cooktop. If not, this scraper can be bought in hardware stores.

▶An immaculate countertop

Sprinkle half a lemon with some table salt, and then rub onto the countertop. Concentrate on the stains. Leave to act for a few minutes before rinsing in cold, clean water with the aid of a sponge. Dry with a clean cloth.

• If the joints are gray, giving them a little scrub with a toothbrush sprinkled with baking soda will do the trick. You don't need to do this every day; once a month will be more than enough.

The monthly clean

Good maintenance ensures that domestic appliances work well and also prolongs their life span. So let's make the most of a quiet weekend to do those essential little bits of cleaning that are so often neglected.

▶A cooker hood free of grease

Remove the grease from the cooker hood with a sponge dipped in liquid black soap by making small circular movements and rinsing your sponge regularly. Rinse with clean water and dry with a microfiber cloth.

Before putting the grilles in the dishwasher, leave them to soak in soapy water or in baking soda. Rinse. Are there some grease deposits left? Scrub them with a brush and some liquid black soap.

▶A refrigerator and freezer in great form

Is your refrigerator empty? Make the most of this situation to clean it. Wash the insides and shelves (don't forget the bottom of the shelves) with a sponge dipped in a mixture of 1 part white vinegar to 1 part lukewarm water. No need to rinse. There you go—it's ready to welcome your next grocery shopping.

For those who are not big fans of white vinegar, clean the insides and shelves with a sponge dipped in liquid black soap. No need to rinse but do dry with a nonfluffy cloth.

▸Beware of bad smells if the drain becomes clogged up

Little by little, garbage accumulates in the kitchen pipes and bad smells start to appear. To avoid this, mix 1 cup (235 milliliters) of soda crystals or baking soda, 1 cup of coarse salt, and 1 cup of vinegar. Pour the mixture down the drain, leave it for at least an hour, and rinse with boiling water.

The every-3-to-6-months clean

▸An odorless drain trap

To avoid bad smells coming up from the drain, empty the P-trap by unscrewing it. No need for pliers; you can do it all by hand. Remember to place a bowl underneath before unscrewing to collect any stagnant water. After cleaning the P-trap, screw thread, and washer with black soap, replace the washer on the P-trap, and then screw it tightly back on, but not too much to avoid crushing the washer.

TIP

Down with bad smells

To remove bad smells in the refrigerator, place three or four natural corks in different corners of the refrigerator and they will absorb them.

The yearly clean

▸Sparkling terra-cotta floor tiles

All you need to do on a daily basis is to give a sweep with a microfiber push broom dipped in a bucket of water with liquid black soap. However, as time goes by, terra-cotta floor tiles lose their shine. Once or twice a year, clean them with a brush and with either a mixture of lukewarm water and soda crystals or with baking soda. Rinse. Once they are shiny, scrub them again but this time, dip the brush in a bucket filled with hot water and soft black soap (1 teaspoon per half quart [half liter] of water).

For a beautiful shine, leave until completely dry, and then slather them in flaxseed oil.

Cleaning as you go along

Doing short, regular bouts of cleaning avoids having to do long, tedious stretches.

▶ **An impeccable broom**

To avoid it leaving more germs than it collects, every 2 months leave it to soak in a bucket filled with water, 1 cup (235 milliliters) of hydrogen peroxide, and half a cup (120 milliliters) of black soap.

▶ **A fryer free of grease**

• **If you want to clean it using heated products:** Choose the white vinegar recipe. Fill the inner pot with it. Switch the fryer on and bring the vinegar to a boil. Unplug, leave to cool, then empty. Remove the rest of the grease on the inside with a sponge dipped in dish soap. Rinse and dry with paper towels.

⚠ WARNING: Open the windows to ventilate the room because vinegar can be an irritant.

👉 Did you know?

To make sure that the P-trap is not leaking, place a paper towel underneath it and turn the tap on. If a drop lands on the paper towel, unscrew the P-trap once again and check that the washer and screw thread are clean.

💡 TIP

Detecting a gas leak

Is there a vague smell of gas in your kitchen? To make sure that the gas cooker pipe has not become porous, mix 3.5 fluid ounces (100 milliliters) of soap shavings with a bit of water until you obtain a paste that is almost sticky. Adjust the quantity of water and shavings accordingly. Wipe this "glue" onto the pipe with your hand or with a sponge. Bubbles will form if it's leaking.

• **If you want to clean at room temperature:** Choose the flour recipe, which will also save you from getting burned. Sprinkle a generous quantity of flour on the whole inner pot, as it will absorb the fat. Leave it to stand for an hour or more. Remove the surplus with the help of paper towels. Repeat if necessary. Then wipe with a sponge dipped in soapy water, rinse with clean water, and dry.

▸**Impeccable aluminum pans**
• **To get rid of stubborn stains,** cook rhubarb or sorrel in them.
• **To make your aluminum items shiny again,** wipe them with a cloth soaked in some vegetable oil mixed with a few drops of denatured alcohol.

▸**A limescale-free kettle**
Slip a cleaned and scrubbed oyster shell into your kettle to avoid it getting coated with limescale. Limescale deposits will collect on the oyster shell rather than on the inside of the kettle.

IN THE LIVING ROOM

Thanks to the advent of home cinema, game consoles, and so on, the living room has established itself as the culture hub of the family. We go there to recharge our batteries and relax, and when we eat there, it's

Help, my wooden floor squeaks!

TIP

To put an end to it, insert talcum powder or melted paraffin between the wooden slats. Some cabinetmakers use Marseille soap flakes.

in front of the TV with a dinner tray. So, we need to take care of it to make sure that this space remains our sanctuary.

The weekly clean

▸**A gleaming stained wood floor**
Stained wood flooring requires little attention. Water should be banned, as it can make it turn gray. It should simply be dusted regularly with a lightly dampened mop. To avoid it looking dull, reapply a layer of oil approximately every 6 months.
• **Oh no, stains!** Wipe immediately. If the stain is already dry, opt for a sponge lightly dampened with lukewarm water to which you will have added two drops of black soap.

▶ **A lustrous varnished floor**

• **Is your varnished floor dull and blackened in places?** Dilute the equivalent of a capful of liquid black soap in a large quantity of hot water and clean your parquet floor with a damp mop.

• **Is this method not enough?** Add a few drops of white vinegar, rinse, and dry quickly. Above all, do not use an abrasive sponge, as it will scratch it.

▶ **Spotless Plexiglas and plastics**

These are trendy materials that can be used everywhere in the house. They have the beauty of glass and come in a large array of colors, which add some fun to the décor. The disadvantage is that they become dull if they are not taken care of.

• **To retain their shine,** cleaning them with a sponge dipped in a dime-sized amount of black soap or Marseille soap will do the trick. Rinse then polish with a soft cloth.

TIP

Protective oil

To protect them from water and to avoid stains, polish Plexiglas or plastic with vegetable oil. Leave them to dry, and then polish to make them shine.

• **Get rid of static electricity.** Depending on their quality, these materials can generate static electricity. This means that as soon as the dust has been removed, it comes back right away. To remove it, clean these items with a sponge dipped in a mixture made from 1 cup (235 milliliters) of white vinegar, 1 tablespoon of black soap, and 2 cups (475 milliliters) of hot water. No need to rinse. Leave to dry.

▶ **A pristine TV**

Dust the edges, and then clean them with a nonfluffy cloth moistened with soapy water (a dime-sized amount of black soap in a quart of water). Clean the screen with some denatured alcohol.

The monthly clean

▶ **Luminous lampshades**

These are the main light diffusers and yet we let them become dull and dusty, not realizing that they let less light through.

• **To dust a fabric lampshade,** you just need to vacuum delicately with the dusting brush. No vacuum cleaner on hand? Use the hairdryer.

• **Has the fabric become yellow?** Just rub it with soft bread pellets. Is it stained? Give it a lukewarm shower with a sink sprayer, soap delicately with a special wool detergent, and rinse off. You have to act fast so that the glue does not have time to dissolve.

• **Glass or plastic lampshade?** Unscrew it and clean it with baking soda sprinkled on a damp sponge. Rinse with clean water and dry with a nonfluffy cloth.

▶ Squeaky clean light switches

To eliminate fingerprints on light switches, doors, and window frames, rub them with a potato cut in two while making small circular movements; then dry with a nonfluffy cloth.

🛈 WARNING: Make sure to switch off the electricity to avoid any risk.

▶ Happy houseplants

Are your houseplants not looking happy? It could be because of dust. As it accumulates on the leaves, dust gradually suffocates the plant. Once a month get into the habit of rinsing your plants in your bathtub or shower.

Once every 3 months, clean the leaves, one by one, with a sponge soaked in a mixture made from a quart of water and beer, vegetable oil, makeup remover, or a teaspoon of baking soda.

🛈 WARNING: Baking soda should not be used to water indoor plants.

▶ Transparent windows

Do not clean your windowpanes when it is very sunny. It leaves streaks and the products dry too quickly. Remember to clean both sides.

• **To get rid of streaks,** rub the windows with a sponge lightly dipped in liquid black soap (half a capful for a quart of water), dry them with a squeegee, and finish off with a microfiber cloth. Despite its thick and oily consistency, black soap does not need to be rinsed, which is convenient.

• **Did you know that there is no better cloth than damp newspaper for windows?** The secret? Printing ink is an excellent cleaner.

• **You will make windows and mirrors shiny again** by cleaning them with a sponge dipped in white vinegar diluted with a bit of hot water. To avoid leaving marks, make circular movements and of course ensure you dry completely with a nonfluffy cloth.

The every-3-to-6-months clean

▸ An immaculate sofa

• **Leather sofa.** To restore springiness and shine to your sofa while removing stains, dab it with a nonfluffy cloth lightly dampened with a mixture made from 1 tablespoon of liquid black soap per half quart (½ liter) of water.

• **If it is covered in fabric,** clean it with a damp sponge lightly dipped in hydrogen peroxide (2 teaspoons of hydrogen peroxide per quart of water). This will revive colors as well. Leave it to dry.

TIP

Antiglass bread

Broken glass? To collect any minute shards of glass, which are often invisible, place a piece of sliced bread on the floor: They will stick to the bread thanks to its compact consistency.

▸ Translucent sheer curtains

After the windows come the curtains. They protect privacy from the neighbors but if they become too dusty, they also make the room darker. To brighten them, put them in the washing machine on a warm wash and add the juice of one lemon and 2 tablespoons of baking soda to the laundry detergent. Run out of baking soda? Add some baking powder to the laundry detergent. Hang them while still wet to avoid creasing.

▸ A healthy carpet

It is cozy but also a magnet for dust and dust mites. Vacuuming every week is not enough; you should give it a deep clean on a regular basis. So stock up on baking soda! It is a powerful dust mite killer and deodorizes and revives colors. Sprinkle it everywhere on the carpet and leave it for 2 hours. Vacuum it all away.

Are there still some stubborn stains? Rub them with a heavy-duty scrub brush soaked in a mixture made from 2 parts sparkling water to 1 part white vinegar.

▸ Glinting marble

• **For daily care,** a damp mop dipped in a mixture of black soap and lukewarm water will do the trick (one capful per 1.5 quarts [1.5 liters] of hot water). Rinse and make it shine with a soft cloth and a few drops of flaxseed oil.

▸**Rugs fit for a king**

• Our ancestors used to clean their rugs with snow to remove the dirt once a year. Unfortunately this is not always possible nowadays!

• **A simpler method** is to vacuum the dust away, scrub with a brush and black soap, and then rinse with clean water.

• **You can also revive colors** by spreading finely chopped herbs or damp used tea leaves. Roll the rug, and then leave it in a dark, dry place. Then vacuum the herbs or tea away. This is a bit cumbersome but worth it if you have the time.

🄸 WARNING:

• The dyes on a rug are not always well set. Before dampening it, always test on a hidden area.

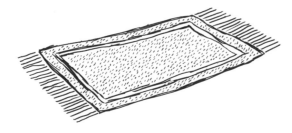

• A boiled plant-based liquid (coffee, tea, saffron sauce, etc.) spilled on a rug can act as a colorant. It is imperative to scrub the stain with black soap very quickly

TIP

Brush it away

If the feet of furniture have left a mark on the carpet, place a damp cloth on it and briefly apply a hot iron. Remove cloth and iron then brush to raise the pile. The marks will disappear.

and then rinse it with a large quantity of clean water.

The yearly clean

▸**A chimney as good as new**

Is the time for wood fires over? Take the time to give your fireplace insert a thorough clean. Using a short brush, sweep up the ash (keep it, as it is useful!), and finish off with the vacuum cleaner. Clean the inside with a hard bristle brush dipped in a mixture made from a quart of hot water and 3 cups (700 milliliters) of white vinegar at regular intervals.

• **As always,** baking soda is your ally. You can scrub the inside with baking soda sprinkled on a damp brush. Repeat until stains disappear, rinse, then dry.

• **Don't forget the mantelpiece!** Brush it by making circular movements with a hard bristle brush dipped in a mixture made from 4 tablespoons of liquid black soap, 2 tablespoons of baking soda, and 2 quarts (2 liters) of water.

• **Rinse with clean water,** and then dry with a nonfluffy cloth or balls of crumpled newspaper.

• **The fireplace glass.** The fireplace insert glass should not be dirty and black if you want to admire the flames in the evening. To restore its transparency, use the ash removed from the chimney, taking care to remove the solid pieces.

• **Crumple some newspaper into a ball,** moisten it with lukewarm water, and press it into the ash. Rub the ball in small circular movements against the fireplace insert window.

• White vinegar combined with a few grams of coarse salt also works very well. Rub the fireplace insert window with this mixture with a sponge. Rinse with clean water and dry with a nonfluffy cloth.

• **For the cast-iron back plate,** use an iron brush or coarse grain emery board then use extra-fine steel wool to finish off. Once it is clean, wipe with a cloth soaked in Vaseline oil to make it shine.

▸ **Dust-free books**

Vacuum them with the dusting brush regularly to prevent the dust from settling. Once a month, hold the book very tightly and rub the edge of the pages with a flat nail file to remove any yellow or grayish tinge.

Cleaning as you go along

▸ **Shiny silverware**

• **To restore their original color,** leave your silver cutlery and dishes in a bowl of lukewarm water with 4 tablespoons of liquid black soap for about 5 minutes. Clean the engraving with a soft tooth-

TIP

Antirust

To get rid of rust stains, rub them with half an onion, and then slather them with vegetable oil.

brush. No need to rinse, but do dry them and wipe them with a soft, nonfluffy cloth.

• **Is it impossible to soak your silver chandelier** with its imitation wax candle? Then rub the silver part with a quarter-sized amount of black soap paste with a damp sponge and polish with a soft cloth.

❶ WARNING: Do not ever use the abrasive side of the sponge or your items will become scratched.

▶Glossy bronze items

• **On a daily basis,** a nonfluffy cloth dipped in soapy water (1 tablespoon of black soap per quart [liter] of lukewarm water) will be enough to add shine to your bronze items, such as furniture legs and handles. No need to rinse but dry and polish.

• **They will recover their gloss** if you wipe them with the water used for cooking dried beans!

• **Are they very grimy?** Once a year, apply a mask of dried beans or fava beans to give them a boost. Cook then mash two big handfuls of beans (adjust according to the number of bronze items). Sieve them. Leave them to cool briefly. Wipe this paste on the bronze with a nonfluffy cloth, then wipe off. The ideal thing is to let everything dry in wood shavings. Granted, it's not that easy. So a simpler method is to brush with a toothbrush dipped in lemon juice. Rinse carefully with clean water, and then polish with beeswax to make it shine.

• **To remove verdigris from bronze,** rub it with a cloth soaked in a tablespoon of white vinegar mixed with a pinch of table salt.

• **To polish bronze items,** a few drops of Worcestershire sauce on a soft cloth works marvels.

▶Perfect copper

• **To restore shine,** leave them to soak for 5 minutes in a bowl of lukewarm water with 4 tablespoons of liquid black soap, rinse, and then wipe off.

• **For a deeper clean,** pour 5 tablespoons of flour and 5 tablespoons of table salt in a bowl. Mix and add white vinegar until you obtain a paste that is sufficiently creamy for it not to run. Spread the paste on the copper item with a flat brush with circular movements. Leave it to dry, rinse, and dry off with a soft, nonfluffy cloth.
• **Has it become oxidized?** Combine 2 cups (475 milliliters) of vinegar and half a cup (120 milliliters) of salt and bring to a boil. Place the item in the mixture. Leave it for a few minutes, rinse with clean water, and dry.

▶**Luminous tin**
• **On a daily basis:** Cleaning with soapy water or with the water used for cooking onions will do the trick. Don't forget to rinse.
• **To restore their shine,** rub your tin items with a cloth dipped in warm beer, leave to dry, then polish.
• **Do you prefer not using warm liquids?** Use raw cabbage leaves, and then polish your tin items with a soft cloth.

IN THE BATHROOM

This most intimate of spaces must always be pristine, whether we spend 5 minutes for a quick wash, or 2 hours luxuriating in a hot bath.

The weekly clean

▶**A welcoming bathtub**
We like to luxuriate there for hours, with a book in hand and music in the background. A bath is the perfect opportunity to relax and unwind. It would be a shame for this little treat to be spoiled by nasty stains.
• **If it's enamel,** to prevent it from getting grimy, the best thing is to rinse it with the showerhead after each bath while wiping with a sponge dipped in black soap to avoid stains becoming ingrained on the sides. For best results, repeat weekly.
• **Do you want it to shine brightly?** Wipe the sides with a cloth dipped in turpentine.
• **Leave it to dry,** and then rinse with clean water and polish with a clean cloth. Repeat this every 2 to 3 months.

• **As time goes by,** does your bathtub look gray rather than white? To restore its shine, rub the sides with half a lemon covered in salt, and then wipe with a cloth dipped in hot white vinegar. Leave it for a few minutes, rinse, and dry.

• **Have ugly brown stains appeared around the drain?** Make a miracle paste from baking soda: 2 parts baking soda for 1 part hydrogen peroxide. Adjust the quantities to obtain a thick paste. Apply the paste onto the stains and leave it for an hour. Then scrub with a lightly dampened sponge that is nonabrasive so as not to scratch. Rinse with clean water.

• **If it's resin,** do not rub it with abrasive products. Resin needs to be handled with care. So for regular maintenance, just wipe it with a sponge or soft cloth dipped in liquid black soap or dish soap. Rinse with clean water.

• **Is it a really stubborn stain?** Rub it delicately with multipurpose cleaner and a sponge. If it's really stubborn, then use dish soap, diluted white vinegar or half a lemon. Rinse quickly with a large quantity of water.

▸Glossy chrome faucets

Cleaning them every week will prevent them from getting dirty, losing their shine, and becoming covered in limescale. With a brush or old toothbrush, scrub the faucet with a mixture of 1 part white vinegar and 1 part water. Dry the area with a clean, dry cloth.

• **Too late,** has the limescale built up on the edges? Scrub it with a toothbrush dipped in hydrogen peroxide, white vinegar, or the juice of half a lemon.

▸Spotless toilets

• **Hunt down the limescale!** If it builds up inside the toilet bowl, it will quickly acquire a nasty brownish color.

• **To get rid of it,** pour half a quart of boiling white vinegar into the bowl and leave it for an hour. Before rinsing by flushing, scrub the sides with a lightly abrasive sponge, making sure you protect your hands with gloves. Be careful, vinegar fumes can cause irritation, so remember to open the windows or to ventilate the room. Have you just cooked potatoes? Instead of throwing the water away in the sink, empty it in the toilets and wait an hour before flushing. This will eliminate any limescale.

• **What about the tank?** Place a quarter-sized amount of black soap paste in the tank. As the days go by, the soap will melt and clean the inside, and even better, the limescale particles will disappear every time you flush.

The monthly clean

▶ Sparkling wall tiles

Have your tiles lost their shine? It is time to get rid of the limescale to smarten them up.

Black soap has mighty powers for removing surface deposits. Wash them with a sponge dipped in soapy water. Be careful with the dosage: a quarter-sized amount of black soap in a bucket of hot water is enough or it might leave streaks. No need to rinse. Leave it to dry and wipe with a soft cloth. The benefit of this is that black soap leaves a film on the surface, preventing limescale from building up.

• **Stubborn stains can be removed with a damp sponge** sprinkled with baking soda, while the most ingrained ones can be scrubbed off with lukewarm white vinegar. Be careful, however, as it is best used cold on colored tiles. If the smell bothers you, then swap the vinegar for a sponge dipped in lemon juice and sprinkled with coarse salt. Leave it for a few minutes and rinse with clean water.

▶ Fog-free mirrors

Clean your mirrors with soap to avoid them fogging up! Apply black soap paste on the surface with a soft, nonfluffy cloth and rub it until the soap disappears completely. Your mirror will shine bright.

▶ A transparent shower door

Is your shower more white than see-through because of limescale? To eradicate it without using too much force, soap the shower door with a sponge dipped in a mixture of black soap and denatured alcohol. Leave it for a few minutes, rinse, and dry with a microfiber cloth. You can also add a drop of citric acid to increase brilliance.

• **Prepare your mixture in advance**. Mix a tablespoon of black soap, half a teaspoon of denatured alcohol, and a cup of lukewarm water.

About scent

Leave a few drops of vanilla extract in the inside of the toilet roll. The paper will absorb the scent, which will be diffused every time you unroll it.

The half-yearly clean

▸ Odorless drains

To put an end to those annoying little smells, mix a generous handful of coarse salt, a smaller handful of baking soda, and 1 cup (235 milliliters) of white vinegar (watch out for the chemical reaction). Pour the lot down the drains before going to bed. Leave overnight and rinse in the morning by turning the faucet on.

▸ A powerful shower

What a pain! Over time, has the water flow in your showerhead become less powerful? Look up: Some of the spray holes have probably become clogged with limescale. Unscrew the showerhead and soak it in undiluted white vinegar for 15 minutes. Scrub the holes with a toothbrush to remove any scale residue. Leave it to soak for another 15 minutes before rinsing with clean water.

▸ A spotless shower curtain

Is your shower curtain dotted with black stains? To eliminate those mold stains, scrub them with the abrasive part of a sponge dipped in hot vinegar, and then put it on a cold cycle in the washing machine, adding 3 tablespoons of baking soda to the wash.

▸ Clean joints

It's inevitable that, with time, bath and shower joints become grimy and even moldy. As a result, they become less waterproof and this is when water can start to leak in. To avoid this, rub them with a toothbrush dipped in black soap paste and no water. Then dry with a microfiber cloth.

 Did you know?

Has your soda gone flat? Pour it into the toilets. Leave it for 2 hours; scrub with a brush, paying special attention to any stubborn stains; and rinse. It's a fantastic limescale remover!

• **Have you run out of black soap?** Replace it with white vinegar or denatured alcohol.

◆

IN THE BEDROOM

As we spend nearly half our lives here, our bedroom deserves its fair share of cleaning . . .

The every-3-to-6-months clean

▶A seagrass rug

Seagrass is made of fibers from woven aquatic plants, so it needs to be moistened to keep its luminosity. So once every 2 or 3 months, wipe it with a damp mop, and then dry it with a hairdryer or fan heater.

• **For a deeper clean,** mix half a capful of ammonia with a teaspoon of black soap in 5 quarts of lukewarm water. Rub with a brush or mop, with particular attention given to the most grimy areas. Rinse and dry with the hairdryer, as seagrass is susceptible to white marks and mold.

❶ WARNING: To avoid white marks: Wipe off any drops of water immediately with paper towels and dry with a hairdryer while making circular movements from the outside to the inside.

▶An impeccable mattress

It is necessary to clean it regularly to ensure a good night's sleep.

Dust the mattress and box springs regularly with the vacuum cleaner, making sure you clean the dusting brush beforehand.

• **To prevent dust mites,** it is important to give it a deep clean every 3 months. Spray a mixture of 5 fluid ounces (150 milliliters) of denatured alcohol, 12 fluid ounces (350 milliliters) of water, and 5 drops of lemon essential oil. Leave it to dry naturally. If you don't have any denatured alcohol left, replace it with flavorless vodka; it will be just as effective.

• **For a deeper clean,** mix 1 cup (235 milliliters) of baking soda with 1 quart (1 liter) of white vinegar in a bowl. Watch out for the chemical reaction. Leave it to foam; once the mixture has gone down again, scrub the mattress with a sponge dipped in this solution. Remember to wear gloves. Let it dry naturally.

• **To remove dried bloodstains,** squeeze some lemon onto the stain and leave it for 5 minutes. Then soak your cloth in the rest of the lemon juice and rub

Antimold

Before hanging up your shower curtain, leave it to soak in heavily salted water, as it will prevent mold from building up.

the stain. To prevent it from spreading, make small circular movements from the outside to the inside. Rinse with a sponge and let it dry naturally. Is the stain still there? Prepare a slimy paste by mixing water and starch in equal parts. Spread the paste onto the stain, leave it for at least 2 hours, and then scrub with a hard bristle brush to make it disappear. Rinse with a sponge lightly dampened with water and let it dry naturally. You can also replace starch with talcum powder or cornstarch.

• **To remove a urine stain,** the best thing is to rinse with water, and then rub it with hydrogen peroxide. Dry the mattress with a hairdryer, carefully making small circular movements from the outside to the inside.
• **Too late, has it become set?** Dab it with a cloth dipped in hydrogen peroxide and rinse with a sponge.

Sprinkle with baking soda to remove any smell. Let it dry naturally, and then vacuum the powder away.

The yearly clean

▶ **An odorless closet**

If you've put away a sheet while it was still damp, an unpleasant smell of mold can permeate the whole closet. To get rid of it, clean the shelves with a sponge soaked in a blend of white vinegar and water (10 fluid ounces [300 milliliters] of white vinegar, 7 fluid ounces [210 milliliters] of water, and, for its disinfectant and purifying properties, 5 drops of tea tree essential oil). Pay particular attention to the mold, and then dry carefully. Leave the door open for several days to let the air circulate.

❶ WARNING: Do not use tea tree essential oil near a pregnant or breastfeeding woman, children, or pets.

▶ **Preventing the appearance of dust mites**

To prevent them from settling in, vacuum inside the cabinets and under the furniture regularly. Plus as they hate being disturbed, move things around in your cabinets and closet. Open them, ventilate them, move your piles of clothing and the coat hangers around, and so on.

At the end of winter (March or April at the latest), empty your shelves and clean them with a sponge dipped in a mixture made from the juice of 3 lemons, 8 fluid ounces (210 milliliters) of water, and 2 drops of eucalyptus essential oil. Give particular attention to the corners. Leave it to dry before putting your clothes back in. Finally, place lavender or camphor sachets in the closet to repel them further.

TIP

Deodorizing cabinets

To get rid of bad smells, place a few pieces of charcoal in a small linen bag. They will absorb the smells in a day or two. If you don't have any charcoal, you can replace it with a small bowl filled with baking soda, as it is also a great way to absorb odors.

2
WHITE VINEGAR

Clean · Degrease · Disinfect
Make it shine

WHITE VINEGAR

. . . THE CLEANING AGENT WITH A BAD REPUTATION

Are you fed up with storing a multitude of household products in your cupboards? Swap them all for a single bottle of white vinegar—it will wow you in just a few wipes of a sponge.

From floor to ceiling and through to the backyard, vinegar works wonders. It cleans, removes grease, disinfects, and brightens colors. It's easy to use and can do practically everything—it alone can replace all the detergents, grease-removal products, disinfectants, and different weed killers. It's also a powerful antibacterial agent, as it kills 99 percent of bacteria, 82 percent of mold, and 80 percent of viruses. Even though it's naturally colorless, nontoxic, biodegradable, and above all super economical (usually less than $2 for a gallon), white vinegar has been overshadowed by baking soda and clay products. What's the drawback of white vinegar? Its smell. It's strong, lingering, and stings the eyes (without irritating them). Many people can't tolerate it, even though it evaporates quickly. However, by following a few tips, its smell can be minimized.

▸**What is it?**
White vinegar is industrially produced by the acidification of beet or corn alcohol.

☞ *Did you know?*

Whether it is called distilled spirit, virgin, or white vinegar, white vinegar is made industrially by acetification, the process of turning corn or beet alcohol into vinegar. Although it is produced industrially, white vinegar is in fact a 100 percent green and natural product, which deteriorates quickly and has no environmental impact.

• **Paradoxically,** although industrially produced, white vinegar is a 100 percent natural, eco-friendly product, because it degrades rapidly and doesn't leave any trace in the environment. White vinegar is a valuable household addition, as it can also be used to preserve gherkins, pickles, and canned food.

• **Unlike other vinegars that are made from alcohol** (wine, cider, etc.), white vinegar is made from corn and even some malts that are fermented to produce a highly concentrated alcohol (90 percent). This alcohol is then processed into acetic alcohol, filtered, and finally mixed with some water. That's why alcohol content isn't listed on a bottle of white vinegar, but the percentage of acetic acid (usually 8 percent) present in the bottle usually is.

▸**Can I cook with it?**
Due to its lack of flavor, white vinegar's more fragrant and colorful cousins are a better option. But chefs use it as their secret weapon in the preparation of mayonnaises and vinaigrettes. To preserve vegetables, you need to dilute it with white wine

or water and a little sugar, because undiluted white vinegar is too strong. It's ideal for rinsing salads, as it kills all the insects.

▸ How do you preserve it?

The best way to preserve the translucence of white vinegar is to store it away from direct light, at room temperature. If it becomes cloudy over time, use a strainer to filter it—this will restore its translucent color.

Warning:

IMPORTANT!

WHITE VINEGAR DOES NOT TOLERATE BEING COMBINED WITH CERTAIN PRODUCTS, SO YOU NEED TO PLAY IT SAFE.

▶ Make sure that you always open the windows when using it, especially if you're heating it. Its strong smell can cause coughing and eye irritation. It is not too serious, but nevertheless unpleasant.

▶ It should never be used with bleach because this mixture releases toxic fumes.

▶ Be careful when you use it with baking soda, as the mixture causes a chemical reaction. The mixture becomes frothy due to the carbon dioxide. This is not harmful, but to avoid any irritation (nose and eyes), open the windows or dilute it.

▶ As it has a powerful stripping action, never use it on marble surfaces, slate, or other porous materials because it will damage them.

▶ Exercise caution, because the strength of undiluted vinegar increases when hot and it turns to acid. So, dilute it with water when you clean your coffee maker or else you'll have to throw it away.

▶ Carry out a test in an inconspicuous corner of the room you want to clean to check that it can withstand this treatment. If you have any doubt, stop the treatment and seek advice from a specialist.

▶ Never swap cider vinegar for white vinegar and vice versa, as the results would be disastrous, if not dangerous. Use white vinegar for household chores; cider vinegar is used for beauty care, and wine vinegar is reserved for cooking.

▶ Protect your hands by wearing protective gloves, specifically for do-it-yourself projects or housework.

From floor to ceiling, it cleans, disinfects, and makes everything gleam around the house. Effective and inexpensive, white vinegar has everything going for it.

WHITE VINEGAR: THE KING OF CLEANLINESS

HOMEMADE PRODUCTS

Making these products in advance is practical and makes day-to-day life easier.

▸**A quick tip when making them**
Like a cook, you'll learn to adapt recipes to your own requirements. You can adjust the amounts to achieve the right quantity or the right consistency. Old recipes are not an exact science but are the result of many trials and experiments.

☞ *Exercise caution with essential oils*

Essential oils must be used with caution. Wear protective gloves and avoid direct contact with the skin. Follow the recommended dosages (if necessary, check the manufacturer's instructions), or else they can very quickly become toxic and noxious. Also, they should be avoided, and above all not used, if you live with allergy sufferers, children, and pets.

❶ CAREFUL PACKAGING
• **Never keep white vinegar in water bottles** or soda bottles. Use the original container or a jerrican.
• **Clearly label the products** you make and list the ingredients. If anyone other than you uses it, they must know what they are handling. And in case of an accident, it allows them to react more quickly.

▸**A stain remover**
A fast response is often the secret of stain removal. Therefore, to avoid wasting time, prepare your "special task" bottle.
You will need:
• **1 part white vinegar**
• **3 parts sparkling water**
Mix the water and vinegar in a spray bottle. Moisten the stain and leave it to act for a few minutes. Then rub it in a circular motion with a sponge, starting at the outer edge and working inward. Rinse in clean water.

▸**A specially formulated floor polish**
You will need:
• **5 tablespoons white vinegar**
• **4 tablespoons olive oil**
• **3 tablespoons turpentine**
Mix all the ingredients and then apply the polish with a brush or cloth.

▸ **Dishwashing liquid**

Known as a grease removal agent, white vinegar is an excellent product for obtaining grease-free, gleaming tableware.

You will need:

• ½ cup (120 milliliters) green Marseille soap (olive oil soap), grated or flaked
• 1 quart (1 liter) hot water
• 2 tablespoons soda crystals
• 1 tablespoon baking soda
• ½ cup (120 milliliters) white vinegar
• 10 drops orange, tea tree, and lemon essential oils

Melt the Marseille soap in the water, while stirring continuously. Remove from the heat and add the baking soda, then the vinegar (exercise caution, as it will froth). Next add the soda crystals and finally the essential oils. Leave to cool and then pour this preparation into a labeled spray bottle.

▸ **A rapid clean**

For everyday cleaning of furniture, doors, and painted walls, in complete safety.

You will need:

• 1 part white vinegar
• 4 parts water

Pour the vinegar and water into a spray bottle and it's ready. Give the surface you want to clean a quick wipe over, then wipe again with a slightly moistened cloth and it's done.

⊘ CAUTION: Never use on untreated wood.

▸ **A multipurpose cleaning agent**

Practical, it can be used on every surface, except of course those surfaces that don't tolerate white vinegar.

You will need:

• 1 tablespoon baking soda
• 2 tablespoons white vinegar
• 2 quarts (2 liters) of water
• ¼ cup (60 milliliters) white Marseille soap, flaked or grated

Mix the Marseille soap in a saucepan of boiling water until it completely dissolves. Remove from the heat, add the white vinegar, and then the baking soda. Exercise caution, as it will froth. Leave to cool before transferring to a spray bottle. You can add a few drops (5 to 6) of essential oil to reduce the smell.

▸ **A multipurpose cleaning agent**

No problem if you don't have any Marseille soap; just adapt the recipe!

You will need:

- **½ cup (120 milliliters) white vinegar**
- **¾ quart (¾ liter) water**
- **1 tablespoon baking soda**
- **10 drops essential oil**

Mix all the ingredients in a spray bottle while taking care to dilute the vinegar in the water before adding the baking soda. This will reduce the amount of frothing produced by the vinegar and baking soda.

▶ **A product for wooden furniture**

To nourish and give wood a shine, this quick recipe will surprise you.

You will need:

- **7 tablespoons white vinegar**
- **7 tablespoons olive oil**
- **20 drops lemon essential oil**

Mix the three ingredients in a small bottle fitted with a stopper and take care in labeling them. Lightly soak a clean lint-free cloth and start rubbing!

❶ **ATTENTION:** Always experiment on a hidden corner first!

▶ **A glass-cleaning product**

You will need:

- **13.5 fluid ounces (400 milliliters) white vinegar**

Make your own "special housework" cleaning wipes

💡 TIP

Making your own cleaning wipes for stain removal means that you always have them at the ready. Once you've used these squares of cloth, you just need to wash them before you use them again.

1. Blend 3 tablespoons of white vinegar, 1 tablespoon of black soap or Marseille soap, and 2 cups (475 milliliters) of water in a salad bowl.

2. Cut about 20 pieces of white cotton fabric into squares measuring 4 x 4 inches (10 x 10 centimeters) and then immerse them in this liquid.

3. Leave to soak for at least 1 hour. Take them out of the liquid and gently squeeze them out.

4. Fold them into four and store them in an airtight container to prevent them from drying out.

- **3 fluid ounces (90 milliliters) water**
- **5 drops tea tree essential oil**

Mix all the ingredients in a spray bottle, and it's ready!

THE SECRET TO CLEAN, FRESH LAUNDRY

White vinegar is inconspicuous and doesn't leave a trace of color behind; it gets your laundry whiter than white again or ensures a fade-resistant wash.

▶ Softening

A chemical fabric conditioner is unnecessary, as white vinegar is an excellent alternative. Pouring ½ cup (120 milliliters) into the rinse compartment will suffice. If you're worried about the smell, add about 10 drops of essential oil of your choice.

▶ Whitening

Over time and successive washes, white discolors and turns gray. To remove this film spoiling your best cotton shirt, pour 2 to 3 tablespoons of baking soda into the washing detergent compartment or straight into the drum. Run your usual program and it's done. To keep your whites white, soak them regularly in a mixture made with equal parts water and white vinegar. Leave soaking for at least 10 minutes and then put in the washing machine.

▶ Descaling the iron

You're ironing your shirt and it's a disaster: There are traces of black on the fabric because of the limescale that has been deposited in the iron. So to avoid spoiling your clothing and bed linen, take action and unblock the holes in the sole plate. To do this, pour a solution made with equal parts cold water and white vinegar into the water reservoir. For safety reasons, stand above the sink and turn the iron toward the wall. Switch it on and when it starts to steam, leave the iron for 5 minutes in a vertical position and then direct it toward the sink. To remove the limescale, wipe with an old, clean cloth while it's steaming. When the reservoir is empty, fill it with clean water (exercise caution with jets of water from the steam vents and be careful not to burn yourself). Repeat the operation (rinsing and ironing on the cloth) several times until any residue has been completely removed. Leave the iron to cool down.

• **Are there some stubborn traces of limescale** on the holes? Scrub them with a slightly moistened toothbrush soaked in baking soda. Rinse off with a sponge and clean water.

⚠ CAUTION: Never use white vinegar to descale a new iron, as the acidity could damage it.

▶ Removing yellow stains

With the advent of duvet covers, the superb cotton sheets of our grandmothers are of little use. Also, just when they're needed, they reveal ugly yellow marks in the folds. To remove them, arm yourself with a soft, flat brush and either a bowl of skim or part-skim milk. Daub the folds briskly. Allow to dry in the sun, weather permitting. Machine wash on a normal cycle.

▶ Disinfecting

White vinegar is an excellent antibacterial agent. Pour ½ cup (120 milliliters) into the washing detergent compartment and it's done. Or better still, you can reduce the amount of washing detergent by half and the result will be equally good.

▶ Removing pieces of lint

The process of washing or drying creates small pieces of lint that mainly disperse in the machine. To remove them, pour ½ quart (½ liter) of white vinegar straight into the drum and 5 fluid ounces (150 milliliters) into the fabric conditioner compartment. Run the washing machine empty at the cold or warm setting.

• **Take the opportunity** to clean the washing machine too. Pour white vinegar into the drum and it will also be undiluted at the end of the wash.

▶ Fade-resistant laundry

Blue jean dye that remains on the hands, T-shirts that fade . . . nowadays, the quality of clothing is sometimes disappointing and dyes are not always fade-resistant. So before you increase the number of loads you wash, find time to make your clothes fade-resistant. It's easy—just immerse the garment in a bowl containing a mixture of 8 parts cold water to 2 parts white vinegar. Leave soaking for about 10 minutes while making sure that you move the garment around so that every part is covered. Rinse in clean water and avoid drying it in the sun. To improve the result, you can add a good handful of coarse salt to this mixture.

• **Is the item of clothing too big?** Don't be afraid to run it on a cold cycle in the washing machine. Use 5 tablespoons of white vinegar instead of washing detergent.

Don't forget the washing machine
🔔 **TIP**

Caring for your laundry is all well and good, but you should also consider maintaining the washing machine. Once every 2 months, pour 1 quart (1 liter) of white vinegar into the drum and run it empty at the warm setting. In the process of cleaning the drum, the vinegar will descale the circuits.

❗ **CAUTION:** Fabrics made from acetate do not tolerate direct contact with undiluted vinegar. The fibers could melt.

▶Combating perspiration stains

Even after several washes, perspiration odors persist on certain materials such as Lycra. Worse still, the heat of the iron makes them more obvious. To remove these stains, pour some white vinegar onto the armpit area of the garments before putting them in the washing machine. Then slip the garments into the drum, but before turning the machine on, leave to act for 5 to 10 minutes. The garments will emerge odor-free, but you can still pour a few drops of tea tree essential oil into the rinsing compartment if you'd like.

• **If you don't have any vinegar,** cut a lemon in half and dab the marks or use a clean, lint-free cloth soaked in lemon juice. Allow to dry, preferably in the sun. Then put the washing machine on without any washing detergent, but make sure you add 1 tablespoon of hydrogen peroxide at 30 percent to the washing detergent compartment.

⚠ CAUTION: Never replace white vinegar with a colored or a different type of vinegar, as the garment will emerge marked or stained.

THE KING OF THE STUBBORN STAIN

Whether you heat up white vinegar or use it cold, those who are prone to burning and staining everything can rely on it.

⚠ CAUTION: Always remove stains from clothes before putting them in the washing machine...otherwise there's a risk that the stains will be "cooked" and become permanent.

▶ Beer
• **For cotton or wool:** If the stain doesn't come out when you wash it in water, dab it with a solution made with equal parts white vinegar and cold water.
• **For silk, satin, or velvet:** You need to use a clean, lint-free cloth, soaked in alcohol at the warm setting.

• **For synthetic textiles, suede and leather:** Use denatured alcohol.

▶ Chocolate
Here, too, the stain normally fades in cold water. If it's deeply ingrained, dab it with a cloth soaked in undiluted white vinegar.
• **To remove a milk chocolate stain,** pour some sparkling water onto it, let it sit, and then sponge off as much as possible with some paper towels. Then carefully dab with some alcohol at the warm setting. Next, rub a tablet of black soap onto the stain. Finally, put the item in the washing machine.

▶ Wax
Greasy, colored wax stains are insidious because they become ingrained inside the fibers like a dye. With the exception of delicate fabrics, sprinkle some baking soda onto them. Let it sit and then dab with a cloth moistened with white vinegar. Then put in the washing machine.
• **If you don't have any white vinegar,** use a toothbrush with some black soap and then rinse in sparkling water.

• **For delicate materials and fabrics** that are not suitable for washing, such as suede, wood, fur, or silk, remove as much of the wax as possible by carefully scraping it off. Absorb the grease with some paper towels and then apply some turpentine.

• **For leather:** Dab the stain with some paper towels and run a tepid iron over it to lift the grease.

• **For wool:** Dab with a cotton swab soaked in acetone.

Glue

You may well be the king of home improvement and do-it-yourself projects, but hanging wallpaper and making things without spilling a few spots of glue on your clothes is an almost impossible task.

• **To avoid fixing the stains** on cotton, denim, or linen clothes, dab them with a soft, lint-free cloth soaked in a few drops of warm, white vinegar. Rinse and dab with another cloth, this time soaked in clean, hot water.

Ink

Absorb as much of the stain as possible with some paper towels. Then soak with white vinegar. Leave to act and then dab again with some paper towels. Put in the washing machine on a normal cycle.

• **The acidity of white vinegar** has an adverse effect on leather. A cotton swab soaked in cleansing milk and a drop of white vinegar is all you need to remove the stain.

• **Wool:** It cannot tolerate the acidity of white vinegar, so just soak the stain with milk.

TIP

Silverware and silver jewelry

To restore your silver to its former glory, beat one or two egg whites until stiff, and then add a few drops of white vinegar. Use a paintbrush to apply this mixture to the items you want to clean. Allow to dry and then wipe with a cloth and they will be as good as new. Soak your jewelry (except if the items have been bonded with glue) in a bowl filled with white vinegar for 2 hours. Rinse in clean water and wipe dry.

And how about your carpet?

TIP

Rub ink, coffee, rust, and wine stains with a cloth soaked in white vinegar. No need to rinse.

▶ Grass

• **For nondelicate, fade-resistant fabrics:** Dab the stain with a mixture made with 1 part white vinegar to 2 parts water. Rinse in clean water and put in the washing machine.

• **For delicate fabrics and colored fabrics:** Use denatured alcohol instead.

▶ Makeup

Avoid pure water, as it will fix the stains in place.

• **To remove mascara:** Rub it with white vinegar.

• **Lipstick can be removed** with a mixture made with 1 part white vinegar to 2 parts water.

▶ Tannin stains on porcelain

To remove tea stains from porcelain bowls: Rub gently with a sponge soaked in a mixture made with 1 part table salt to 1 part white vinegar.

▶ Clay

Let the clay dry and then brush it. If the stains have been made damp or if they've left behind traces, clean them with a mixture made with 1 tablespoon of white vinegar, 1 tablespoon of black soap, and 1 quart (1 liter) of tepid water. Scrub gently. Rinse in clean water with a damp cloth.

• **If the stains are proving hard to shift,** repeat the process, using more white vinegar this time.

• **You can use lemon juice** instead of white vinegar.

• **If, despite all your efforts,** the orange-colored stains persist, dab them with a cloth soaked in ammonia. Don't forget to rinse.

▶ Tea

• **If the stain is still damp,** quickly clean it with some soapy water (1 tablespoon of black soap to 1 quart [1 liter] tepid water). Rinse in water and white vinegar (two-thirds to one-third mixture).

• **If the stain is dry,** dab it with a lint-free cloth soaked in a mixture made with equal parts white vinegar and alcohol at the warm setting.

• **To remove an ingrained stain,** soak the laundry for 5 to 10 minutes in a mixture of tepid water and white vinegar before rubbing it with a tablet of black soap. Then rinse.

🛈 CAUTION: For wool: Dab the stains with a cloth soaked in lemon juice. Don't forget to rinse.

▶ **Urine**

• **Is the stain still damp?** Sprinkle it immediately with talcum powder. Let it dry until it has been completely absorbed, and then remove the surplus with a brush. Then wash in liquid black soap. The stain and smell will quickly go.

• **For delicate fabrics:** Dab the stain with a cloth soaked in white vinegar and then put it all in the washing machine.

TIP

Does the smell persist?

Cover the stain area with some baking soda. Leave to act overnight before dusting or vacuuming.

BAKING SODA

▶ **Vomit**

To avoid a lingering smell, clean the stains carefully and thoroughly. Spray them with sparkling water. Leave to soak. The bubbles will remove the vomit from the fibers. Next clean with some paper towels. Then scrub with a brush soaked in white vinegar. Rinse and finally, if possible, machine wash with some black soap.

◆

KITCHEN

Pipework, limescale, black marks—nothing can withstand white vinegar.

▶ **Absorbing the smells from the trash can**

Pour a few drops of white vinegar into the garbage bag to eradicate all the unpleasant odors.

▶ **Unblocking the pipework**

Is your sink blocked? Does the water drain too slowly? Is an odor rising up? Then it's time to "purge" the pipework.

First, empty the drain trap. Make sure you place a bowl underneath before you unscrew it. Clean inside by scrubbing the sides with a toothbrush soaked in white vinegar. Make sure that all the debris drops out. Once you've tightened the trap, slide a paper towel underneath and then flush through with water, to make sure that you've put the joint back correctly. If droplets of water form, you'll find that the paper towel gets wet. If this is the case, start again and make sure that you put the joint back properly this time (if it's showing signs of wear and tear, replace it).

☞ *Did you know?*

Which direction should you unscrew the trap? Practically all everyday objects are unscrewed like the lid of a jelly jar—counterclockwise. However, as the trap reservoir points downward, it is unscrewed like a jar held upside down.

• **But emptying the trap and cleaning** a section of it with a toothbrush is not enough. You now need to tackle the sides of the inaccessible pipework. To do this, pour a mixture made with 6.5 fluid ounces (190 milliliters) white vinegar, ¾ cup (180 milliliters) coarse salt, and ¾ cup (180 milliliters) baking soda where the water discharges from the sink. Leave the mixture to work for at least 30 minutes and then rinse through with boiling water. Repeat the process, if necessary.

▶ **For gleaming burners**

To remove cooking traces from induction or ceramic burners, rub with a nonabrasive sponge (if you don't have one, be careful not to scratch the burners) soaked in a mixture made with 1 teaspoon of white vinegar and 2 teaspoons of white Marseille soap. Rinse and dry with a soft cloth.

• **To tackle stubborn stains,** ideally cover them with black soap and leave to act for 5 to 10 minutes, depending on the surface. Then just rub gently using a scraper specially designed for ceramic burners;* rinse

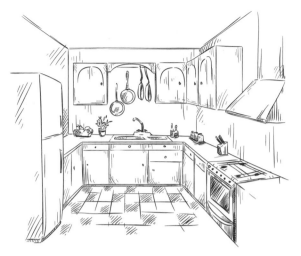

in clean water and finish by wiping with a sponge soaked in white vinegar.

 * It's generally delivered with the ceramic burners, but if not, then this scraper can be purchased in hardware stores.

▸**Removing grease from the deep fryer**
Unplug the machine and let it cool down. Drain the oil and then wipe the sides of the inner chamber with paper towels. Next fill the chamber with white vinegar (one-third). Plug in the fryer and switch it on to heat the white vinegar. Switch off, unplug it, and leave to cool down. Now clean the sides again with paper towels. Rinse with a sponge soaked in clean water and dry with paper towels.
• **To restore the sheen on the outer chamber,** use a damp sponge and a tablet of black soap and rub in a circular motion to avoid spreading the grease. Rinse with

tepid water mixed with 1 to 2 tablespoons of white vinegar, which will prevent any buildup of grease becoming ingrained when you use the fryer again.

❶ CAUTION: Open the windows so that you're working in a ventilated room, because white vinegar can be an irritant.

▸**Removing grease from a microwave**
Have any deposits formed over the weeks? To remove them and eliminate unpleasant odors at the same time, heat a bowl filled with 1 cup (235 milliliters) of white vinegar at maximum temperature for 5 minutes. Leave the glass for another 5 minutes without opening the microwave door. Wipe everything with a damp sponge, then wipe with a dry cloth.
• To enhance the effect and eliminate all odors, add the juice of a lemon to the mixture.

▸**Disinfecting and deodorizing the refrigerator and freezer**
To maximize the performance of your refrigerator and prevent unpleasant odors or bacteria from establishing themselves

in there, clean the interior once a month. Take all the food out, sort through it, discard anything that is past its expiration date, and remove any packaging. Then lift out the racks and wash them in the sink, making sure that you rinse them in water and 1 cup (235 milliliters) of white vinegar afterward. Next, rub the internal surfaces of the refrigerator with a nonabrasive sponge, moistened in tepid water and soaked in white vinegar. No need to rinse but dry them with a lint-free cloth.

• Whether your refrigerator has an automatic defrost or not, once every 3 months use the same recipe to clean the freezer too. Then, to prevent the ice from building up again too quickly, wipe down with a dry, lint-free cloth soaked in white vinegar.

▸ Descaling small appliances

For tea makers, coffee makers, and kettles, white vinegar is the ultimate descaler. But exercise caution—it should never be used undiluted, because when exposed to heat, it becomes a powerful acid.

• **For a coffee maker:** Pour 1 part vinegar to 5 parts water into the reservoir. Switch on the appliance. Let the mixture trickle through until it reaches the halfway point. Turn it off, and leave the product to act for 15 minutes. Switch it on again to empty the reservoir. Wait another 15 minutes

before rinsing it through twice with clean water and making a coffee.

• **For a kettle or tea maker:** Fill them with 5 parts water to 2 parts vinegar. Bring to a boil, switch off, and leave to act for at least 20 minutes. Are there any stains proving hard to remove? Gently bring back to a boil and then leave to act for 10 minutes before rinsing. As with coffee makers, rinse through at least twice with clean water before drinking the water again.

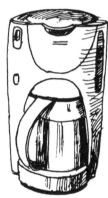

 Did you know?

Where does limescale come from? Faucet water contains calcium, magnesium, and other mineral salts that crystallize into calcium carbonate, which is more commonly known as limescale. The acidity of white vinegar converts this calcium carbonate into calcium bicarbonate. So what's the difference? Calcium carbonate is water resistant while calcium bicarbonate is soluble and therefore can be removed.

A limescale-free kettle

To prevent the kettle from furring up, wash and scrub an oyster shell and slip it inside. The limescale will attach itself to the oyster shell and no longer to the surfaces.

▸ Removing verdigris (patina) from copperware

Copperware is beautiful, but over time verdigris takes hold. To restore your copperware to its former glory, remove the verdigris with a soft, nonabrasive, dampish sponge. Then rub it with a sponge soaked in a mixture made with 1 cup (235 milliliters) of white vinegar and 1 tablespoon of coarse salt. Rinse in clean water and wipe dry.

• **If the white vinegar bottle** is down to its last few drops, use a mixture of lemon juice and salt instead.

① CAUTION: This treatment is not suitable for gilded bronze.

▸ Shiny chrome

In the process of descaling your chrome, restore the shine and remove unsightly stains. To achieve this, rub them with a cloth soaked in undiluted white vinegar.

• **If this doesn't do the trick,** wrap a cloth soaked in white vinegar around your faucets, and leave it for about 10 minutes. No need to rinse, but rub with another clean, dry cloth to give them a shine.

▸ Cleaning the cooker hood

Remove the filter grids, but before putting them in the dishwasher, scrub with a brush and some black soap to loosen the buildup of grease in the crevices. Make sure you rinse them well before putting the dishwasher on. Meanwhile, use a sponge soaked in undiluted white vinegar to combat greasy deposits on the surfaces. To avoid spreading the grease,

☞ *Did you know?*

Verdigris can cause burns and release toxins. If it contacts the skin, wash immediately in soapy water and then rinse thoroughly with plenty of clean water.

always use a circular motion, working from the outside inward.

• **If your cooker hood is very greasy,** gently heat up the white vinegar.

▶Making your glasses sparkle

Over time, glasses discolor and become cloudy. To restore their crystalline appearance, add 2 to 3 tablespoons of white vinegar to your dish water. Rinse in cold, clear water and dry with a clean, lint-free cloth.

• **If this doesn't do the trick,** soak for 15 minutes in a bowl of warm water and white vinegar with a proportion of 3 parts water to 1 part white vinegar. Rinse thoroughly with plenty of clean water and then dry carefully.

• **If your glasses are really dirty,** it's time to give them a makeover. Soak them in very warm water with a handful of soda crystals. Rinse thoroughly in clean water and then dry carefully to remove any traces.

▶Rescuing the preserving pan

Scrubbing your preserving pan is not always an easy task. To clean it without too much effort, make a paste with 1 part white vinegar to 1 part flour and add a ½ part of salt. Take a soft, lint-free cloth to work in thoroughly, using a circular motion. Leave for several hours before rinsing and polishing with a wool cloth.

• **If you don't have any white vinegar,** use lemon juice instead.

▶Scouring the sink

You wash the dishes and clean the vegetables in it, so it must always be clean. If it's made from stainless steel, never use abrasive products, as they're guaranteed to cause scratches. Sprinkle a mixture made with 1 part baking soda to 1 part coarse salt over the sink. Rub with a nonabrasive sponge. Use a toothbrush to remove all the grime from around the drain. Rinse in hot water and then wipe with a cloth soaked in white vinegar.

• **If it's made from resin,** a sponge soaked in soapy water (1 teaspoon of white Marseille soap) or dish detergent will suffice to remove the grease. Rinse in clean water and dry with a cloth. Are the stains proving hard to remove? Use black soap. Mix a tablet of black soap in a small bowl of tepid water. Rub, leave in for a few minutes, rinse, and wipe with a soft, dry cloth.

⊘ CAUTION:

• **Resin sinks, washbasins, and bathtubs** don't tolerate abrasive products. So never use bleach, anti-limescale products, detergents, and even abrasive sponges equipped with scouring pads on them.

TIP

A clean sink

To restore the spotless sheen to your stainless-steel sink, sprinkle it with 1 heaping tablespoon of flour and then polish with a cloth.

• **Be careful** before you empty pans of boiling water down your sink. Some resins are less resistant than others to intense heat.

• **If you have an enamel sink,** soak a sponge with baking soda and rub it until you've removed the unsightly black marks that form on the back and the sides after washing a pan or a pot in it. To remove the yellowish film and restore the original whiteness to the enamel, you can also use white vinegar. Leave to act for 5 minutes, rinse in clean water, and polish with a dry, lint-free cloth.

▶ Scouring a dish or saucepan

You no longer need to use elbow grease to remove burned-on food that sticks to the bottom of gratin dishes and various rice dishes. Pour some white vinegar into the saucepan or the dish (cover the bottom with at least a centimeter of liquid), and bring to a boil for 5 minutes. When the food starts to loosen, rub it gently with a thin spatula or a knife with a rounded blade to remove it completely. Rinse in clean water. If necessary, repeat the process.

▶ Removing deposits from carafes, pitchers, and bottles

If your carafes, pitchers, or bottles have unsightly deposits, it's time for a cleaning. Pour 2 cups (475 milliliters) of hot white vinegar (not boiling hot) into the carafe and then add ½ cup (120 milliliters) of uncooked rice. Leave for 10 minutes and then shake vigorously. The white vinegar will remove the deposits and the rice will absorb them. Empty and rinse.

• **If the deposits are proving hard to remove,** fill the carafe with hot white vinegar (but not boiling hot) and crushed eggshells. Leave overnight. The next day, shake vigorously, and then empty out the mixture. Rinse in hot water and wipe dry.

▸Cleaning the gas range

If the burners on your gas stove switch off in dramatic fashion, then it's time to remove the grime. Soak them overnight in a bowl filled with undiluted white vinegar and then rinse in clean water and wipe them thoroughly.

• **If the burned-on stains have become ingrained,** spray some undiluted white vinegar onto paper towels and clean around the rings where the grime is attached. Leave and in the morning you'll be pleasantly surprised to see that these deposits have disappeared effortlessly.

• **To polish the gas range,** soak your sponge with soapy water and add a few drops of white vinegar.

▸Taking care of your linoleum

Practical to maintain, the new plastic or PVC linoleums look great, provided they

Using an eraser on linoleum TIP

To remove black streaks and fine scratches on linoleum without scraping it: Erase them with the traditional two-tone ink eraser. Use the soft pink side for the streaks and the more abrasive blue side for the scratches.

aren't stained or discolored. So to clean and protect them, use water mixed with white vinegar and white Marseille soap to remove grease on a regular basis.

BATHROOM

You relax, unwind, and chill out in the bathroom, so if you want to pamper yourself, you should first look after this room, which is often small but very private.

▸Tile joint whitener

Without effective sealant (grout), tile joints can gather dirt, start lifting off, and get moldy, which opens the door to seepage. To avoid these problems, find time to scrub the tile joints with a toothbrush soaked in undiluted white vinegar and then wipe them with a microfiber cloth.

• **If you've run out of white vinegar,** use black soap instead.

❶ CAUTION: If, despite your best efforts, the tile joints are still black, it's because the mold has been allowed to grow unchecked. So you will need to renew them.

▶ For gleaming floor tiles

For a spotless floor, a bit of elbow grease is required. Rub the ingrained marks with tepid white vinegar. But take note, it's better to use it cold on colored floor tiles. Leave to soak in for a few minutes and rinse in clean water.

• **If the smell of white vinegar troubles you**, use a sponge soaked in lemon juice and sprinkled with coarse salt instead. Leave the mixture on for a few minutes and rinse in clean water.

▶ Removing stains from the shower curtain

If the shower curtain is dotted with black marks, these are mold stains. To remove them, rub the curtain with the abrasive side of a sponge soaked in warm white vinegar. Do not rinse, but put it in the washing machine. Set the washing machine on cold, making sure you add 3 tablespoons of baking soda to the washing detergent compartment.

▶ Cleaning the toilets

Overnight is a good time to disinfect, clean, and descale the toilets. Pour a liter of extremely hot white vinegar onto the sides and into the bowl. Leave in overnight and then scrub the sides with a sponge (making sure that you clean under

Eliminating unpleasant odors

If foul odors are rising up from the pipework, clean the drains on a regular basis because hair, pieces of soap, and so on, accumulate down there. Prepare some ice cubes made with a mixture of 3 parts water to 2 parts white vinegar. One night a week, before you go to bed, place two ice cubes over the drains. As they trickle along the sides of the pipework, they'll melt very slowly and will remove unpleasant odors.

❶ CAUTION: To differentiate between the vinegar ice cubes and the normal ice cubes and to avoid any problems, pour a colorant into the vinegar cubes, a few aromatic herbs such as thyme, and label them very clearly, or put them into a sealed bag.

the rim, which is where limescale builds up the most). Flush the toilet to rinse it away. Are there any traces of limescale left? Repeat the process several times.

If traces of limescale are still proving hard to remove, scrub the sides with a slightly damp sponge covered in baking soda. Leave to act. Then add 1 quart (1 liter) of white vinegar. Be careful the mixture doesn't bubble up and into your eyes. Leave the mixture in overnight. The next day, scrub the entire bowl with a sponge before flushing the toilet to rinse it all away.

❶ **EXERCISE CAUTION** with fumes rising from the white vinegar, as they can be an irritant. Make sure you open the windows or ventilate the bathroom.

▶**For a pristine shower screen**

Is your shower screen more often white than transparent because of the effects of limescale? Soap it with a sponge soaked in a mixture of black soap and denatured alcohol. Leave in for a few minutes, rinse, and dry with a microfiber cloth. To enhance the shine, you can add a drop of citric acid.

☞ *Did you know?*

Do you have leftover soda? Even if it's gone flat, pour it into the toilets. Let it sit for 2 hours and then scrub with a brush while concentrating on the edges. Flush the toilet and the limescale traces will disappear and the toilet bowl will shine.

• **TIP:** Prepare your mixture in advance. Pour 1 tablespoon of black soap and ½ teaspoon of denatured alcohol into a cup of warm water.

▶**A gleaming bathtub**

Has your enamel bathtub become more gray than white over time? Rub it with half a lemon covered in salt and then wipe with a cloth soaked in warm white vinegar. Leave to act for a few minutes, rinse and dry.
• If you have a resin bathtub, using abrasive products is not an option. Always use mild products. To keep it clean, just wipe with a sponge or a soft cloth soaked in liquid black soap. Rinse in clean water.

▶**A gleaming mirror**

Letting your mirror become smeary is not an option. Soak a ball of newspaper in a solution made with 1 part white vinegar to 4 quarts (4 liters) of water. No need to rinse. Allow to dry. The vinegar will leave a film that is invisible to the naked eye but will prevent condensation from settling too quickly.

A detangling conditioner

To restore vitality and softness to your hair and above all to enable you to untangle it easily, shampoo it with a mixture made with 1 to 2 tablespoons of white vinegar and 1 tablespoon of water before you give your hair a final rinse. Leave on for 3 minutes and then rinse thoroughly in tepid water. Be careful to protect your eyes!

▶ **For a powerful shower jet**

We descale faucets, but showerheads are often forgotten even though their nozzles quickly clog up with limescale. To remove it, unscrew the showerhead and soak for 30 minutes in a bowl of undiluted white vinegar. Make sure that the nozzles are thoroughly submerged. Before rinsing, scrub them with a toothbrush to remove the limescale deposits. Soak for an additional 15 minutes and rinse in clean water.
• Is the showerhead impossible to unscrew? Pour 1 quart (1 liter) of white vinegar (or more, depending on size) into a plastic bag and secure this around the showerhead with a rubber band. Leave to act overnight. Remove the plastic bag,

scrub the nozzles with a toothbrush, and then turn on the water to rinse them. Finally, wipe with a sponge soaked in clean water.

❶ CAUTION: Make sure that you protect your eyes.

MAKING ROOMS MORE APPEALING

Even if you're not a fan of housework, a bit of cleaning is necessary. How fortunate, then, that white vinegar removes grease,

Lice repellent

If these nasty little bugs have taken up residence in your kids' hair (or in yours), wash it once with a mixture made with 1 part white vinegar to 2 parts warm water. Leave in for 5 minutes. Although it's not strong enough to kill lice, its acidic action dissolves the egg envelopes of the nits. By preventing them from reaching maturity, it slows down their proliferation, which is something at least.

disinfects, deodorizes, and even gives a shine with just the wipe of a cloth.

··

▸ **For sparkling windows and mirrors**

Mix 1 part white vinegar to 5 parts tepid water to make a very effective cleaning product for glass and to restore windows and mirrors to their former glory. To prevent marks, wipe in a circular motion and in particular make sure you dry them thoroughly with a lint-free cloth. And above all, never wash windowpanes on sunny days, as this will leave streaks and the products will dry too quickly.

▸ **Say goodbye to diaper odors**

To reduce baby diaper odors, pour 1 tablespoon of undiluted white vinegar into the diaper bin.

▸ **Cleaning the insert glass (fireplace)**

White vinegar and a few grams of coarse salt work very well. Rub with a sponge soaked in this mixture. Rinse in clean water and wipe dry with a cloth.

CAUTION: Sweep the chimney regularly to avoid any risk of fire.

▸ **Removing dust from a mattress**

To prevent nighttime becoming less appealing than daytime, regular cleaning is necessary. Make sure that you clean the upholstery attachment before you start and then remove the dust from your mattresses and bedspring with the vacuum cleaner.

• **To ward off dust mites,** spray a mixture made with ⅔ cup (160 milliliters) denatured alcohol, 1½ cups (350 milliliters) water, and 5 drops of lemon essential oil evenly onto the mattress every 3 months. Allow to dry naturally or use a hairdryer.

• **Have you run out of white vinegar?** Use natural vodka instead, which will be just as effective!

• **To disinfect the mattress more thoroughly,** mix 1 cup (235 milliliters) of baking soda and 1 quart (1 liter) of white vinegar in a bowl. Be careful, as this will set off a chemical reaction; let it froth and

☞ *Did you know?*

The best cloth for glass is moistened newsprint (from newspapers and not from magazines).

TIP

Adding fragrance to your white vinegar

Do you find the smell of white vinegar pungent? No problem! Just pour about 10 drops of essential oil into the bottle. If you'd prefer to make your own fragrance, put some fresh flower petals—ideally scented—or citrus peel (orange, grapefruit, lemon) into an empty white vinegar bottle. Then fill the bottle with undiluted white vinegar. Close the bottle and leave it all to steep for at least a week before use.

then once the mixture has subsided, take a sponge soaked in this solution and rub the mattress vigorously. Make sure that you wear protective gloves. Absorb the excess with kitchen towels. Allow to dry naturally or use a hair dryer.

▶ Disinfecting baby toys

Babies constantly carry their toys in their mouth and leave them lying around all over the place; not to mention the kind of toys that end up in the bathtub have a tendency to be grubby. Clean the toys with a sponge soaked in a tablet of black soap or Marseille soap. For the hard-to-reach

areas, use a toothbrush. Rinse in clean water and then soak them for about 10 minutes in a bowl of cold water mixed with 1 or 2 cups (235 to 475 milliliters) of white vinegar. For large toys, rub them regularly with a cloth soaked in white vinegar.

🛈 CAUTION: Take the baby out of the room while you're cleaning the toys so that the smell doesn't upset them, and ventilate the room.

▶ Deodorizing a closet

A damp sheet has been put away too soon and an unpleasant musty smell fills your closet or dresser. To combat it, clean the shelves with a sponge soaked in a mixture made with 10 fluid ounces (300 milliliters) of white vinegar and 6.5 fluid ounces (200 milliliters) water. Add 5 drops of tea tree essential oil for its effectiveness as a disinfectant and purifier. Concentrate on the mold stains and then dry thoroughly.

Leave the door open for several days to let the air circulate.

❶ CAUTION: Never use tea tree essential oil near pregnant or lactating women, or near children or pets.

▶ Removing deposits from flower vases

To restore your vase to its former glory, fill it with 1 part tepid water to 2 parts white vinegar. Leave to act overnight. At this point, empty out a little of the liquid and shake the vase over the sink so that all the deposits come loose.

• **Are some residues proving hard to remove?** Rub them either with a toothbrush or a bottle brush. Empty out the water and rinse in clean water. If necessary, repeat the process.

▶ Cleaning the fitted carpet

To deep-clean it, mix 2 parts sparkling water to 1 part white vinegar. Rub with a scrubbing brush. In the event of stubborn stains, use undiluted white vinegar.

▶ Cleaning wood floors

To clean your wood floors, all you need is a cloth or a microfiber floor cloth and a mixture made with 1 part cold water to 1 part white vinegar. To give it extra freshness, you can add 5 to 10 drops of pine, eucalyptus, or tea tree essential oil to the mixture.

❶ CAUTION: Unsealed or unsprung wood floors are not washed, but polished!

▶ Reviving cut flowers

To prolong the life of your splendid bouquet of cut flowers, for every quart of water add a mixture made with 2 tablespoons of white vinegar and 2 tablespoons of superfine sugar.

▶ Polishing your gold frames

Eggs are not only used in the kitchen, but they also revive gold paint. First thoroughly remove the dust from the frame, and then use a paintbrush to apply a mixture of egg whites beaten until stiff and 1 tablespoon of warm white vinegar. Rinse as you go along with the aid of a damp cloth and then wipe dry.

❶ CAUTION: For antique gilt frames, it's better to seek advice from a specialist.

Whether doing odd jobs around the house, gardening, treating all kinds of aches and pains, looking after pets, or cleaning and maintaining vehicles, white vinegar is an essential ally.

WHITE VINEGAR: THE EVERYDAY ALLY

HOMEMADE VINEGAR PRODUCTS

You no longer need to resort to toxic solvents for small everyday jobs, as white vinegar is often a viable alternative.

▸**Removing wallpaper**
• **No wallpaper stripper on hand?** Pour 1 part water to 1 part white vinegar into a spray bottle. Mix, and then spray onto the wallpaper. Leave to act for 5 to 10 minutes, depending on the thickness of the paper. Then peel it away gently with a scraper.
• **TIP:** To enable the mixture to penetrate more easily, particularly through thick wallpaper, detach it lightly with the scraper. Proceed square by square and

lift the paper starting from the bottom, working your way up to the top.

❶ CAUTION: Spraying water onto the surface doesn't work on vinyl wallpapers, and with good reason, as they're intended to be used in humid rooms (bathrooms, kitchens) and are renowned for their impermeability. To tackle them, first you need to rub vinyl wallpapers with sandpaper, in order to remove the waterproof layer.

▸**Stripping a cement floor**
To get a cement floor looking as good as new, rub it with a scrubbing brush soaked in cold, undiluted white vinegar. Rinse in fresh water with a clean floor cloth.

▸**Rust removal**
Do you have some old tools or rusty scooter parts? Soak them for 24 hours in a bowl filled with undiluted white vinegar, or diluted with 2 parts water to 8 parts white vinegar. Make sure that the item for cleaning is completely submerged. To speed up the process, add a handful of coarse salt. Rinse in clean water.
• **If it isn't possible to soak them,** take a brush soaked in white vinegar and coat the items until the rust marks have vanished. Rinse them with a clean cloth soaked in fresh water.

• **Have you run out of vinegar?** Try soda! In the battle against rust on chrome and stainless steel, it's infallible. Pour some soda on the area to be cleaned and leave to act for a few minutes. Rub gently, and if necessary use a nonabrasive sponge (but be careful not to scratch it). Rinse in clean water and dry with a lint-free cloth.

Itchy hands TIP

Have you got itchy hands? It's not surprising when you renovate a kitchen or a bathroom. Irritations can occur after touching plaster, cement, and other construction materials. To alleviate the itching, rub your hands with a solution made with 1 cup (235 milliliters) of white vinegar and 2 cups (475 milliliters) of cold water, and then wash your hands with Marseille soap. The acid in the vinegar will neutralize the alkaline content of these materials.

Tendinitis TIP

To alleviate tendinitis, soak a compress in a mixture made with 1 cup (235 milliliters) of vinegar and a handful of coarse salt, and then apply to the affected area. Leave on for 15 minutes. Repeat three to four times a day.

▸**Diluting glue**

Has your white wood glue or fabric glue become too thick? Dilute it with a few drops of white vinegar to restore its uniform texture.

▸**Eliminating paint odors**

Although most paints are odorless nowadays, some smells are nevertheless emitted during the drying process. To reduce the odors as quickly as possible, put out one, two, or three bowls (adjust the amount depending on the surface area) of undiluted white vinegar, open the window a little, close the door, and wait a few hours.

Can you still smell it? Renew the white vinegar and change the bowls.

▸**Bonding the paint**

Do you need to repaint the metal chairs in the garden? Make sure that you rub them down with fine sandpaper first, and then take a clean, lint-free cloth soaked in white vinegar to wash down each chair (make sure you tend to the joints and the exposed parts). The acidity of the vinegar will eventually clean and remove grease from the surfaces, and it creates a micro-porosity that enables the paint to adhere better. Allow to dry. Result: The paint will take longer to peel off.

▶ Looking after your brushes

To restore dry brushes or brushes impregnated with glue, boil some white vinegar and pour it into a container. Soak them for 24 hours. They'll emerge clean and silky.

THE BACKYARD'S ALLY AND AN INSECT'S ENEMY

Eliminate ants and control slugs with 3 tablespoons of white vinegar, and you'll find that cultivating your backyard will virtually become child's play.

▶ Repelling bees

There's nothing more enjoyable than eating outdoors in summer, except that most of the time bees do everything they can to spoil it. So to avoid getting stressed, drive them away. Place a few small bowls on the table half filled with a mixture made with 1 tablespoon of honey, 3.5 fluid ounces (100 milliliters) of white vinegar, and 13.5 fluid ounces (400 milliliters) of water to reduce the odor.

▶ Repelling spiders

Whether you view them as a sign of hope or grief, there are no two ways about it, spiders often cause fear. To avoid getting stressed, prevent them from coming into your house. It's simple: Take a sponge soaked in white vinegar and rub around the doors and windows on a regular basis.

• **Have they already moved in?** Send them packing with lavender. They can't abide it, whether in the form of bouquets or essential oil.

▸Is your soil chalky?

Armed with a spade in one hand and a rake in the other, you're all set to turn over the soil all through the backyard to mix the nutrients. A good idea provided that you plant the right plants in the right soil. Marguerites, campanula, and honeysuckle need an alkaline soil and don't thrive in an acid soil. So before you buy everything in sight at the garden center, assume the role of the alchemist and check the quality of your soil.

• **Divide a handful of soil** between two bowls. Put ½ cup (120 milliliters) of white vinegar in one bowl, and then ½ cup of water mixed with 2 tablespoons of baking soda in the other and watch what happens. Does the mixture containing the white vinegar become frothy? If so, you have a chalky and alkaline soil. Is the mixture containing the baking soda bubbling? If so, you have an acid soil. Nothing's happening? Then you undoubtedly have a neutral soil (pH 7).

☞ *Did you know?*

To enhance the effect of the white vinegar, ideally carry out the weeding when the sun is out, before your annuals go to seed, or when they are at their weakest, to prevent them from spreading too quickly.

Sunburn TIP

Dab the area with a compress soaked in white vinegar to soothe the effects of sunburn.

▸Effortless weeding

Are weeds invading the paths and patios? White vinegar can do the job of eradicating them—in two stages. First, it burns off the parts of the plant exposed to the air that it comes in contact with. Second, as the vinegar is being conveyed by the sap, it destroys the plant completely. For this purpose, you either spray a solution made with 1 part water to 1 part white vinegar directly

onto the plant, or spray it around the base of the plants. To improve the chances of success, add a small piece of black soap to the mixture to help it adhere to the plants.

⚠ CAUTION: Do not misuse this recipe, because if the white vinegar rapidly biodegrades, any mishandling could acidify the soil.

▶ Cleaning the pots

Pots protect plants, but over time, watering, rainwater, sand, and wind tarnish them and limescale deposits can start building up. To restore them to their former glory, scrub them with a stiff bristle brush soaked in a mixture of warm water and white vinegar, using 2 parts white vinegar to 5 parts water. If the pots are small, immerse them in a bowl.

▶ Dispersing ant colonies

Although appealing and inoffensive, ants are annoying. When you find one, you can be sure that you'll discover a whole colony. To send them packing, just pour some white vinegar, lemon juice (discard the peel), coffee grounds, or fireplace ash in their path.

• **Are you afraid they'll colonize the cupboards?** Place an envelope of green sage or camphor in your cupboards, as they can't abide these odors.

• **And if you really can't tolerate these convoys of ants,** locate the nest and flood it with 10 quarts (10 liters) of hot water mixed with 6.5 fluid ounces (200 milliliters) diluted black soap.

▶ Catching flies

While, as the old saying goes, you catch more flies with honey than with vinegar, thanks to vinegar, you can put them to flight once and for all. Pour some white vinegar into a small dish and it's done. If you find the odor offensive, reduce it by simply adding 1 tablespoon of grated Marseille soap.

• **If you don't want to leave small dishes** around the house, clean the windows with a cloth soaked in white vinegar. It will not only give them a brilliant shine, but it will also prevent insects from approaching.

TIP

Insect bites

If you're bitten by a mosquito, a spider, a flea, or even an ant, just dab the bite with a compress soaked in white vinegar for a few minutes to stop yourself from scratching it later.

Spray in the early morning or early evening. Never spray during the hottest times of the day, in direct sunlight, or when it's raining, because you risk damaging the plants.

▸ **An end to mosquitoes**

To eradicate them, spray white vinegar mixed with a few drops of eucalyptus essential oil directly onto them.

▸ **Repelling aphids**

Without warning, they colonize plants. To eradicate them, spray them with a liter of water mixed with 5 to 6 tablespoons of white vinegar. Make sure that you specifically target the infested plants to avoid harming insects that are allies of the backyard, such as the ladybug.

▸ **Replenishing rosebushes**

Have you noticed that your rosebushes are not looking their best? Are the flowers losing their color and perfume? Over several consecutive evenings, spray them with a solution made with 1 quart (1 liter) of water, 1 tablespoon of milk, and 1 tablespoon of white vinegar, and they will be restored to their former glory. However, be careful not to drown them—spray each flower just once.

AN ANIMAL'S ALLY

We adore our four-legged friends, but they leave their mark all around the house.

▸ **Tackling cat urine odors**

Mimi may be clean, but urine odors linger even if you wash and rinse her litter box on a regular basis.

To eliminate these odors from fabrics or the carpet, mix 5 tablespoons of sparkling water and 3 tablespoons of white vinegar. Soak the affected area with this mixture and leave to act. No need to rinse. Repeat the process until the odor has completely gone. Then absorb the excess with some paper towels.

• **Have you run out of sparkling water?** Use 3 teaspoons of baking soda instead. Be careful when you're mixing it in, as it will froth.

• **On hard floors** such as cement and concrete (with the exception of marble), prepare a mixture made

with 3 tablespoons of white vinegar and 1½ tablespoons of lemon. Scrub the stain and then rinse with clean water. Dry with a clean cloth in a circular motion working from the outside inward, so that you don't spread it.

▶ Protecting the walls from dog urine

Fido is adorable but not a single wall is spared. So this time, resort to drastic measures. Mix 1 part white vinegar to 1 part water and add 3 tablespoons of black pepper, whole mustard, baking soda, and lemon juice. Pour the mixture into a spray bottle and apply to the bottom of the walls. The odor will put him off.

▶ Protecting electric wires

It's not easy to train a kitten. Turn your back for a second and there he is gnawing through the computer cables in the blink of an eye. To prevent him from stripping them bare, wipe them with a cloth soaked

Eliminating fleas

These unpleasant little bugs love hiding on pets. To remove them, apply a solution made with 1 cup (235 milliliters) of water and 1 cup (235 milliliters) of white vinegar to his coat. Make sure you work it in well. They'll scuttle away in no time, as they can't stand this odor.

❶ **WARNING:** White vinegar is used to deodorize and keep your dog's coat in good condition, but use cider vinegar for other parts of his body (e.g., ears).

in white vinegar. He'll be stopped in his tracks, because he can't stand the smell.

PAMPERING YOUR CAR

Taking your vehicle through the carwash or high-pressure water jets is not always

enough to maintain it, and you often need to use a bit of elbow grease to protect it.

....

▸ Shiny bodywork

Does your car simply need a good rinse to get it looking pristine again? Rub it with a nonabrasive sponge soaked in a mixture made with 5 parts water to 2 parts white vinegar, and then dry with a microfiber cloth. It will give the bodywork a shine and remove traces of limescale at the same time.

• **Does it need a more thorough clean?** Before soaping it, be sure to park it in the shade: The bodywork paint doesn't tolerate being washed in full sun and you'll risk creating indelible limescale deposits.

☞ *Did you know?*

The damage done to a car's bodywork is not due to the corrosive effect of acid substances contained in bird droppings, but to the combination "duration and heat." In practical terms: The longer the droppings remain on the bodywork, and the more the exterior temperature rises (beware of the sun), the harder the deposit will become, and the more the paint will form a solid mold that is impossible to remove without damaging the paintwork, once it has cooled down.

A gleaming bodywork

TIP

Make sure that your car stays in shape. From now on, regularly treat it with a polish that is "specially designed for bodywork." This will not prevent the pigeons from forgetting themselves, but the paintwork will "cook" more slowly and the droppings can be removed more easily.

• **To remove bird droppings and greasy marks,** clean your car with a nonabrasive sponge soaked in 1 part black soap to 5 parts tepid water. No need to rinse, but wipe with a microfiber cloth.

▸ Shiny wheel rims

To restore them to their former glory, rub with a soft, dry brush to remove leaves, debris, and other muddy traces. Then wash them with a damp sponge and a tablet of black soap. Rinse in clean water

Insect-free headlights

To remove insects from your headlights, rub them with a toothbrush soaked in toothpaste. Rinse in clean water and dry with a lint-free cloth.

with a microfiber cloth soaked in undiluted white vinegar. No need to rinse the vinegar, but wipe the wheel rims with another cloth to give them a shine. Remember to rinse the sponge out regularly.

⚠ CAUTION: Never apply white vinegar to aluminum wheel rims. Use a mixture made with 1 cup (235 milliliters) of soda crystals and 2 quarts (2 liters) of warm water instead. Rub them with a soft brush and rinse immediately. Then dry with a cloth.

▶ An amazing demister and an excellent deicer

To prevent condensation forming too quickly on the inside of the car windows, rub them with newspaper rolled into a ball and soaked in white vinegar.

It will leave behind a light protective film that will prevent them from misting up.

• **Have you run out of white vinegar,** but do you own a cat? Use some of her cat litter! Fill a knee-high stocking with a good handful of litter, preferably made from silica. Knot it and then place it near the windows. After a few days, the condensation will disappear.

• **If you rub the exterior** of the car windows with vinegar in winter, it will prevent ice from building up, so that you can remove it more easily.

▶ Cleaning the windshield wiper blades

If your windshield wipers struggle to clean the windshield and you don't have the time or money replace them, give them a second lease on life. Use a dry cloth to remove all the dirt, and then finish with a cloth soaked in water and white vinegar for the blades.

▶ Removing stains from car seats and floor mats

It's difficult to keep a car clean with children dropping chocolate and crackers all the time. To revive your fabric seats, vacuum them first and then rub them with a soft brush soaked in a mixture made with 2 cups (475 milliliters) of sparkling water and 1 cup

TIP

Absorbing odors

TIP

You can of course open the windows, but it's generally not enough to eliminate all the odors that fester in a car. Pour 4 drops of essential oil onto a clay pebble and place or attach it somewhere. Make sure you choose an oil that doesn't have too strong an odor or it will be overpowering.

(235 milliliters) of white vinegar. No need to rinse but you can wipe them down with some paper towels to speed up the drying time.

• **The faster you clean a stain,** the easier it is to remove. The only exception to that rule is mud stains. You need to let mud dry before cleaning it, so that it can be easily eliminated. Remove as much of the mud as possible with a knife and then pour some sparkling water over it. Then rub with a brush soaked in a mixture

made with 1 teaspoon of black soap, 1 teaspoon of white vinegar, and 1 quart (1 liter) of warm water. No need to rinse, but dry with paper towels.

• **For leather seats:** Use a cloth soaked in cleansing milk instead of white vinegar and water.

▸ **Give your bicycle tires a better grip**

Do your tires fail to grip properly, especially on wet surfaces? Remove the dust with a soft brush and then rub with some white vinegar.

◆

THE VINEGAR FAMILY

▸ **Light malt vinegar**

This is white vinegar that has been colored. It gets its amber color from added caramel.

▸Red wine vinegar

This vinegar is the oldest. Gourmet versions are reminiscent of the wine flavors from which it's produced, and so it's particularly prized in the kitchen. Nowadays, it's adapted in a thousand and one ways. Aside from the traditional wine vinegar (young or old), some are flavored with shallots, tarragon, garlic, and fruit (raspberry, blackcurrant, etc.).

• If **"traditional wine vinegar"** is printed on the label, it means that it's been formulated in accordance with the French Orleans Method; however, if nothing is mentioned, it means that it's been formulated in accordance with the submerged fermentation method and then aged in oak barrels. The term "aged wine vinegar" indicates that it has been formulated with a fermented wine before its conversion to vinegar.

▸Sherry vinegar

Made in Spain, sherry vinegar is aged in oak barrels that have contained sherry wine. This is what gives it such a distinctive nutty flavor. The logo "Sherry Vinegar" must appear on the label, which is the only guarantee of origin and product conformity. Of course, although it's a perfect accompaniment to Spanish cuisine, surprisingly it's also used to make chocolate desserts.

▸Cider vinegar

Derived from the fermentation of cider, its degree of acidity is reduced. Its light odor and flavor go with delicate dishes such as fish. Cider vinegar is also used for body care, beauty care, and animal care.

▸Balsamic vinegar of Modena

Originating from the Modena region of Italy, it's made from the grape juice of the sweet Trebbiano grape. The process of producing it requires numerous manipulations and it must age for a period of 12 to 25 years in wooden barrels.

In addition, the genuine "aceto balsamico tradizionale di Modena" (traditional balsamic vinegar of Modena) is safeguarded by a protected designation of origin (PDO) and is expensive. Indeed, most inexpensive balsamic vinegars are in reality made with a mixture of grape juice, vinegar, and caramel. With a balanced sweet and sour flavor, it reigns supreme over Italian cuisine, but also over desserts. A dash of this vinegar gives figs, strawberries, and melons a real kick.

▸Banyuls vinegar

Delicate with warm spicy notes, rich in aromas and typically Mediterranean, this vinegar must age for 4 years in oak barrels exposed to the sun. Once it has converted to acetic acid in accordance with a traditional method, it is then refined in barrels for 12 months.

▸Reims (champagne) vinegar

This is produced with an ounce or two of the sediment collected from champagne bottles. It needs 4 years of filtration and aging before it reaches the marketplace (3 years in the champagne cellars and 1 year in their barrels).

▸And vinegars are available in every country . . .

• **Whey vinegar** is made from skim milk that is first converted to alcohol and then to acetic acid. Amber-colored and made in Switzerland, it has a distinctive flavor.

• **Malt vinegar** is of course enjoyed by the British. Made from cereals (mainly barley), there's nothing like it when it comes to giving the famous fish and chips a kick.

• **Rice vinegar** is made with rice wine or sake. The Chinese and Japanese use it a lot in their cuisine, but also for healing, as it's renowned for its medicinal qualities.

3
BAKING SODA

Clean · Deodorize · Descale

BAKING SODA

. . . MAGICAL AND NATURAL

Once you've discovered baking soda, you'll never want to be without it. A true miracle product, it's very inexpensive and versatile. It makes your laundry whiter, removes stains, freshens the air, and eliminates unpleasant odors. And that's not all—its fine consistency and alkaline properties are great for beauty care and staying healthy; and in cookery, it gives all our dishes a hint of perfection.

Edible, biodegradable, nontoxic, preservative-free, water soluble, odorless, an antacid, anti-limescale, and a gentle abrasive, this fine white powder stacks up a host of advantages in its own right.

A deodorizing agent, disinfectant, and stain remover, baking soda can be used instead of most household products around the home. Sometimes, it must be combined with other miracle products such as white vinegar, lemon, and salt.

In the kitchen, it's renowned for making dishes more digestible, for helping pastry to rise, and helping vegetables retain their color.

For beauty care, it softens bathtub water and skin, replaces exfoliating products, whitens the teeth, and reduces dandruff.

The health benefits of baking soda include tackling mouth ulcers and bad breath and aiding digestion and reducing stomach acid.

BAKING SODA OR BICARBONATE OF SODA?

Baking soda, sodium bicarbonate, bicarbonate of soda, bicarbonate, sodium hydrogen carbonate—these are five names for the same product. Baking powder, however, is mostly used in baking. It is a mixture of baking soda, an acidifying agent (cream of tartar), and a drying agent (usually starch).

▶ **Back to school**

The chemical formula of *Natrii hydrogeno-carbonas* (Latin name) is $NaHCO_3$, which is not to be confused with sodium carbonate, Na_2CO_3 (soda crystals), or caustic soda, whose formula is $NaOH$.

Na is the chemical symbol of sodium, H is the chemical symbol of hydrogen, and CO_3 is the chemical symbol of carbonate (ion formed from an atom of carbon and three atoms of oxygen).

Sodium bicarbonate is a chemical compound composed of sodium (Na) and the ion bicarbonate (HCO_3).

It is this ion "bicarbonate" that does everything. Naturally present in nature and in our body, it intervenes in many necessary mechanisms for the survival of all things. Slightly alkaline, bicarbonate facilitates a healthy pH (hydrogen potential) balance of the body (blood, saliva), water, and many other environments.

Because of this ion, baking soda is called a "buffer" substance. Its ability to balance the pH makes it just as effective in combating aches and pains as tackling acid corrosion in the pipework or removing grime that is often composed of fatty acids. For the same reason, it's also a water softener.

The chemical structure of bicarbonate also makes it something of a miracle product: When it comes in contact with an acid product such as vinegar or lemon, it releases carbon dioxide (CO_2) in the form of bubbles. This property also makes our cakes or pastries rise. Bicarbonate can be

found in the ingredient list of many food products and carbonated drinks under the code E 500 (ii).

▸**Where does it come from?**
Originally, it was extracted from natron, a mineral that is formed on the surface of lakes rich in sodium and in dried-up riverbeds. Nowadays, it is derived from the industrial transformation of a mixture of chalk and rock salt, coming from deposits in Africa or North America.

In 1791, the French chemist Nicolas Leblanc formulated sodium bicarbonate from the sodium carbonate of plants, by way of an artificial process. But it was not until 1846 that bicarbonate became industrialized, due to the method developed by two New Yorkers: John Dwight and Austin Church. Back then, bicarbonate was manufactured from sodium carbonate and carbon dioxide.

In the 1860s, Belgian chemist Ernest Solvay developed a new, more economical method with a rock salt and chalk base. Nowadays, this is the most widely used manufacturing method, although baking soda is primarily extracted from natron in the United States.

It is said that the Ancient Egyptians were already using this white powder for the purpose of embalming, as well as for hygiene and cleaning. They extracted the powder from the mineral natron from evaporated African salt lakes.

HOW SHOULD YOU STORE IT?

If you've forgotten all about your baking soda at the back of a damp cupboard and it's now as hard as wood, all you can do is throw it away, as it will have lost all its properties; worse still, it will already have absorbed odors and relatively innocuous substances, which could render it harmful.

One of the main properties of this powder is its absorptive capacity. Therefore, you'll understand the importance of storing it in its tightly sealed packaging away from damp and odors. Under these conditions, it can keep for up to 4 years. However, don't be alarmed if a few bubbles form in the packet—the bicarbonate is said to be "clumping" (binding together).

Shake it a little and its normal appearance will be restored.

❶ CAUTION: Most of baking soda's properties come from its great capacity for absorption. For this reason, it cannot be reused. It must be discarded, even if the baking soda has retained its pristine white appearance. And don't feel bad about throwing it away, as baking soda is a biodegradable product and very cheap.

BAKING SODA'S ALLIES

Baking soda is mostly used on its own or with water. But you can enhance its strength by combining it with other products that are just as natural. It's mainly combined with lemon, coarse salt, and, above all, with its great accomplice, white vinegar.

▶ White vinegar

Adding white vinegar to baking soda enhances its scouring action. This is a perfect combination for unblocking sinks or any clogged pipework or sluggish drainage, or for removing traces of limescale that are proving hard to remove.

⚠ CAUTION: Mixing white vinegar with baking soda causes a chemical reaction. The mixture becomes frothy and swells because of the carbon dioxide released. It isn't harmful but to avoid any irritation (nose and eyes), open the windows and dilute it.

▶ Lemon

Lemon blends perfectly with baking soda. Mixing baking soda (1 teaspoon) and lemon juice (1 teaspoon in a ½ quart [½ liter] of warm water) make a much more effective deodorizing agent than a store-bought product. Both a descaling agent and a disinfectant, lemon sprinkled with baking soda becomes a powerful weapon against limescale.

▶ Salt

Sea salt is rich in iodine and has antibacterial properties. It's also a whitening agent. It enhances the power of the baking soda, but be careful—table salt is not as gentle as baking soda. Unlike baking soda, it should always be dissolved in water.

A little test

To ascertain whether your baking soda is still effective, pour 1 tablespoon into a glass of water and add a few drops of lemon or white vinegar. Does it froth? If so, it has retained all its properties. If it doesn't, it's lost them.

Cleaning, scouring, removing grime, polishing, deodorizing . . . baking soda is an added asset for household jobs. Nontoxic and economical, it's a multipurpose product that can be used on all surfaces, except aluminum [see below].

HOUSEHOLD USES FOR BAKING SODA

CLEANING, REMOVING GRIME

Baking soda not only dissolves grease but also absorbs it. Another benefit is that it neutralizes limescale from your water and enhances the efficiency of cleaning products. Ultimately, its abrasive action works wonders and without the risk of scratches.

▶ Spotless tableware

Do you wash dishes by hand? Sprinkle a little baking soda into the water. You'll boost the efficiency of the dishwashing soap and you won't have to scrub as much.

• **Has your pasta stuck to the bottom of the saucepan?** Pour a mixture made with 2 tablespoons of baking soda and one glass of water into the saucepan, to a depth of

½ inch (1 centimeter). After a good hour, all the grease and residue will have come away.

• **Are your porcelain cups stained with tea or coffee?** Fill your cup with water mixed with 1 tablespoon of baking soda and soak. The stains should disappear by themselves. If they're resistant, sprinkle baking soda over a sponge and rub them.

• **If the stains are proving hard to remove,** bring the mixture to the boil for 5 to 7 minutes, and then leave to cool. The baking soda will loosen the residue. Finish off with a sponge (the nonabrasive side) or remove the residue with a wooden spoon.

▶ Putting an end to stubborn grease

Use this method for your oven, microwave, or barbecue grills. Prepare a mixture made with 2 teaspoons of baking soda and 1.5 fluid ounces (45 milliliters) water. Apply the mixture over the surfaces and leave on overnight. Rinse with a tepid sponge.

• **Plastic salad bowls and the deep-fryer:** Sprinkle plenty of baking soda over the inside. Leave on for at least 30 minutes (that's how long it takes for the baking soda to absorb the oil). Clean with a slightly damp sponge, rinse, and then wash with a traditional washing-up product.

▶ Is your ceramic cooktop stained?

Baking soda works by loosening grease particles, and you can scour with it because it doesn't scratch surfaces. Ideally, moisten the burner and sprinkle with baking soda. Leave it to act for at least 1 hour. Then scrape with a wooden spatula. Or, better still, with the small device specially designed for this purpose: Composed of a razor blade set in a support (ceramic burner scraper), it enables you to scrape the surface in a precise and effective way without any risk of scratching.

▶ Cleaning your household appliances

Baking soda helps your appliances stay clean—both interior and exterior surfaces—whether they're made from white or colored melamine or stainless steel. Its distinctive feature is one of whitening appliances and reviving colors. Sprinkle baking soda over a damp sponge and rub gently. Leave to act for a few minutes and then wipe clean: Your

Did you know?

Baking soda can be used on most surfaces. Aluminum is the only surface that doesn't tolerate it.

appliances will sparkle and be restored to their former glory.

• **Interior surfaces:** Both the dishwasher and the refrigerator deserve a thorough cleaning to prevent microbes and mold from forming. Clean the inside regularly with a damp sponge sprinkled with baking soda. Don't forget the seals. Dry it all thoroughly with a soft cloth.

• **A stronger treatment is required for the refrigerator two to three times a year:** Put a small teaspoonful of black soap in a bowl of water mixed with baking soda (50/50). Clean with a sponge, and then rinse with warm water mixed with 1 tablespoon of white vinegar.

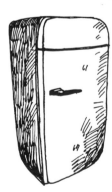

▶ A clean sink at all times

• **Whether made of stoneware or porcelain,** sinks can tolerate abrasion and scouring without any ill effects. Just make sure that you rinse it after using a scouring powder or dish soap.

• **Remove grease from resin sinks** by using a sponge soaked in a mixture of 1 part water to 1 part baking soda to restore it to its former glory. If it's really greasy, you can add a drop of dish soap. Rinse and make sure you dry it.

• **To tackle stubborn marks on stainless steel,** baking soda diluted in water (1 part water to 3 parts baking soda) is the order of the day. Polish it with a soft cloth sprinkled with dry baking soda to restore its clean, shiny appearance.

⚠ CAUTION: Never use a scour pad or any abrasive product on a stainless steel or resin sink.

▸ **Gleaming bathroom fittings**

Like white vinegar, baking soda helps your bathroom fittings stay clean. It has no equal when it comes to removing traces of limescale and polishing and whitening, but above all it has the great advantage of stopping mold growth. It's an indispensable aid in keeping damp rooms spick-and-span.

• **For really white tile joints:** Toothpaste whitens them. You only need to put a dab of it on an old toothbrush and scrub the tile joints, and then rinse. For heavily stained tile joints, mix 4 tablespoons of baking soda with 3.5 fluid ounces (100 milliliters) of white vinegar in a spray bottle and clean the tile joints. Leave on for 24 hours, scrub, and then rinse.

• **Finishing touch:** Make full use of the abrasive properties of baking soda. Just put a little of it on a dry cloth and polish until you obtain the desired level of shine.

• **Can you see any brown stains around the drains?** Make a mixture with baking soda. Mix 2 parts baking soda to 1 part hydrogen peroxide and stir well. Apply the paste to the stains and leave to act for 30 to 60 minutes. Rub the stains with a soft sponge.

▶ **Is your shower curtain stained black?**

If your shower curtain is dotted with black stains, it's no reason to discard it. You can remove this mold by rubbing the stains vigorously with the abrasive side of a sponge soaked in hot white vinegar. Then you just need to machine wash it at the warm setting and add 3 tablespoons of baking soda to the wash cycle. The baking soda stops mold and bacteria from forming.

▶ **A natural descaler**

Baking soda is no substitute for white vinegar, which is the king of descalers, but it will fit the bill perfectly when it comes to loosening everyday grime.

• **Chrome:** Mix 3 teaspoons of baking soda with 1 teaspoon of tepid water. Apply this mixture to the chrome. Leave on for 5 minutes and then rub gently with a sponge. Rinse in clean water and dry with a lint-free cloth.

• **Washing machine and dishwasher:** To prevent a buildup of limescale in the washing machine or the dishwasher, once a month, pour 5 ounces (140 grams) baking soda into the washing machine's drum or sprinkle across the bottom of the dishwasher and run them empty.

• **Small appliances:** Baking soda helps to reduce the buildup of limescale in tea makers, coffee makers, and kettles. Every 3 months (depending on the hardness of your water), boil 2 teaspoons of baking soda mixed with 1 liter of water. The limescale will come away from the sides and the bottom in thin patches. Rinse in clean water and then repeat the process once or twice, depending on how furred up the appliances are.

TIP

Lemon and baking soda— unity is strength

If you've had a glass of lemon juice in the morning (it's good for the health), keep the squeezed lemon halves. Use them as a sponge to scrub limescale while sprinkling them with baking soda. The combined effect of the two products will be doubly effective.

• **The iron:** Descale your iron regularly by pouring 2 teaspoons of baking soda mixed with 1 quart (1 liter) of water into the reservoir. Rub the sole plate with a damp sponge soaked in baking soda (approximately 1 tablespoon).

• **Bathroom fittings:** Effective and non-toxic, baking soda is ideal for descaling faucets and bathroom fittings. Mixing 3 tablespoons of baking soda with 1 quart (1 liter) of water will get your bathroom fittings looking pristine. In areas where limescale is proving hard to remove, such as around faucets, use the baking soda in the form of a paste. Half fill a moistened mustard jar with baking soda, until the powder is saturated. Smear this paste around the faucets and leave on for at least 30 minutes. Scrub the hard-to-reach corners with an old toothbrush.

• **To clean:** If you use baking soda in the form of a paste, the limescale will disappear and the faucets will emerge clean and shiny. Mix some baking soda in a small bowl of water until it's the consistency of a paste. Better still, use lemon juice instead of water, as it contains properties that "feed" on limescale, whiten it, and give it a shine. Rub this mixture over bathroom fittings. No need to rinse. Allow to dry.

• **Do your toilets need a clean?** Use 1 tablespoon of baking soda and within 5 minutes the deposit should disappear. If the deposit is proving hard to remove, you'll have to do it the hard way: pour 3 tablespoons of baking soda, 3 tablespoons of table salt, 8.25 fluid ounces (240 milliliters) of white vinegar, and some boiling water into the toilet bowl. Leave in for a few minutes and then scrub with the toilet brush.

▶ Ultraclean windows and mirrors

Wash your windows and mirrors with a damp cloth soaked in baking soda mixed with water (3 tablespoons of baking soda in a large glass of tepid water) and rub. Allow to dry and then wipe with a dry lint-free cloth.

• **If the marks are proving hard to remove,** make full use of the abrasive properties of baking soda and sprinkle some dry baking soda onto a damp sponge to rub the windows or mirrors. Wipe with a clean cloth.

▶ A method for antioxidation

Most metals cannot tolerate being exposed to the air and blacken over time; others such as stainless steel or brushed steel tarnish and become smeared with marks. To prevent this from happening, it's better to keep them in good condition. As a general rule, you just need to rub them regularly with a damp cloth sprinkled with baking soda. Then rinse and dry with a soft cloth.

TIP

A quick recipe for cleaning silverware

Put a sheet of aluminum foil at the bottom of your sink. Place your silver items on the foil, while preventing them from touching one another. Cover them with boiling water and add three handfuls of baking soda. The silverware will immediately turn white and all you need to do is rinse it thoroughly and dry with a soft cloth. The baking soda triggers the electrolysis phenomenon and the silver turns white, while the aluminum sheet turns black.

❶ **CAUTION:** Do not use the above method if your silverware is decorated with precious stones.

• **If the marks are ingrained:** You can wash copper, chrome, steel, stainless steel, gold, and silver and any other metal by making a paste with 3 tablespoons of baking soda and water. Apply the mixture, leave on for a moment, rinse in hot water, and then polish with a soft cloth. To give it a shine, use newsprint: the composition of ink cleans and polishes metal.

▶ Maintaining wooden furniture

The gentle cleaning properties of baking soda make it suitable for cleaning and dusting wooden furniture, whether varnished, waxed, or untreated. Lightly dampen a clean sponge with water and sprinkle it with a pinch of baking soda. Always follow the grain of the wood as you sponge.

• **Musty furniture:** The previous method should be enough to remove light traces of recent mold growth. If the problem is more serious, soak the sponge in white vinegar before sprinkling with baking soda. Rinse and dry immediately.

• **Soiled rattan furniture:** Prepare your solution in a spray bottle by pouring 2 tablespoons of baking soda and 1 teaspoon of dish soap into 1 quart (1 liter) of tepid water. Remove the dust with a dry cloth, spray the mixture onto the piece of furniture, and rub with a brush, following

TIP

A neat trick for cleaning beams

Washing the feet of exposed wooden beams with a sponge is not an easy job and you'll need to watch out for splinters. Try using an oven glove. Its double thickness will reduce cleaning time by half and your hands will be protected. Just soak the glove directly in a mixture of water and baking soda (1 teaspoon of baking soda to 1 quart [1 liter] of water).

the grain of the wood. Rinse with clean water. To clean all the parts that are difficult to reach, rub with an old toothbrush.

• **Is there a patch of water on your solid wood sideboard?** Rub it gently with a paste made with 1 part toothpaste to 1 part baking soda. Use a circular motion, working from the outside inward, taking care not to go beyond the stain.

❗ CAUTION: Valuable furniture items require special care. Seek the advice of a specialist before embarking on their maintenance.

▶ Transparent plastic furniture

Nowadays, the quality of plastic furniture has improved significantly and it's much more resistant to yellowing caused by UV light. But these plastics tend to become dull and stained. Never scrub them, as you risk scratching them. Use baking soda—since it's a mild abrasive, there's no risk of leaving marks behind. Add 2 tablespoons of baking soda to 1 quart (1 liter) of water, and you'll have a solution to restore the translucence, cleanliness, and spotlessness of your plastic furniture.

Also, the plastic furniture's vivid colors will be restored to their former glory. If there are any old stains, add a small teaspoonful of dishwashing liquid to the mixture and rinse thoroughly with clean water.

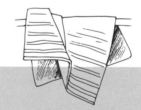

TIP

And how it sparkles!

As is very often the case, the brightness of a material is primarily the result of thorough cleaning. Wash the item, and always wipe carefully with a microfiber cloth afterward.

▸ Nice clean floors

Baking soda is suitable for all your floors. With or without black soap (1 teaspoon per 1 quart [1 liter] of hot water), it is a good alternative to the commercial products that are available for cleaning and removing the toughest stains. Use 3 parts baking soda to 1 part hot water. Clean with a long-handled scrubbing brush and then rinse with clean water. Wipe dry.

• **Bring back the shine to your tiled floor:** It will be restored to its former glory when you apply a mixture made with 1 part water to 1 part baking soda. Leave to act for 1 hour, and then rinse in clean water.

• **Concrete and cement stains:** Scatter baking soda directly onto the stains and leave to soak. Then wash and scrub with a mixture of water and baking soda (3 tablespoons of baking soda in 1 quart [1 liter] of hot water). Rinse in clean water.

▸ A fireplace as good as new

Find a bit of time to clean your insert glass from top to bottom. Empty out the ashes with a small brush (keep them, as they'll come in handy) and finish off with the vacuum cleaner.

• **Clean the mantelpiece** by rubbing in a circular motion with the aid of a stiff bristle brush, soaked in a mixture made with 4 tablespoons of liquid black soap, 2 tablespoons of baking soda, and 2 quarts (2 liters) of water. Rinse in clean water and then dry with a lint-free cloth or with a sheet of newspaper rolled into the shape of a ball.

• **To clean the sides,** scrub them with a stiff bristle brush and soak it regularly in a mixture made with 1 quart (1 liter) of hot water and 3 cups (700 milliliters) of white vinegar. Sprinkle baking soda onto the brush. The same goes for the insert glass. If you rub the insert glass with a sponge moistened with white vinegar and sprinkled with baking soda, it will look pristine again. Rinse with clean water and dry.

❶ PLEASE NOTE: Residual dirt will come loose even more easily if the glass is tepid.

▸A wash accelerator

Baking soda can't clean your laundry on its own. However, it makes the washing detergent more effective so that you need use only half as much of it. As a softening and whitening agent, it's an excellent substitute for any laundry products. It's perfect for deodorizing clothes soiled by unpleasant accidents like urine or vomit. Baking soda also produces a whiter than white wash and brightens colors.

❶ CAUTION: Never use on wool and silk.

• **Whiter than white laundry:** Pour 2 to 3 tablespoons of baking soda into the washing detergent compartment or directly into the drum, and then run your usual program.
• **If your whites have turned really gray,** add 10½ ounces (300 grams) of baking soda per medium load to the washing detergent compartment on the last rinse.

This is a healthy alternative to bleach.
• **Are your curtain sheers grubby?** Soak them overnight in your bathtub and add 2 cups (475 milliliters) of baking soda. You'll get them looking pristine again and smelling clean. Another benefit is that they won't crease.

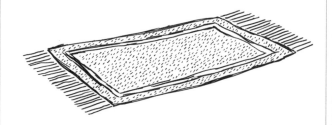

• **Strong colors:** Here's a yearly cleaning option for your carpets. Thoroughly dampen the carpet and then sprinkle it liberally with baking soda. Rub with a scrubbing brush to work the baking soda into the carpet. After 1 hour, brush with clean water to rinse.

❶ CAUTION: Turn your carpet over to make sure that it hasn't made the floor wet to avoid any risk of mold forming. As a precaution, sprinkle a layer of baking soda onto the floor before replacing the carpet.

Express drying

TIP

To speed up the drying process, rub the carpet with a microfiber cloth to absorb as much moisture as possible.

▶ Baking soda feeds on stains

Baking soda can defeat any grease stain and many others besides. All materials can tolerate it, except for wool, silk, and aluminum. However, always test the recipe on an inconspicuous corner of the item before starting.

You should act as quickly as possible when treating stains. The longer you wait, the more the stain will set and the more difficult it will be to get out.

• **Fat stains:** Baking soda excels at these. First remove the surplus fat with the blade of a knife and a paper towel, and then sprinkle baking soda directly onto the stain. Leave to act for at least 5 hours. Next brush it gently. Finally, soak the stained fabric in a mixture of water and baking soda (2 teaspoons of baking soda to 1 bowl of cold water).

• **Other stains:** For grass, fruit, ink, and so on, the principle is practically the same. As a matter of priority, rinse the stain under cold running water as quickly as possible.

This usually removes the bulk of it. Baking soda should do the rest, but not always. Soak the fabric in a mixture of water and baking soda (2 teaspoons of baking soda per 1 bowl of cold water) before washing, as this will remove most of the grime. Then put in the washing machine and add some baking soda (1 tablespoon) to the rinse compartment. This will complete the job and remove the last traces.

❶ CAUTION: Never use baking soda on wool and silk.

• **Stubborn stains:** Lipstick, deodorant, foundation, perspiration stains, and many other marks merit a prewash treatment. Prepare a paste with a mixture of 1 part water to 1 part baking soda and apply to both sides of the fabric. Leave to act for at least 1 hour, or even overnight. Then put in the washing machine.

• **Removing mold stains.** Is it a recent stain? Moisten it slightly and then apply a paste made with 3 tablespoons of baking soda and 1 tablespoon of water. Rub with a toothbrush, using a circular motion. Rinse in water mixed with vinegar and then machine wash.

⊙ CAUTION: To prevent it from "cooking" and fixing the stain in place, treat the stain before putting the item in the washing machine.

• **A wax stain?** There's no need to rush to remove the wax the very moment it drips onto the fabric, because you'll only make it worse by spreading it. Bide your time and allow it to dry. Once it has hardened, remove the bulk of the wax with the blade of a knife. Put two or three paper towels onto the remaining wax and iron the stain. When exposed to heat, the wax will be absorbed by the paper. Repeat the process until there's no trace of grease on the paper towels.

• **Has the wax gone but a greasy stain remains?** No problem. Sprinkle it with baking soda. Wait until it has been completely absorbed, dust the residue off, and repeat the process if necessary. This works not only on fabrics but also on wood and marble.

▶ **Cleaning with dry baking soda**

Regular upkeep of furniture avoids a build-up of grime that is difficult to get on top of. Sofas, armchairs, cushions, and carpets should be treated to a quick clean approximately every 2 weeks. If you give it a thorough brush, you'll remove the dust and recent stains, revive the colors, and above all eradicate dust mites, or even potential mold growth. To do this, sprinkle with baking soda, rub gently, and leave to act for at least 1 hour. Then vacuum carefully.

• **If the stain is proving hard to remove** or if the material is really soiled, use a slightly moistened sponge.

⊙ CAUTION: Always test on an inconspicuous area before starting. If the material is leather, don't rub it; then apply a nourishing cream, such as a cleansing milk.

▸ Cleaning your walls

Baking soda is great for cleaning your walls. As a grease remover, whitener, and deodorizing agent, it simplifies the washing of large areas. Mix 1 heaping tablespoon of baking soda per quart (liter) of hot water in a bucket. Wash, rinse, and it's done. For your walls: Remove the grease, dust off, and if necessary prepare them for wallpaper adhesive or paint. If the walls are really gray, add a small teaspoonful of dish washing liquid to the mixture.

▸ Tackling smears

Use baking soda to remove finger marks, pencil marks, and felt-tip pen marks from painted surfaces (walls, furniture, doors), as well as from varnished, laminated, or melamine-coated surfaces. Its grains generate a very gentle scrubbing action that doesn't leave a trace. Sprinkle the baking soda onto a damp sponge and simply rub. Don't dampen the sponge too much, because the grains remain effective as long as they're not dissolved in water.

▸ Making it shine

The gentle, abrasive properties of baking soda are a gift for any surface needing a light polish. Stainless steel, steel, glass, and PVC will be restored to their former glory if you just polish them with a soft, damp cloth sprinkled with baking soda.

• **Is your glassware cloudy?** Mix 1 tablespoon of baking soda in a glass of tepid water. Rub your glasses or your vases with this mixture and they should be restored to their former translucence. If the dishwasher is responsible for this gray appearance, it's doubtful whether you'll ever be able to retrieve it. The chemical reaction occurring between the lead entering their composition and certain products used in a dishwasher irreversibly whitens glasses and vases.

It's clear!

TIP

The above method also applies to eyeglasses. Rub your glasses with a little moistened baking soda and you really will see clearer!

THE BEST DEODORIZING AGENT

This is one of baking soda's greatest properties. It not only "neutralizes" odors due to its great capacity for absorption, but it also prevents them from developing in the first place. It acts as a buffer, meaning that it rebalances the pH and destroys the bacteria responsible for unpleasant odors.

Moreover, its natural composition renders it harmless when exposed to the air because it doesn't release VOCs (volatile organic compounds) that are actually indoor air pollutants. Use it to eliminate musty odors, tobacco odors, mold odors, and more.

☞ Did you know?

To be effective, the contact area between the baking soda and the surrounding air must be as great as possible. For example, choose a tapered dish rather than a narrow bowl.

TIP

Making deodorizer shoe balls

Wear protective gloves. Mix 1 tablespoon of baking soda, 1 tablespoon of corn starch, and 1 tablespoon of clay. Work these ingredients, adding 20 drops of tea tree essential oil (for its disinfecting and antifungal properties) at the same time. Take two squares of old pantyhose and put a little of this mixture on each square. Squeeze very tightly to join the edges to form small, compact balls, and then seal them with rubber bands. Slip these balls into the shoes.

▸ **Tobacco odors**

There's nothing more unpleasant than the smell of stale cigarette smoke. Put a thin layer of baking soda at the bottom of the ashtray and say goodbye to odors.

▸Mold odors

Has your kitchen been flooded and is there a persistent moldy odor? Once you've checked that the leak has been properly repaired, spray with white vinegar to eliminate the odor and then put a bowl of baking soda in a corner away from any splashes. The odor will disappear.

• **If a bag has absorbed an off-putting odor**, sprinkle the inside with baking soda and leave it for at least 2 weeks away from any moisture.

▸Musty odors

Place a bowl filled with baking soda in a corner to eliminate the odor. Better still, frequently place small cups of baking soda in strategic corners of stuffy rooms to prevent any unpleasant smells.

▸A clean refrigerator

A bowl of baking soda placed in the refrigerator will prevent odor buildup. The baking soda should be renewed every 2 months. But be careful, as a refrigerator that doesn't "smell" does not mean it's clean. Clean your refrigerator every week. How? With baking soda! Ideally, use baking soda 1 week and white vinegar the next.

▸Washing machine and dishwasher: The same battle

To prevent unpleasant odors and to protect the pipework from limescale, run your dishwasher and washing machine empty approximately once every 3 months. One cup (235 milliliters) of baking soda instead of dishwashing liquid or washing detergent and it's done.

▸Are unpleasant odors rising up from your pipework?

Whether in the sink, the washbasin, or the shower, residues build up on the interior of the pipework. Pour 1 cup (235 milliliters) of coarse salt, 1 cup of baking soda, and 1 cup of white vinegar into the pipework. Be careful, as a chemical reaction occurs and the mixture will froth. Leave overnight and then rinse with clean, hot water. Cold white vinegar is used for this, but if the dirt is heavily ingrained, you can heat the white vinegar before pouring it in.

▶Sanitize your vacuum cleaner

Our odor trapper is also extremely useful for preventing the vacuum cleaner from circulating unpleasant odors and allergens. Pour ½ cup (120 milliliters) of baking soda onto the floor and vacuum it up. The powder will block the formation of odor and will prevent the spread of dust mites and other allergens.

▶Deodorizing curtains and bedding

Mix 2 tablespoons of baking soda and 6 tablespoons of hot water. Spray this magic deodorizing potion onto the curtains and your mattress. This will eliminate any odor and eradicate dust mites. You can also add 10 drops of true lavender or tea tree essential oil for their scent and their purifying and disinfecting action.

❗ CAUTION: Never use essential oils near pregnant or lactating women, or near children or pets.

• **For the mattress:** Spray with the solution and rub with a sponge. It's better to do this in the morning so that it can dry thoroughly. You can speed up the drying time by sprinkling some baking soda onto the mattress after you've sprayed it with the solution. You'll just need to vacuum it before remaking the bed.

❗ CAUTION: Always test it first on an inconspicuous area, as some fabrics can have a bad reaction. Silk and wool, in particular, do not tolerate baking soda.

▶A remedy for shoes

There's nothing better. Sprinkle a little baking soda into each shoe and it's done: No more odor! Better still, one of baking soda's amazing properties is that it blocks the development of microscopic fungi.

▶Musty old books

Have your books been lying around in a basement for a while? Do the pages give off a musty smell? Sprinkle them with baking soda. Leave overnight before dusting it off into the sink.

▸ The trash can

Even though you've washed the trash can, it can eventually absorb an unpleasant odor. It doesn't have to be that way. Clean it and then dry thoroughly. Next, sprinkle the bottom with a thin layer of baking soda that will prevent odors.

• **If you throw a foul-smelling product** into the garbage bag, sprinkle it with baking soda, as this will prevent the odor from spreading, until it's time to change the bag.

▸ The laundry basket

To combat dirty socks and perspiration smells, sprinkle every new layer of laundry with a pinch of baking soda on a regular basis. Baking soda is not only a deodorizing agent but it can also tackle stains.

Clean hands — TIP

After you've been cooking, do you find that you can't get rid of the smell of onions or maybe you have traces of oil and grease on your hands? Pour a small amount of baking soda into your palm and rub your palms together. No more smells and your hands will be clean and soft.

COMBAT DUST MITES

These micro-arachnids love moving into our beds, our bedding, our carpets, and any other fabric for that matter. They are one of the main causes of respiratory allergies in our homes. They feed on our skin flakes and love moist heat and confined spaces. Our grandmothers' solutions to combat them were as follows: a daily airing (30 minutes each morning) and putting the fabrics out in the sun. These are habits that we should keep, to the best of our ability.

But there's something simpler and more radical: baking soda. As effective, if not more so, than specific insecticides, it has the great advantage of being harmless to our health, even for babies. The method is simple but rather laborious because it requires tracking them down in every nook and cranny and taking meticulous action. Plan a shock treatment over the course of one day, with the windows open, and carry this out approximately every 3 months; later, a light weekly treatment will suffice.

Baby's soft toys

Baby's cuddly toys are not immune to dust mites—far from it. If the soft toys are too bulky to put in the washing machine, wrap them in a plastic bag with 10½ ounces (300 grams) of baking soda. Shake and leave for 4 hours. Remove the toys and brush them over your bathtub or out in the fresh air.

▸Shock treatment

Duvet cover, sheets, undersheet, cushion cover, curtains (if possible), should all go in the washing machine. Next use the vacuum cleaner, which must be free of dirt with an empty filter: vacuum the carpets, the fitted carpet, the mattresses (including the grooves) and the bedsprings thoroughly. Then sprinkle them liberally (4 tablespoons per square yard or meter) with rather fine alimentary baking soda: It will penetrate deep into the fibers. Leave for at least 4 hours. Rubbing with a brush is recommended for high-pile carpets and mattresses. Empty and clean the vacuum cleaner before vacuuming thoroughly.

▸Preventive treatment

Every week, get into the habit of sprinkling bedding, carpets, and fitted carpets with baking soda before vacuuming to make dust mites a thing of the past.

▸Extra-large washing machines

It's time to wash your bulky items (pillows, bedspread, curtains, duvet, etc.). Take advantage of the Laundromat just around the corner from you, as their extra-large machines can accommodate big items and also dry them.

Prepare your washing detergent at home by adding 2 tablespoons of baking soda. Also put 1½ tablespoons of baking soda into the fabric softener compartment. The residue of the baking soda in the fibers will delay the onset of these unpleasant bugs.

☞ Did you know?

Dust mites cannot tolerate heat exceeding 140°F (60°C), hence the value in ironing as much of your laundry as possible.

ANIMAL'S ALLY

Completely harmless and odorless, baking soda promotes the well-being of our pets, without disrupting their keen sense of smell. As a trapper of odors, an insect repellent (particularly lice and fleas that don't tolerate the rough texture of grains), and a grease remover, baking soda helps to preserve the environment of our animal companions. Choose a baking soda type with a fine grain that is used for alimentary use.

▸ Dry shampoo

Has your dog come home drenched? Sprinkle him with some baking soda—alimentary, of course—and then rub him down with a towel and brush him. The baking soda will neutralize the odor.

▸ Bathtime

Sprinkle your dog's coat evenly with baking soda. Leave to act for a few minutes. Then wash him and rinse him in clean, tepid water. Finally, brush him thoroughly. His glossy coat will be restored and it will be protected from parasites for a while, because most of them can't abide baking soda grains.

❶ CAUTION: If your dog becomes infested with parasites or has a persistent odor, you should consult a vet.

▸ Fresh breath

Soak a compress with a mixture of baking soda and water (1 teaspoon in a bowl of water). Wind this compress around your finger and gently rub your dog's teeth. The abrasive effect of the baking soda will remove the tartar along with the bad breath. Generally, once a week is enough.

❶ CAUTION: There can be several reasons for bad breath and it's better to seek advice from the vet if the problem persists.

▸ Deodorizing the litter tray

A thin layer of baking soda at the back of the litter tray (approximately 3 tablespoons) will minimize the spread of odors and slow the rate at which you need to change it.

❶ CAUTION: An absence of odor doesn't mean that the litter tray is clean. Make sure you clean and disinfect it each time you change the litter.

▸Cleaning the baskets

Whether the basket belongs to Rex the dog or Fluffy the cat, it's the same challenge. A weekly clean is essential. Sprinkle with baking soda (1 tablespoon), leave for at least 4 hours, and then vacuum thoroughly. Not only will the basket not smell anymore but also all the undesirable parasites will have been eradicated.

❶ CAUTION: After you've completed this job, make sure that you empty out and clean the vacuum cleaner; otherwise you'll propel all this dust into the atmosphere when you next use it.

▸Cleaning bird or hamster cages

Cleaning the cages couldn't be easier. Scrub the bars and the bottom of the cage with a sponge moistened in hot water and sprinkled with 1 tablespoon of alimentary baking soda. Rinse in clean water and then thoroughly dry. Sprinkle 1 tablespoon of baking soda onto the bottom of the cage

before putting newspaper down. This will neutralize the odors and repel parasites.

▸Cleaning the cage items

Tin dish, toys: Washing them with a mixture of hot water and baking soda (2 tablespoons per quart [liter] of water) will eradicate grease deposits, dirt, and unpleasant odors.

▸Has your pet had a "fragrant" accident?

Has your pet had an accident on the carpet? Once you've cleaned the stain, spray it with a mixture of water and baking soda (3 tablespoons per 1 quart [1 liter] of water). Leave it to act for 15 minutes, and then allow to dry naturally. The last traces of the offense, and the odor, will be gone.

❶ CAUTION: Avoid using bleach to clean a urine stain made by a cat. Cats are mad about the smell and are only too pleased to reoffend in the same place! Use white vinegar instead, as it's less toxic.

Used in organic farming, baking soda helps in the battle against harmful pests, prevents certain plant diseases, and is an excellent weed killer. It can impede mold growth, which actually makes it an indispensable antifungal treatment. The product is both safe for gardeners and for nature.

BAKING SODA: THE BACKYARD'S ALLY

WEEDING YOUR PATHS AND PATIOS

Spray weeds with a mixture of water and baking soda (4 to 5 tablespoons per quart [liter]).

▶ For your patio

Water your paving stones with a mixture of water and baking soda (3 tablespoons per liter of water) to eliminate weeds, moss, and blackened joints. Leave on for a few minutes and then brush with a long-handled scrubbing brush.

⚠ CAUTION: Don't let it spill onto your flower beds. Concentrated baking soda can "scorch" plants.

On account of its buffering action, baking soda reduces the acidity of the soil, which is a bonus, as this will ensure plenty of flowers and the growth of healthy vegetables.

A little test — TIP

How do you know if you have an acid soil or a chalky soil? Put a little soil into two different containers. In one container, add ½ cup (120 milliliters) of white vinegar, and in the other container add ½ cup of water mixed with 1 large tablespoon of baking soda. The soil is alkaline if the mixture froths in the container with the white vinegar; if it froths in the container with the water and baking soda, the soil is acidic.

▶ Combating parasites

• **Baking soda stops the spread of parasites.** Pour 1 teaspoon of baking soda per 1 quart (1 liter) of water (do not use a more concentrated mixture of baking soda on your plants) into a spray bottle. Avoid spraying over the flowers. Carry out this treatment once a month.

• **You can add olive oil** (5 teaspoons) to the mixture so that it can spread slowly over the foliage.

▸ A preventive treatment for mildew

Enemy number one of vines, mildew is a fungal disease (plant damage caused by a fungus or another filamentous organism). This disease mainly affects vines, tomatoes, and potatoes. Initially, it is characterized by the appearance of a few spots on the leaves, before it spreads slowly to the rest of the foliage, which eventually falls to the ground.

To prevent mildew, add 2 teaspoons of black soap and 1 teaspoon of baking soda to 2 quarts (2 liters) of water. Spray this treatment onto the rosebushes, fruit trees, and vegetables.

▸ A preventive treatment for powdery mildew

To tackle powdery mildew, a fungus also referred to as "white rot" that attacks many plants in the garden—particularly grapes and plants of the gourd family, such as squash—add 5 teaspoons of olive oil to the mixture as mentioned above.

💡 **TIP**

Cleaning garden furniture and tools

The cleansing and abrasive power of baking soda and its antifungal properties make it particularly suitable for cleaning garden furniture and tools. Scrub them with a mixture of tepid water and baking soda (2 tablespoons per 1 quart [1 liter] of water). If the grime proves hard to remove, leave the mixture on for a good hour before scrubbing again. Then rinse and wipe dry.

HAPPY HOUSEPLANTS

Are your green plants wilting? It could be dust.

When dust accumulates on the leaves, it gradually suffocates the plant. Don't

Ants put to flight

Ants always follow the same route. If they deviate from it, they get lost and are completely disoriented. They find their way by detecting traces of pheromones that they leave en route. To compel them to do an about-turn, you need to disrupt these odorous traces. Baking soda will do the job. Find time to observe their movements, in order to identify their route. Once you've tracked it down, sprinkle it with baking soda. Repeat the process at least three times a month.

allow this to happen. It'll take a bit of work—you have to remove the dust from each leaf! Use a sponge to wipe 1 teaspoon of baking soda mixed in 1 quart (1 liter) of water over the leaves to give them a glossy shine.

❶ CAUTION: Baking soda must not be used to spray houseplants.

▸ Longer-lasting cut flowers

A pinch of baking soda added to the vase water will prolong the life of your bouquets. Another benefit: The water will stay clean and will not smell.

A CLEAN CAR

You should always keep a little pot of baking soda in the trunk of your car. Your car will stay clean and odorless, due to its efficiency at dissolving and removing grease and organic material, alongside its cleaning power and deodorizing properties.

▸ The exterior

• **A nice, clean windshield:** Mix 2 tablespoons of baking soda in 1 quart (1 liter) of hot water. Soak a sponge in the mixture and wet the windshield thoroughly. Leave on for 10 minutes and then rub. Rinse in clean water and wipe with a microfiber cloth. This mixture removes insects that have flown into the windshield, grease, sap, and more.

• **The bodywork:** Chrome and wheel rims tolerate baking soda mixed with water just fine. The same treatment as for the windshield works wonders.

▸The interior

• **Sprinkle the seats and carpet** with baking soda to maintain them. Brush and then vacuum thoroughly. Has a soda pop tipped over? Is there a smell of wet dog? Has a baby wet themselves? Mix 2 table-spoons of baking soda in 1 quart (1 liter) of hot water. Moisten and rub the stain.

• **To combat the smell of stale cigarette smoke:** Pour a layer of baking soda into the ashtray. This will absorb all unpleasant odors.

4
LEMON

Descale · Disinfect · Deodorize

LEMON . . .

IT CAN BE USED FOR NEARLY ANYTHING

....

This small, lightweight, sun-colored citrus fruit measuring about 3 inches (8 centimeters) long is essential for cooking, for beauty care, and of course for looking after the house. Antiseptic, cleansing, antibacterial, an antioxidant, health-giving, and packed with vitamins—it can do anything.

....

▸ A slice of history

Legend has it that the first lemon trees appeared in Kashmir, on the borders of China and India more than 3,000 years ago. These were the first steps on a long journey. After Persia, the lemon turned up in Mesopotamia and then the Mediterranean basin, notably in Spain in the tenth century, thanks to the Arabs. However, it was not until the fifteenth century that the Spanish and the Portuguese planted it in Florida in the United States.

▸Identity card

The fruit as we know it today is called "lemon" but the scientists call it *Citrus limetta*. There are several varieties. An expert will recognize it by the color of its peel, varying from bright yellow to golden yellow. Similarly, it has different flavors and can be tart, sour, or even sweet.

It's a hybrid citrus descended from the citron and the Seville orange (bitter orange). Reaching 16 to 33 feet (5 to 10 meters) in height and evergreen, lemon trees produce fruit several times a year.

▸A few varieties

In France, the varieties are selected according to their juiciness.

• **The Eureka:** An intense yellow color when ripe, with an oblong shape, and juicy, tart, scented pulp, this lemon produces fruit all year round and is the most readily available in supermarkets. It's also one of the sourest.

• **The Lisbon:** This variety is Portuguese in origin and resembles the Eureka. It's very juicy and stays on the tree for a long time.

• **The Meyer:** This popular domestic plant is mainly grown in California. A hybrid of a lemon and an orange, it is yellow and rounder than a Eureka lemon. It is sweeter and has a less acidic flavor than the more common Lisbon or Eureka supermarket lemon varieties.

• **The Sorrento:** Native to Italy, these lemons are available all year-round. They can be difficult to find throughout the United States, as they are mostly grown in California. This fruit's zest is high in lemon oils. It is the variety traditionally used in the making of limoncello. They are

What about limes?

There are many different varieties of limes. Those with small fruits come from Mexico and the West Indies, while those with large fruits come from Tahiti or Persia. The limes dry out more quickly than traditional lemons, so it's better to buy them in small quantities.

TIP

Store lemons in the right place

To keep them longer, put whole lemons into a glass jar, cover them with water, and store them in the refrigerator. They'll stay juicy this way. Don't seal the jar.

medium-large and very acidic, and their peels are extremely fragrant, as they are packed with a high concentration of essential oils.

• **The Ponderosa:** a hybrid of a citron and a lemon. This variety is more cold-sensitive than other lemons and the fruit is thick-skinned and very large.

▶ A health benefit

Lemons are full of vitamin C (52 mg per 100 g), but also in vitamin P, organic acids, selenium, fiber, and so on, with a low caloric value, making them an essential part of a healthy diet.

▶ The king of storage

Lemons keep for up to several months in the vegetable compartment of the refrigerator. However, as soon as you cut it, the vitamin C content begins to oxidize.

LEMON COUSINS

They look and smell like a lemon, and sometimes have the same color and properties... So what do they have in common?

▶ Citric acid

It's safe and naturally present in the lemon. Citric acid is used in the domain of nutrition (it's an additive better known under the label E330), medicine, and everyday life. Biodegradable and nontoxic to humans, it's antifungal, antibacterial, and antialgae. This white powder keeps

☞ *Did you know?*

The yellower the lemon, the shorter time it can be kept.

for years and is ideal for removing lime-scale, rust, algae, mold, and lichens. But be careful—it's not suitable for enamel, marble, and any surface that doesn't tolerate acids. It can be used in many recipes around the house instead of lemon juice.

▶Essential oil

Lemon essential oil is not made with the pulp of the lemon but with its peel. You need 3,000 lemons to make 35 ounces (1 kilogram) of essential oil. It has a pale, greenish-yellow color, and its fresh lemony scent is renowned for its deodorizing properties. Essential oil is ideal for cleaning floors, toilets, washbasins, and so on, because of its antiseptic and disinfecting properties.

• As an antibacterial and antiviral agent, it can be used as a spray (with an essential oil spray bottle) to purify the air in the room.

▶And how about citronella?

Citronella is often likened to the lemon family, but that's not the case. Citronella, also known as Indian verbena, Madagascar, or Java verbena, is in fact a grass-like plant with green, slender leaves (lemongrass). It's a perennial plant due to its rhizomes (underground stems), and the only thing it has in common with the lemon is the scent it releases when you rub the leaves. Citronella is best known for its ability to repel mosquitoes.

❶ CAUTION:

Essential oils must be handled with caution. Wear protective gloves and avoid direct contact with the skin; follow the directions for use and the advice of the manufacturer, otherwise they can very quickly become toxic and harmful. Above all, never use them near people with allergies, pregnant women, children, and pets.

ADVICE

Materials suitable for successful cleaning

TO ACHIEVE THE BEST RESULTS, EQUIP YOURSELF WITH THE RIGHT TOOLS:

▶ Clean, lint-free, microfiber cloths
▶ A chamois leather (they're becoming rare, but you can still find them in hardware stores)
▶ An all-purpose sponge for large areas
▶ Soft sponges for every surface
▶ A soft toothbrush (for getting into the gaps)
▶ A slightly used knife for gentle abrasion
▶ A scrubbing brush for rubbing without scratching (Plastic ones are less effective, because the bristles quickly start to bend under pressure.)
▶ Newsprint from a newspaper (glossy paper from magazines is not suitable)
▶ A clean floor cloth
▶ Extra-fine steel wool for removing small scratches
▶ A scraper for windowpanes
▶ And of course a broom, a bucket or bowl, a shovel, a vacuum cleaner, and protective gloves

To avoid wasting time preparing all these recipes when you need them, it's best to make them in advance. Like traditional products, most keep for a long time provided you protect them from light.

HOMEMADE PRODUCTS USING LEMON

A HOMEMADE DEODORIZING AGENT

Make your own air freshener by mixing the products in a spray bottle.

You will need:

- **1 teaspoon lemon juice**
- **1 teaspoon baking soda**
- **2 cups (475 milliliters) warm water**

Mix the ingredients together and pour them into a small spray bottle. Make sure that you label it. Shake before each use and then spray as needed.

A little bit of guidance on making the recipes

ADVICE

Adapt the recipes according to your requirements. Adjust the dosages to achieve the right quantity and consistency. Recipes made in the traditional way are not an exact science, as they are the result of many tests and experiments.

A HOMEMADE FABRIC CONDITIONER

To soften the laundry, there's no substitute for white vinegar, but some may be turned off by the odd smell. You just need to perfume it with citrus peel.

You will need:

- **2 lemons**
- **4 cups (950 milliliters) white vinegar**

Infuse the lemon peel and white vinegar for at least 24 hours in an airtight container. Filter into a bottle, taking care to remove the peel, and it's ready: 2 tablespoons in the fabric softener compartment and your laundry will emerge from the washing machine all soft with a lovely fresh scent.

A LOTION FOR POLISHED FURNITURE

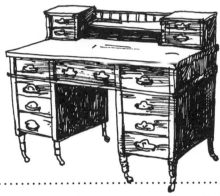

To restore the shine to all your polished furniture, nourish them with a homemade product.

You will need:
- **2 tablespoons lemon juice**
- **2 tablespoons white vinegar**
- **6 tablespoons olive oil**
- **4 tablespoons peanut oil**

Filter the lemon juice to remove the pulp and seeds. Then mix all the ingredients in a bowl. Pour the mixture into a bottle and label it clearly.

Use a soft brush to spread 1 tablespoon of the lotion onto the furniture, and then polish with a clean, lint-free cloth.

A PRODUCT WITH WOOD IN MIND

A quick "spray" on polished or varnished wood and a wipe with a lint-free cloth will remove stains and grime and restore it to its former glory.

You will need:
- **5 tablespoons lemon juice**
- **5 tablespoons olive oil**
- **15 drops lemon essential oil (Citrus limonum) for its perfume and anti-parasitic properties**

Filter the lemon juice to remove all the pulp and seeds. Mix it with the olive oil and then the essential oil. Make sure you label the bottle clearly. This mixture will keep in the refrigerator for 15 days.

---◆---

A TRADITIONAL MULTIPURPOSE PRODUCT

It can do anything and is prepared in advance.

You will need:
- **½ quart (½ liter) of water**
- **2½ tablespoons grated or flaked white Marseille soap**
- **juice of ½ lemon**

Heat the water without allowing it to boil. Add the soap and blend it until it has completely dissolved. Filter the lemon juice to remove the pulp and seeds. Remove from heat and add the lemon juice to the saucepan. Mix thoroughly. Pour into a pre-rinsed, prelabeled old spray bottle.

- **If the mixture is too thick,** dilute it with about 3 tablespoons of hot water (you can judge its consistency).
- **Shake it before each application** and spray directly onto the surface you want to clean. Then rub with a slightly damp sponge. Rinse in clean water and wipe with a dry, lint-free cloth.

---◆---

AN ANTI-LIMESCALE PRODUCT FOR THE TOILET

To descale your toilets regularly, prepare this mixture in advance.

You will need:
- **6 tablespoons baking soda**
- **3 tablespoons sodium percarbonate**
- **1 teaspoon water**
- **6 tablespoons citric acid**
- **5 drops tea tree or lemon essential oil for their antiseptic properties**

Mix the different powders, water, citric acid, and the essential oil with some water to obtain a thick paste. Distribute the paste in a large ice-cube mold. Allow to dry for 1 hour.

Remove from the mold and put the tablets in an airtight container, taking care to label it clearly. Put a tablet into the toilets when necessary, preferably in the evening before you go to bed.

Leave overnight before flushing the toilet to rinse it away.

A DISHWASHING PRODUCT

Why buy an industrially perfumed product when you can make it yourself in 5 minutes?

You will need:
- **4 lemons**
- **½ pound (250 grams) coarse salt**
- **1½ cups (350 milliliters) white vinegar**
- **4½ cups (1 liter) water**

Cut off the ends of the lemons, and then slice into rings, without peeling them. Put them into a saucepan and then add the coarse salt, white vinegar, and water. Stir and then warm up the mixture for 15 minutes on medium heat, while stirring constantly. Remove from the heat and stir again for 20 seconds. Leave to cool. Filter

to remove the pulp and seeds and then pour into an old, prerinsed and carefully labeled dish-detergent bottle.

◆

DISHWASHER TABLETS

To avoid dropping powder everywhere, you can prepare these water-soluble tablets.

For 18 tablets, you will need:
- **6 tablespoons citric acid**
- **6 tablespoons soda crystals**
- **6 tablespoons grated or flaked white Marseille soap**
- **3 tablespoons sodium percarbonate**
- **30 drops lemon essential oil**
- **2 teaspoons water**

Mix all the ingredients until a thick, smooth powder is achieved. Pour into an ice-cube mold and leave to harden. Remove from the mold and store in an airtight container, taking care to label it clearly. Use 1 tablet per wash.

From the kitchen to the bathroom,
this little citrus fruit delicately
perfumes the house
while deodorizing and disinfecting
it thoroughly.

COMPLETE CLEANING USING LEMON

LAUNDRY ESSENTIALS

To restore whiteness or tackle stubborn stains, there's no substitute for lemon.

⊘ **CAUTION:** Don't forget to always carry out a test on an inconspicuous area of the garment you want to clean, to make sure that it tolerates this treatment. If in doubt, don't proceed and seek advice from a specialist.

▸Whitening

Has your favorite top turned gray? To get it whiter than white again, soak it in a bowl of boiling water mixed with the juice of 2 lemons. Rinse in clean water. If it's made of cotton, put it into a saucepan of boiling water and add 1 tablespoon of white Marseille soap and 2 lemon rings. Make sure that the whole top is immersed. Rinse in clean water before putting it in the washing machine.

If you can't find the time to do this, put it all in the washing machine, cut a lemon into rings, and place them directly into the drum. Wrap the lemon rings in a knee-high stocking to avoid clogging up the machine.

▸Putting an end to gray collars

Do your shirt cuffs and collars remain hopelessly gray or yellowish? To remove these marks, dab them with a mixture

made with 1 part lemon juice to 1 part ammonia to 1 part white Marseille soap. Leave on for 1 minute and then scrub with a toothbrush. Rinse.

▸Perspiration stains?

Before putting it in the washing machine,

Not on leather

Leather doesn't tolerate the acidity of lemon. It needs something less abrasive. So to remove stains, dab gently with a lint-free cloth soaked in 1 part denatured alcohol to 9 parts water. Rinse with a slightly moistened cloth.

pour some lemon juice and then salt on it. Dab with a cloth. Allow to dry. Rinse in clean water.

▸Chewing-gum stain

First and foremost, make sure that you remove it all before putting the garment in the washing machine; otherwise the outcome will be the very opposite to the one you are expecting, because the chewing gum will be fixed permanently in place and will sully the other fabrics at the same time.

• **To combat this,** attach a small plastic bag filled with ice cubes to the chewing gum to harden it. Leave for 30 minutes. Has it hardened? Remove it carefully with the flat blade of a knife until it is completely gone. Clean the blade each time you do this on paper towels.

• **If the chewing gum has left behind a colored stain,** rub some toothpaste on it with the aid of a toothbrush. If it's a greasy stain, clean it gently with a cloth moistened in black soap. With synthetic fabrics, use

TIP

And how about washing the machine?

Once a month, pour 9 tablespoons of citric acid directly into the drum and run it empty on the cold or warm setting to remove all the impurities left behind through successive washes.

lemon juice, and with delicate fabrics, apply glycerine or alcohol at 194°F (90°C) and leave for 30 minutes. Whichever remedy is necessary, rinse thoroughly in tepid water.

▸Ink stain

Act as quickly as possible by absorbing as much of the stain as you can with some paper towels. Then dab the stain with water mixed with lemon juice (juice of half a lemon per bowl of water). However, with wool, use milk instead of lemon.

▸Red berry stains

Dab the stain with a lint-free cloth soaked in lemon juice and leave to act for a few minutes. Then rinse in clean water.

• **If the stain proves hard to lift,** dab it with a tablet of black soap. Leave to act for a few minutes, and then rinse.

• **If the stain is ingrained,** apply some hydrogen peroxide (1 part hydrogen peroxide to 10 parts water) and rinse thoroughly.
• **For silk,** dab with a cloth soaked in alcohol at 194°F (90°C), and then rub gently with a clean cloth.

▸Grass stain

For nondelicate fabrics, generally you just need to rub the stain with very hot water mixed with white Marseille soap, moving in a circular motion, working from the outside inward. Then rinse in clean water.
• **If the stain proves hard to lift** and there's no risk of the fabric fading, dab it with a cloth soaked in lemon juice. If in doubt, use a mixture made with 1 part white vinegar to 2 parts water.

• **For delicate fabrics and colored fabrics,** use denatured alcohol.
• **To remove stains from satin, silk, velvet, wool, or fur,** use slightly diluted ammonia: 25 percent ammonia to 75 percent water. Rinse in clean water.
• **For suede, use heavily diluted ammonia:** A few drops of ammonia in a glass of water or denatured alcohol are both effective.
• **Leather:** Don't forget that this material doesn't tolerate the acidity of lemon; instead, rub it with cleansing milk.

▸Grease stain

Mix 1 part prefiltered lemon to 1 part white vinegar and apply to the grease

TIP

Cleaning the sole plate of the iron

To avoid staining the laundry, clean the sole plate of your iron regularly. Work on it when it's cold. Rub the sole plate with half a lemon sprinkled with table salt, while concentrating on stubborn stains. Rinse with a damp sponge and then dry with a soft cloth.

System D

If you don't have any stain remover at hand, use toothpaste! Spread a dab of toothpaste onto the stain with your fingers. Leave on for a few minutes, then rinse and wash.

stain. Leave on for about 10 minutes and then remove with paper towels.

▸Mold stain

To remove traces of mold from fabrics, apply some lemon juice and then sprinkle with table salt. Leave on for about 10 minutes. Brush to remove it all. Is some of it proving hard to lift? Repeat the process until the stain has gone.

▸Rust stain

Dab the stain with half a lemon sprinkled with table salt. Rinse in clean water.

▸Tea stain

To remove a tea stain from wool, dab it with a clean, lint-free cloth, soaked in lemon juice. Then rinse in clean water.

• **For cotton:** If the stain is still damp, clean it quickly with soapy water (1 tablespoon of soap to 1 quart [1 liter] of tepid water). Rinse in water and white vinegar (two-thirds white vinegar, one-third water). If the stain is dry, dab it with a lint-free cloth, soaked in a mixture made with 1 part white vinegar to 1 part alcohol.

• **For synthetic fabrics:** Apply some tepid glycerine and leave to act for a few minutes and then rinse. To remove an ingrained stain, soak the fabric for 5 to 10 minutes (judge by eye) in a mixture of tepid water and lemon juice, before rubbing with a tablet of black soap. Rinse.

▶Whitening sneakers

To get your sneakers whiter than white again, rub them with a cloth soaked in lemon juice. Allow to dry.

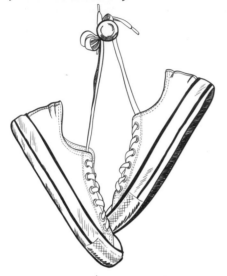

THE KING OF THE KITCHEN

Whether you're rustling up meals, cakes, and fruit juices, or cleaning your floor, sink, and stoves, lemon is indispensable in the kitchen.

▶Disinfecting the trash can

Wash it once a week with 1 quart (1 liter) of hot water mixed with ½ cup (120 milliliters) of lemon juice. Scrub the outside and inside of the trash can thoroughly with a sponge soaked in this mixture. Leave on for a few minutes and then rinse in clean water.

▶A clean sink at all times

• **If your sink is made of resin,** rub it with half a lemon while concentrating on stains or streaks. Leave to act for 3 minutes, rinse in clean water, and dry with a lint-free cloth. Are the stains proving hard to lift? Use some black soap. Mix a cube of soap in a small bowl of tepid water. Apply a little pressure as you rub. Leave to act, rinse, and wipe with a soft, dry cloth. Remember that sinks, washbasins, and bathtubs made of resin do not tolerate abrasive products.

• **If your sink is made of enamel,** use baking soda to tackle these black stains. Use a slightly damp sponge to wipe the baking soda over the sink. Leave to act for 15 to 20 minutes and then rinse. Next, rub it with half a lemon or a sponge soaked in lemon juice to remove the yellowish film that has accumulated and get your enamel looking whiter than white again. Leave on for 5 to 10 minutes, rinse in clean water, and then polish with a dry cloth.

• **If your sink is made of stainless steel,** be careful not to scratch it. Rub the surfaces with a cloth soaked in a mixture of salad oil and lemon juice. Polish it off with a microfiber cloth. For a gleaming finish and to get it looking as good as new, take three paper towels and roll into a ball. Soak the ball in white vinegar mixed with a few drops of salad oil and rub.

• **To remove unsightly black stains,** wipe them with a sponge soaked in a mixture made with 1 teaspoon of black soap, 1 teaspoon of glycerine, and 2 drops of pine essential oil.

▶**Whitening enamel**

To get it whiter than white again with a gleaming finish and to remove stubborn stains such as lipstick and limescale

☞ *Did you know?*

Before squeezing the lemon, roll it two or three times with the palm of your hand on your countertop. The lemon will soften and the pulp will break up more easily. If it's slightly dry, immerse it in hot water for 3 minutes or put it in the microwave for 15 seconds.

TIP

An end to fish odors

The fish was delicious. However, the odors that permeate the living room are far less so...To eliminate them effortlessly, slice a lemon into rings, put them into the bottom of a saucepan, and then cover them with ground cinnamon. Leave the cinnamon to soak into the lemon rings for a few minutes. Then cover them with water. Cook for 15 minutes on a moderate heat and then leave this odor to permeate the room.

---

traces and deposits at the same time, rub the enamel with a damp sponge soaked in a mixture made with 1 part filtered lemon juice to 1 part table salt.

▶**Unblocking the sink**

To prevent the sink from blocking or unpleasant odors from rising up, filter two lemons to remove pieces of pulp and seeds, and then once every 2 weeks pour the juice down the sink before going to work or to bed.

• **If this doesn't do the trick** and the water is sluggish, something must have blocked the trap. To rectify it, roll up your sleeves and empty the trap. Place a bowl underneath before you unscrew it. Remove all the debris, and scrub the sides with a toothbrush soaked in white vinegar and tighten the trap. Then in the evening, before going to bed, pour a good handful of coarse salt, a good handful of baking soda, and 1 cup (235 milliliters) of white vinegar (remember that a chemical reaction is triggered) down the sink. Leave overnight and turn the faucet on to flush it through in the morning.

🛇 CAUTION: Once you've tightened the trap, slide a paper towel underneath and then flush through with water to make sure that you've put the joint back correctly. If droplets of water form, the paper towel gets wet. If this is the case, start again and ensure that you put the joint back properly this time (replace it if it's showing signs of wear and tear).

▸Cleaning the tile joints

To remove black stains and various kinds of mold growth from the tile joints, mix equal parts of lemon juice and baking soda in a small bowl, until a fairly thick paste is obtained. Spread it over the tile joints. Leave on for a few minutes and then rub with a toothbrush. Rinse thoroughly in clean water. Lemon prevents mold from forming because it has anti-fungal properties.

A clean sink with a matte finish 💡 TIP

Your stainless steel sink will be as good as new if you sprinkle it with 1 large tablespoon of flour. Polish it with a soft cloth for a gleaming finish.

▸Removing grease from the range hood

Have you delayed cleaning the range hood for so long that the grease has become ingrained? To loosen it, switch it on and bring a large saucepan of water mixed with the juice of one or two lemons (depending on how big they are) to a boil. As the steam rises, it will act on the grease. If the paper towel did attach to the extractor fan (see tip on the next page), to achieve a good result, you need to stand by the cooker, move the saucepan around, and leave the steam to rise for at least 1 hour. Remove the grease with paper towels, working in a circular motion from the outside inward, to avoid spreading it.

• **As a final touch** to get it looking pristine again, remove the grease from the sides with a sponge soaked in liquid black soap. Then rinse in clean water and dry with a microfiber cloth.

• **To remove grease from the filter grids,** soak them in hot soapy water or in soda before putting them in the dishwasher. Rinse. If the buildup of grease is proving hard to remove, rub them with a brush and some liquid black soap.

• **If your range hood is now spotless,** polish it with a cloth lightly soaked in salad oil to restore its shine. And to prevent the grime from building up again too quickly, you can spray it with a thin layer of silicone.

▸**Disinfecting the refrigerator**
Lemon has antifungal properties and

🔆 **TIP**

Is your range hood extractor fan working efficiently?

To find out how soiled your cooker hood is, switch it on and place a paper towel under the filter grids. If it remains attached, there's no need to clean or change the filters, as the suction is working efficiently. If the paper towel detaches, it's time to act.

combats mold growth. Find time to clean the inside of the refrigerator every 3 weeks by putting the juice of half a lemon, 2 tablespoons of baking soda, and 5 drops of lemon essential oil into a bowl half filled with tepid water. Don't forget to filter the lemon to remove the seeds and other traces of pulp. Soak a sponge and tackle the surfaces of the refrigerator and even the racks, and remember to clean the bottom too.

▸**Removing stains from the chopping board**
For the grill, barbecue, and chopping board: Rub with half a lemon to remove the stains and marks and to eliminate potential germs at the same time. Leave to act overnight before rinsing in clean water.

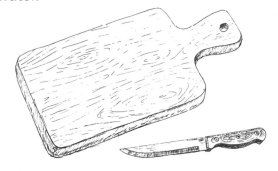

▸**Descaling stainless steel**
To restore the gleam to your stainless steel items, rub them with a cloth soaked in a mixture made with lemon juice and

1 tablespoon of peanut oil. As a finishing touch, polish them with a microfiber cloth.
• **To eradicate unsightly black stains,** wipe them with a sponge or a cloth soaked in black soap, pine essential oil, and glycerine. Be especially careful not to use anything abrasive; otherwise, you'll risk scratching it all.

Deodorizing kitchen utensils
Rub kitchen utensils with the pulp of half a lemon to remove unpleasant fish or garlic odors.

Looking after your cooktops
• **If they're electric:** Over time, unsightly traces of rust appear. Pour 4 to 5 drops of lime onto them and leave on for 5 to 8 minutes. Then rub with a slightly damp sponge. Rinse in clean water.

To slow down the appearance of rust, grease your burners regularly with some paper towels soaked in vegetable oil.
• **If they're ceramic burners or induction burners:** To tackle stubborn stains and get them looking pristine again, rub the burners with half a lemon. Leave on for 5 to 10 minutes before rinsing with a sponge soaked in a mixture made with 1 table-spoon of liquid Mar-  seille soap and 1 tablespoon of white vinegar in a bowl of water. Finally, wipe with a lint-free cloth.

Washing the dishwasher
• **And how about taking care of your dishwasher?** Once every 2 weeks, find time to wash the filter and then pour the juice of two or three lemons into the dishwasher detergent compartment. Make sure that you filter the juice to prevent the seeds and pulp from entering the machine. Run it on a normal cycle, which will not only wash and rinse the interior, but it will also deodorize and disinfect it.

Washing the countertop
Sprinkle half a lemon with some table salt, and then rub onto the countertop. Concentrate on the stains. Leave to act for a few minutes before rinsing in cold, clean water with the aid of a sponge. Dry with a clean cloth.

Cleaning the microwave
• **To both eliminate unpleasant odors** and remove food that has stuck to the surfaces, pour cold water into a bowl until three-quarters full and add three or four lemon rings measuring approximately ½ inch (1 centimeter) thick. Heat the microwave on full power for 3 or 4

minutes until the water turns to steam. Leave to act for a few minutes and don't open the door until the food has come loose. Then scrub with a microfiber cloth.

• **Are the food particles proving hard to remove?** Prepare a fairly thick mixture made with baking soda and liquid Marseille soap. As baking soda is a mild abrasive, it can tackle these stubborn stains. Rinse in clean water and dry with a lint-free cloth.

⚠ CAUTION: Never use a scourer or sponge made of metal, as this will damage the surfaces.

▸ **Cleaning a small electric appliance**
To prevent unsightly limescale stains from furring up the kettle or any other appliance, clean them with a sponge soaked in lemon juice. If the appliance is already heavily coated with limescale, rub directly with half a lemon to clean it.

▸ **Protecting plastic containers**
There's nothing less appealing than a stained or foul-smelling plastic container.

Stain-free hands TIP

It is enjoyable to make blackberry or raspberry jelly, but your hands often get stained with every color of the rainbow. To remove these stains, rub your hands with the juice of half a lemon. Leave on for a few minutes and then rinse in clean water. And to remove strawberry or raspberry stains, simply rinsing in lemon juice is very effective.

To have the pleasure of using them again, soak them in a bowl filled with a mixture made with 1 quart (1 liter) of hot water and 1 cup (235 milliliters) of lemon juice. If the containers are not completely submerged, double the quantities. Leave to act for about 10 minutes. Then rub them with a sponge soaked in baking soda. Rinse in clean water and dry thoroughly.

▸ **Scouring the oven**
You love it when a delicate aroma wafts out of the oven, because it gives you a sense of the dish that's browning in there. But all it takes is a lingering, unpleasant odor to spoil it all. So allowing the oven to get dirty is no longer an option. Whether you have a self-cleaning feature or not, get down to it once a week.

• **Take the racks out of the oven** and pour the juice of two lemons directly into the oven. Spread it over the entire surface. Cut the rest of the lemon into pieces and put them into the oven. Preheat the oven to 176°F (80°C) and leave on for approximately 30 minutes. While taking care not to burn yourself, remove the food deposits with a slightly damp, nonabrasive sponge. They'll come away easily and the oven will smell nice.

• **Are the food deposits deeply ingrained?** Wash the surfaces with a slightly damp sponge soaked in white Marseille soap or black soap, and a little baking soda. Rinse in clean water and then repeat, this time using a sponge soaked in lemon juice.

• **To prevent a film of grease building up on the surfaces,** finish off by using a sponge soaked in white vinegar.

Fragrant hands 💡 TIP

To eliminate the odors of garlic or onion on your hands, just rub them with half a lemon.

▶ **Eliminating odors in the refrigerator**
If you have a lemon left over after preparing your recipe, put it in the refrigerator door and it will eliminate unpleasant odors and release a subtle fragrance at the same time. Make sure you change it every week.

▶ **Cleaning your tiled floors**
• **To remove most stains from floor tiles,** just rub them with a mixture made with 2 tablespoons of lemon juice in 1 quart (1 liter) of water.

• **Greasy stains vanish if you use flour.** Sprinkle them immediately and leave on until they've been completely absorbed. Remove the excess and repeat the process if necessary. Then go over it with a floor cloth.

FROM FLOOR TO CEILING

Antiseptic, cleansing, and antibacterial—lemon is ideal for cleaning the house from floor to ceiling.

▶ **A pleasant moth repellent**
• **A nightmare lurking in our closets,** these little bugs can tackle a pile of sweaters

Lemon, a cook's ally

IT'S USED TO SEASON DISHES,
BUT IT'S OFTEN FORGOTTEN THAT IT'S ALSO A COOK'S SECRET WEAPON.

▸Toning down a spicy dish

Have you gone overboard with the chili? Add a teaspoonful of lemon juice to counteract it. Adjust the amount to taste.

▸Is it too salty?

To counteract the taste of salt, add a little lemon or lime juice.

▸Slowing down oxidization

The acid content of a lemon slows down the oxidization of fruits, guacamole, vegetables, and various fungi. To prevent them from going black, pour some lemon juice onto them and keep refrigerated.

▸Embellishing a green salad

Has the salad wilted? Before throwing it out with the compost, fill the salad spinner with very cold water and add some lemon juice. Then put it all into the refrigerator for 1 hour to revive the salad.

▸Preventing cauliflower from turning brown

Cauliflower tends to turn brown during cooking. To preserve its whiteness, sprinkle with lemon juice before cooking it.

▸Retaining the fluidity of your caramel

As soon as caramel starts to brown, add a teaspoonful of lemon juice to prevent it from hardening at the end of cooking.

▸Washing fruits and vegetables

Lemon is effective against the pesticides found on your fruits and vegetables. Mix 1 tablespoon of lemon juice in some water and pour the mixture into a spray bottle. The lemon juice will add freshness to your vegetables.

▸Protecting an egg

Have you just broken an egg? Rub it with some lemon juice so that it keeps for a few hours; that way you avoid discarding it.

and make six to eight holes in each one. To prevent the moths from moving in, vacuum the backs of the closets and under the furniture regularly. Then make a lot of commotion, as they hate to be disturbed. Open the closets, ventilate them, move your piles of clothes around and shake the hangers, and so on.

• **At the end of winter** (March or April at the latest), empty your shelves and clean them with a sponge soaked in a mixture made with the juice of three lemons, 1 cup of water, and 2 drops of eucalyptus essential oil. Concentrate on the corners. Allow to dry thoroughly before putting your clothes back in the closet. To complete the process, place lavender or aroma sachets in your closets.

• **Put a few cloves inside a lemon** and hang it in the closet. A delicate aroma will greet you every time you open the door, and because moths can't abide this odor, it will drive them away.

Eliminating odors

TIP

Place half a lemon in the top rack of the dishwasher to eliminate cooked egg or fish odors.

▸Polishing furniture

To take care of your wooden furniture, make your own polish. Mix ½ cup (120 milliliters) of filtered lemon juice (to remove seeds and pieces of pulp) with 1 tablespoon of olive oil. Pour this mixture into a bottle and label it clearly. Put a little of this liquid polish on a clean, lint-free cloth. Allow to dry and buff with a soft cloth.

▸Deodorizing an ashtray

• **There's nothing more unpleasant** than the smell of stale cigarette smoke. To prevent the odor from penetrating the walls, wash the ashtray, dry it, and then rub with half a lemon sprinkled with table salt.

• **At the same time,** grate a lemon and then squeeze it to extract the juice. Mix together. Add a teaspoonful of cinnamon. Divide this mixture into two ramekins and place where the smell of tobacco is strongest.

▸Dusting wooden furniture

To dust and restore their shine at the same time, use a clean, lint-free cloth moistened in a mixture made with lemon juice and 1 teaspoon of olive oil. Use a circular motion, working from the outside inward. The cloth must be thoroughly squeezed out before use to prevent droplets from falling onto the wood. Then wipe thoroughly with a clean, dry cloth.

▶Making your windows shine

Filter some lemon juice to remove the seeds and other pieces of pulp; then add this to some tepid water in equal amounts. Soak a ball of newspaper and rub in a circular motion. There's no need to rinse. Allow to dry and polish with a soft, lint-free cloth. And don't forget: For crystal-clear windows, you should avoid cleaning them on sunny days.

▶Eliminating fireplace odors

All log fires have an unpleasant odor. To rectify this, just throw a few pieces of lemon peel into the flames.

TIP

Refreshing a sponge

Once every 10 days, before you go to bed, soak your sponges in a bowl of water mixed with lemon juice. Rinse in clean water and make sure that you squeeze them out thoroughly. Cleaned, disinfected, deodorized—they'll take on a new lease on life.

▶Cleaning brushes

Have you finished painting the living room? Clean your brushes so that you can reuse them. Soak them in a saucepan of boiling water mixed with lemon juice (one lemon per quart [liter]) for 20 minutes. Rinse once in soapy water, and then in clean water.

▶ Cleaning the cupboards

If you have fungi and mold growth in your cupboard, you can use lemon to remove them. The juice is a natural disinfectant. Squeeze two lemons and then pour the filtered juice into a spray bottle. Next add the same quantity of water and mix thoroughly. Then spray the area of the cupboard where the mold is located. But don't make it too wet—you just need to moisten everything. Finally, let it sit for 2 hours. If the odor persists, repeat the process.

▶ Restoring cane chairs

To get them looking pristine again, use the vacuum cleaner to remove the dust. Then prepare a mixture made with water and lemon juice (1 quart [1 liter] of water to the juice of one lemon).

Soak a soft brush in this mixture and then rub (not too hard) in the direction of the cane. Rinse in clean water and allow to dry in the shade.

THE SECRET WEAPON FOR TACKLING THE BATHROOM

Due to its high level of citric acid, lemon is an effective disinfectant. So feel free to use it frequently.

▶ Descaling the toilets

• **Remove these unsightly traces of lime-scale** that build up on the surfaces and in the toilet bowl, by simmering (but don't boil) ½ quart (½ liter) of white vinegar

☞ Did you know?

To restore the shine to your windows, use newspaper rather than magazine paper. Magazine paper is not an option, because it's glossy. Newspaper is effective as a cleaning agent on account of its absorbent properties and printing inks.

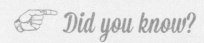

and the juice of two lemons. Once the liquid is warmed through, pour it into the toilets. Rub the surfaces—clean thoroughly under the rim—with a toilet brush and then leave to act for at least 2 hours. Flush the toilet to rinse it through.

• **Has limescale built up under the rims?** Scrub with a toothbrush soaked in lemon juice. Leave to act for at least 1 hour before flushing the toilet.

• **To get the toilet bowl looking pristine again,** clean it with a sponge soaked in a mixture made with 2 tablespoons of lemon juice, water, and white vinegar. There's no need to rinse, but wipe with a clean, lint-free cloth.

• **Don't forget the cistern.** One evening, before you go to bed, pour a mixture made with the juice of two lemons and 2 tablespoons of white vinegar into the cistern. Leave to act overnight before flushing the toilet. The mixture will disinfect, clean, and descale the whole cistern.

▸Descaling the shower

• **To prevent the water pressure from becoming too low,** descale the shower nozzles and spray head regularly. The best way to do this is to unscrew them and rub them with a toothbrush soaked in lemon juice. But to remove the limescale thoroughly, white vinegar is essential. Unscrew the showerhead and soak it in a bowl of undiluted white vinegar for 30 minutes. Make sure that the nozzles are thoroughly submerged. Scrub the nozzles with a toothbrush to remove all the limescale deposits. Soak for another 15 minutes before rinsing in clean water.

• **Are you finding it impossible to unscrew the showerhead?** Pour a quart (liter) of white vinegar (or more depending on size) into a plastic bag and secure around the showerhead with a rubber band. Leave to act overnight. Remove the plastic bag, scrub the nozzles with a toothbrush, and then turn on the water to rinse them. Finally, wipe with a sponge soaked in clean water.

❶ CAUTION: Make sure that you protect your eyes and work in a ventilated room so that the smell of white vinegar isn't troublesome.

▸Mirror, mirror, on the wall

• **To get it sparkling clean,** rub it with a lint-free cloth soaked in a teaspoonful of filtered lemon juice. Allow to dry, and wipe without rinsing.

• **Is it very dirty?** Dilute about 10 drops of lemon essential oil in a mixture made with 90 percent demineralized water and 10 percent denatured alcohol. Wipe over with a cloth.

• **To prevent condensation from forming,** rub your glass and mirrors with black soap. Allow to dry and then remove the excess with a cloth, taking care to wipe in a circular motion, working from the outside inward to avoid leaving streaks. The black soap will leave behind a fine film of glycerine invisible to the naked eye, which will stop condensation from forming.

▸Making your chrome shine

Are the faucets covered in a white film? This is due to limescale. To remove it and get your chrome looking pristine again, scrub them with half a lemon. Leave to act for 5 minutes and then polish with a lint-free cloth. There's no need to rinse. Use a soft toothbrush and a cloth to get the hard-to-reach parts.

▸Scouring the bathtub

A soak in the bathtub wouldn't be very appealing if you allowed it to get dirty or caked with limescale.

• **If you have an enamel bathtub,** rub it with half a lemon, while concentrating on the stains. Leave to act for 10 to

Invisible ink

 TIP

Even in the age of smartphones and game consoles, invisible ink always fascinates young children. So tell them about a trick for playing secret agents. All you need is a sushi chopstick and some lemon juice! Squeeze the lemon and dip the end of the chopstick into it; leave the chopstick to absorb the lemon, and start writing on a piece of white paper. The ink will gradually disappear as you write. To make it reappear and decipher the message, just shine a flashlight under the sheet of paper.

15 minutes and then rinse in clean water. Is it proving hard to lift? Sprinkle the lemon with table salt, rub again, and leave on for at least 30 minutes. Then take a cloth soaked in white vinegar and wipe it over the bathtub. Rinse in clean water and wipe with a dry cloth.

• **If you have a resin bathtub,** never rub it with abrasive products. Just wipe it with a sponge or a soft cloth soaked in liquid black soap or dishwashing liquid. Rinse in clean water.

▶ Restoring the translucence of your shower screen

• **Is limescale the reason why** your shower screen is more often white than transparent? There's no point in scrubbing it, as cleaning products for glass are relatively ineffective. To remove it effortlessly, wash the screen with a sponge soaked in a mixture of black soap, denatured alcohol, and a drop of lemon juice. Leave on a few minutes, and then rinse and dry with a microfiber cloth.

• **Has it turned white** because you've been cleaning it regularly? Tape a few paper towels onto the dry shower screen. Pour some white vinegar into a bowl and bring it to a boil in the microwave. Then trickle it onto the paper towels. Take a sponge

soaked in white vinegar (still hot) to saturate it and make the paper stick firmly to the screen. Leave on for 1 hour, remove the paper, and rinse in clean water.

• **Make sure that you work** in a ventilated room so that the smell of white vinegar isn't troublesome.

▶ Cleaning the tile joints

• **Removing black traces of mold** caused by humidity is quick and easy; it's also important, because tile joints that gather dirt start lifting off and go moldy, thus opening the door to water penetration. Make a paste with lemon juice and a handful of coarse salt. Saturate a slightly moistened toothbrush with this mixture and scrub the tile joints. Leave on for 5 minutes. Rinse with a damp sponge and dry them with a lint-free cloth.

• **If you don't have any coarse salt,** try a different method. Bring a ¼ quart (¼ liter) of water to a boil and add a lemon cut in two. Remove from heat and leave to infuse for 5 minutes. Immerse the toothbrush in this mixture and scrub the tile

joints. Make sure that the mixture is hot; otherwise it will be ineffective. Dry with a clean, lint-free cloth.

• **If despite all your best efforts,** the tile joints are still black, it's because they're too old. It's time to replace them.

Descaling with soda

TIP

Have you any leftover cola? Even if it's gone flat, pour it into the toilets. Leave to act for 2 hours and then scrub with a brush while concentrating on the edges. Then after you've flushed the toilet, the limescale traces will disappear and the toilet bowl will shine.

CLEANING METALS

Metals oxidize and tarnish when exposed to the sun and dust. Clean them regularly to keep them looking pristine.

▶ **Sparkling silver**
Your jewelry and silverware can be damaged by unsightly black. Rub the silverware with a soft toothbrush soaked in lemon juice. Make sure that you filter the lemon juice to remove the seeds, pulp, and other impurities. Rinse and then dry with a lint-free cloth.

▶ **Costume jewelry as good as new**
Rub your jewelry with a soft toothbrush soaked in lemon juice mixed with coarse salt. Rinse with 1 to 2 tablespoons of denatured alcohol mixed in water. Polish with beeswax to give it a shine.

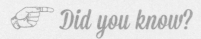

▸ Gleaming bronze

If your bronze objects are very dirty and dull, rub them with a lint-free cloth soaked in a mixture of one-third lemon juice and two-thirds denatured alcohol.

▸ Brass with myriad reflections

• **If it isn't too tarnished,** rub brass with half a lemon sprinkled with salt. Rinse in clean water and then rub vigorously with newspaper to polish.

• **Is it very dirty?** Prepare a smooth paste made with 1 part lemon juice to 1 part flour. Add a half part of table salt. Take a lint-free cloth and rub the brass in a circular motion while concentrating on the stubborn stains. Leave to act for several hours before rinsing and then polishing with a wool cloth.

💡 **TIP**

Grapefruit to the rescue

Grapefruits are as acidic as lemons and will be just as effective in tackling limescale.

▸ Tackling verdigris

• **To remove these greenish stains** defacing your brass and copper objects, brush them with half a lemon sprinkled with salt. Rinse in plenty of clean water and then dry with a lint-free cloth.

• **If your costume jewelry** leaves behind unsightly verdigris stains on your skin, carry out the same treatment: clean the jewelry with lemon juice and then apply some clear varnish to the section that has rubbed off onto your skin.

❶ CAUTION: Verdigris can cause burns and release toxins.

In the event of contact with the skin, wash immediately in soapy water. Then rinse with plenty of clean water.

THE BACKYARD'S ALLY

You often have to leave garden furniture to the whims of the weather, which can damage it.

▸Cleaning white plastic garden furniture

• **If outdoor furniture has turned black,** wash it with a damp sponge soaked in baking soda. Rinse in clean water and then dry with a lint-free sponge.

• **If all the marks have vanished** but there is still a grayish hue, rub with a sponge soaked in lemon juice. Allow to dry and act overnight. Rinse in clean water and polish with a soft cloth.

• **Use beaten egg whites** to get your garden furniture looking pristine again. Beat 4 egg whites until stiff. Take a paintbrush and apply a thin layer of egg white to your garden furniture. Allow to dry and then polish with a soft cloth. They'll be restored to their former glory.

▸Maintaining your deckchairs

• **Winter has taken its toll** on the canvas and as a result it's marked with a number of mold stains. To tackle them, prepare a mixture made with some filtered lemon juice, 1 tablespoon of cornstarch, 1 teaspoon of table salt, and a knob of black soap. Apply liberally to dry stains. Leave on for 1 hour until the paste is dry. Then rub with a stiff bristle brush, taking care to use a circular motion working from the outside inward. There's no need to rinse.

• **Is the mold proving hard to remove?** Rinse with white vinegar mixed in water (2 tablespoons of white vinegar per 6 cups [1.5 liters] of water) and allow to dry in the fresh air.

▸Cleaning wickerwork

As wicker is much daintier than rattan and very lightweight, it is mainly used for making hats, baskets, or children's chairs. Start by dusting it with a lint-free cloth or even with the vacuum cleaner upholstery attachment.

Tip **TIP**

Has your plastic garden furniture been restored to its original color or whiteness? Apply a coat of olive oil to protect it.

Then spruce it up by preparing a smooth paste made with the juice of three filtered lemons and 4 tablespoons of baking soda. Dilute the mixture with 1 tablespoon of cold water to give it a consistent texture. Then rub with a slightly moistened sponge and use a toothbrush to get in between the braids. Allow to dry. Rinse with clean water.

⚠ CAUTION: To prevent rattan or wicker furniture from splitting, dry it in the shade.

▸ **Polishing rattan**

To spruce up your white rattan furniture, rub with a sponge soaked in lemon juice mixed with a teaspoonful of salt. Allow to dry, without rinsing.

▸ **Removing stains from patio paving**

To tackle stains that have become ingrained on your terra-cotta paving slabs, scrub

☞ *Did you know?*

Wicker is often mistaken for rattan. However, they have nothing in common. Wicker is a plant found in cold countries and is a member of the willow family, while rattan is a vine and a member of the palm family. Rattan is found in humid, intensely hot regions such as equatorial Africa, Asia, and more specifically in Indonesia.

Anticreak **TIP**

A rattan rocking chair can often have an annoying creaking sound. You need to nourish these plant fibers to get rid of the creaks. Rub the fibers with a sponge soaked in a mixture made with ½ cup (120 milliliters) of flaxseed oil, 1 tablespoon of turpentine, and 1 quart (1 liter) of hot water.

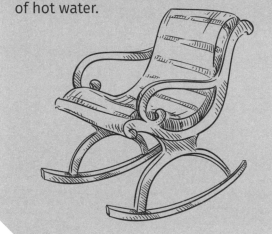

them with a long-handled brush soaked in a bucket of tepid water mixed with lemon juice (4 tablespoons of lemon juice per 1 quart [1 liter] of water).

▸ **Brightening up the patio joints**

• **To get them looking good again,** give them some elbow grease. Prepare a mixture made with 1 part lemon juice to 1 part white vinegar and scrub them one by one with a stiff bristle brush. Leave to act and then rinse in clean water.

• **Is the grime proving hard to lift?** Repeat the process, but this time, sprinkle with baking soda before you start scrubbing. Be careful, as there will be a chemical reaction caused by mixing baking soda and white vinegar. Leave to act and rinse.

⊘ CAUTION: With decking, avoid high-pressure cleaning; even though effective, it's extremely abrasive and in time will likely damage the surface of the wood.

▶ Watering the plants

Plants dislike water that's too hard. So mix some lemon juice into the water before watering them. It will reduce the level of limescale and the plants will thrive.

ANIMALS AND INSECTS, ALLIES AND ENEMIES

Love them or hate them, sometimes you need to act—for or against them.

▶ Keeping cats away from plants

Spray some lemon juice mixed with 1 quart (1 liter) of water on the plants and soil. Cats can't abide this odor.

▶ Diverting cat fleas

Cut a lemon into slices and add to half a quart (liter) of boiling water. Remove from the heat and let the mixture infuse until it's completely cold. Then soak a protective glove in this mixture and gently rub it

over your cat's coat. Repeat the treatment every day if necessary.

❶ CAUTION: Do not apply if the cat's skin is chafed, due to scratching, or if he has any skin lesions.

▶ Neutralizing the cat litter odor

Cut one, two, or three lemons in two and distribute them around the room.

▶ Fighting mice and rats

They can't abide the smell of moldy lemon. So distribute a few slices of moldy lemon in all the places they're likely to hide. You can alternate lemon with peppercorns.

▶ Combating ants

• **Do you have any lemons** that have gone moldy because you left them too long? They're ideal for combating ants. Cut them into slices and then distribute them along their routes (doors, windows). The essential oil present in the peel acts as a repellent. The ants will turn back. Replace the lemon slices every 10 days.

• **Are you afraid the ants will invade your cupboards?** Put a sachet of green sage or camphor on a shelf.

• **And if you really find these convoys of ants troublesome,** locate the ant nest and flood it with 10½ quarts (10.5 liters) of hot water mixed with 7 ounces (200 grams) diluted black soap.

▶ Repelling flies

Instead of distributing slices of lemon on the ground, hang them up high. It's simple: Just pierce the slices and thread a piece of cord through them.

5

REMOVING
ANY STAIN

Tips and miracle products
to get rid of any stains

FROM CLOTHES

. . . TO OBJECTS

Who hasn't raged against the stains on the tablecloth that turn black when you wash them, the white mark on the magnificent solid wood dresser, or the terrible red berry stain on their white shirt? The pharmacy aisles are full of stain removers, but is it really necessary to clutter your cabinets and empty your wallet when there are age-old natural products that are proven to work?

Baking soda, white vinegar, black soap, salt, lemon, and milk are all everyday products that can really help us fight stains. After falling out of use, they are now back in force. In truth, they have everything going for them: biodegradable, green, nontoxic, and they work.

They are also very economical and so save us money. As they are multipurpose, they also save us space in the cabinets, as most of the time, one product combines the properties of various industrial ones. Finally, they are easy to find in local stores, drugstores, and DIY stores.

But the product is not the answer to everything, as removing stains is not the same as cleaning. If all you needed to do was add a miracle product to the wash to get immaculate clothes, that would just be too easy. Most stains are stubborn and appear to disappear after a while but come back grayer, browner, or blacker. This is not only the case with textiles; wood, plastic, upholstery, and tiles attract stains and require particular attention, as the process of removing the stain can end up being worse than the stain when discoloration and white marks appear.

Before attempting, you should know a few rules and follow a specific methodology.

▸ The right technique

Stain removal is a step that requires time and some attention.

▸ Acting quickly

As much as possible, you should act immediately and thoroughly. The longer you wait, the more the stain will become ingrained and will be difficult to treat.

▸ Observing

First, it is necessary to assess the type of material that is stained: untreated wood, waxed wood, silk, colored cotton, and so on. Wool and wood do not like water, while colored fabrics hate stain removers and silk loves gentle care. As much as possible, you should check the composition of the material and read the instructions of the appropriate stain-removing product, especially with regard to dilution. The aim is to remove a stain and keep the material intact.

▸ Doing things in the right order

Don't wash before removing the stain, as hot water and detergent will only set the stain. Stain removal should be done locally. After the stain disappears, then you can wash the product.

Doing it right

TIP

To avoid white marks, always dab the stained area from the outside to the inside.

Getting your hands dirty

It is important to give yourself every chance of success by providing optimal conditions for the stain remover—for instance, by preparing the mixture, scrubbing or dabbing the stain gently, soaking in cold water, and so on.

Moderation is key

There is no point in overdoing it: Use the stain-removing product in small quantities. The aim is to target the stain well and avoid spilling onto the unstained part. It is important to respect dosage or you could get the opposite effect.

Working painstakingly

Unless it is a powder that is scattered directly onto the material, it is advisable to pour the stain remover into a small bowl so that you can use it with more precision with the help of a cotton swab. No cotton swab? A clean cotton cloth will do. However, it must be white: Cleaning a stain with a colored napkin would be a disaster. The color could come out and then you would have two stains on your hands.

Testing first

Whatever the object to be cleaned, always test on a small area to make sure that it can withstand treatment. When in doubt, stop and ask an expert for advice.

Taking your time

This is the hardest thing to do. Few products act immediately. It can take up to 24 hours for them to penetrate, become absorbed, and dissolve.

GETTING STARTED

There are things you should do automatically for each type of stain.

▶ Greasy and liquid stains are absorbed

Don't use water! This could damage materials like wood or will spread the stain. First, you need to absorb the grease by placing a highly absorbent product on the stain, such as talcum powder or cornstarch.

The same goes for liquid stains. Before doing anything, the liquid must be absorbed rather than spread. A paper towel will do the trick and then the stain remover will be able to take effect.

▶ "Thick" stains dry out

If you try to clean out mud, chewing gum, wax, and so on, immediately, you will only make the problem worse! Instead it is best to leave it to dry. Once the stain has hardened, you will only need to brush or rub it out carefully.

SPECIFIC STAIN REMOVERS

Don't let these strange names bewilder you; what counts is their awesome power to eliminate certain stains. These are the only ones that can save our precious belongings because they respect the most fragile of materials. Buy them at your local drugstore or grocery store, or buy them online.

▶ Cornstarch

This is 100 percent natural and safe for humans and the environment

• **Its strength.** It is ideal for removing and eliminating grease and urine marks. Use it on clothes, leather, upholstery, floors, walls, and wood furniture. It has proved to be effective at removing grease and absorbing liquids (it can absorb up to 80 percent of its weight in water). It is easy to use: You just need to sprinkle the stain with this powder and leave it. Then dust it off. It doesn't work straightaway; it is sometimes necessary to leave it overnight, and for some ingrained stains, it will be necessary to machine wash afterward.

• **Its advantage.** It is gentle and adapts to all fabrics and materials: textiles (including silk), carpets, leather, wood, parquet floor, stone, concrete, and so on.

▶The unique ox-gall soap

Its name is unappealing but once you've accepted it, you cannot do without it. As the name suggests, it does contain ox bile extracts. The enzymes they contain are able to digest all organic matter such as urine, blood, and fruit.

• **Its strength.** Not only does it devour grease, but it also feeds on all kinds of stains: motor oil, mayonnaise, fruit, grass, wine, coffee, tea, chocolate, lipstick, blood, ink, and so on. It also does away with sweat stains and is recommended for shirt collars and cuffs. You just need to rub the stain with the soap before machine washing it.

• **Its advantage.** It is the friend of fabrics. Because it is both highly effective against stains and gentle on fabrics, it can be used on cotton as well as synthetics and even on delicates like silk or wool. It will also be safe for the most delicate of colors. Test an inconspicuous spot first. The only disadvantage is you will need to wash afterward.

▶Sodium percarbonate

This granulated white powder, known as solid hydrogen peroxide, is made of a blend of sodium carbonate (soda crystals) and hydrogen peroxide. Sodium percarbonate is biodegradable and nontoxic. It is sold in the United States under brand names such as OxiClean.

• **Its strength.** It has antibacterial, disinfectant, and powerful oxidizing properties and works in warm water. It is the best for white linens and means no more gray shirts and stained collars!

• **Its advantage.** Used mainly on fabrics, it is very easy to use. You just need to add 2 tablespoons to the drum of the machine to get rid of stubborn stains and only 1 tablespoon to obtain radiant white linens.

⓵ WARNING: Handle with care, using gloves and avoiding all contact with skin and eyes. Don't use on aluminum and waxed, painted, or lacquered surfaces (unless you want to strip them down). Because it is a combustible, keep it away from flammable products, including alcohol and essential oils.

▶ Ammonium hydroxide, the destroyer of stains and odors

This is also called ammonia solution or ammonia water. It is an aqueous solution containing ammonia gas (NH_3), and its true name is ammonium hydroxide (NH_4OH).

• **Its strength.** It is primarily a stain remover and eliminates traces of blood, wine, sweat, fruit, wax, varnish, among others. It is used on rugs and carpets, wallpaper, tableware, windows, domestic appliances, floors and walls (apart from cement and concrete), plastics, wood, and all types of fabrics (except wool and silk).

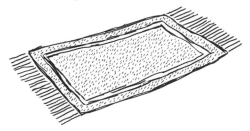

• **Its advantage.** It works immediately and has a deodorizing effect. It is also ideal against urine stains and revives colors. Ammonium hydroxide is diluted in a large quantity of water, then rinsed thoroughly with clean water.

⓵ WARNING: This is a dangerous product that should be used with caution. Always read the instructions, wear gloves, and do not inhale the fumes. Always open the window when using it. Ammonium hydroxide damages linoleum, cement, and concrete.

▶ Turpentine, the antistain champion

This is also called spirit or oil of turpentine. Turpentine is a colorless essential oil, whose smell is reminiscent of pine. It is nonsoluble in water.

• **Its strength.** It dissolves grease, paint, polish, cleaning products, and perfume.

It removes stains from all fabrics, even delicate materials like silk; it removes mold from leather and is as equally effective at cleaning the screens of electronic devices, such as touch screens.

• **It is also the ally of cabinetmakers,** as it removes scratches from furniture. Added to denatured alcohol or olive oil, it works on wood stains. Combined with flaxseed oil, it removes white stains.

• **Its advantage.** The amount varies according to use; follow package directions. It is often used pure to remove stains. It doesn't need to be rinsed.

❶ WARNING: Turpentine is a dangerous product that should be used and stored with caution, away from children and pets and in a well-ventilated room. Avoid all contact with eyes. It is also a mild skin irritant.

Wash hands after each use. Turpentine can be lethal if even small amounts are swallowed by a child. It is highly flammable and should not be exposed to heat.

▶ Rubbing alcohol

An excellent stain remover and antiseptic is 90 percent alcohol, which is sold in pharmacies; 70 percent alcohol is a good alternative found in stores.

• **Its strength.** It dissolves grease, ink, varnish, and resin stains. It is also used to dust furniture and remove fingerprints from walls.

• **Its advantage.** This disinfectant does not leave any trace (but always test an inconspicuous area on colors first). Just dip a cotton pad with 90 percent or 70 percent alcohol and rub the stain. It is therefore suitable for delicate materials that cannot withstand water. It is also not harmful to the environment.

❶ WARNING: Use 70 percent and 90 percent alcohol with caution because they are flammable.

▶ Hydrogen peroxide, the brightener

Also called peroxide, this antiseptic is made naturally from enzymes called peroxidases. It can be found in pharmacies.

• **Its strength.** At home, it is a fantastic stain remover that eliminates almost all organic stains such as blood, fruit, grease, sweat, carrot, tomato, lipstick, grass, and soot. It also gets rid of soap residue and mold.

TIP

Little cleaning nuts

Amazing but true: There is a kind of fruit that can replace industrial laundry and dishwasher detergents. It is commonly known as soapberry and comes from *Sapindus mukorossi*, a tree growing in Kashmir, India. Its shell is full of saponin, a natural soap that is very effective when mixed in water. You just need to slip six shells in a small bag and place them in the drum of the washing machine. You can combine them with a spoonful of sodium percarbonate for very dirty laundry. As they are nontoxic, they are also suitable for washing dishes. They are economical: They can be reused five or six times. You will find them in organic shops.

• **Its advantage.** The dosage varies but it is usually 1 part hydrogen peroxide to 20 or 30 parts water for stain removal. It needs to be rinsed.

THE ESSENTIALS FOR THE WHOLE HOUSE

You don't have any stain removers? No problem—there are basics to have at home for cleaning and removing stains.

▸ **Marseille soap, a safe bet**
True Marseille soap contains at least 72 percent vegetable oil (olive, palm, copra) and caustic soda. It is biodegradable and not made with any perfume, coloring, or additives.
• **Marseille soap is made by hand**. The brown/green soap (made from olive and copra and/or palm oil) is recommended for body care, while the white soap (extracted from the palm oil fruit, peanut oil, or copra oil) is used for laundry and house cleaning.
• **Its strength.** Used dry, it gets rid of most grease stains by absorbing them; in liquid form, it fights difficult stains like fruit, grease, makeup, and drinks.

• **Its advantage** is also its disadvantage. It is gentle so it is suitable for most materials, but sometimes it is not potent enough to eliminate stubborn stains. Like black soap, it removes stains as well as cleans, unlike the other stain removers. The only drawback is that you need to rinse it so it is only suitable for water-resistant materials.

▶ **Essential white vinegar**

White vinegar is made industrially by acetification, the process of turning corn or beet alcohol into vinegar. Although it is produced industrially, white vinegar is in fact a 100 percent green and natural product, which deteriorates quickly and has no environmental impact.

• **Its strength.** Use it as a cleaner, purifier, limescale remover, softener, color enhancer, grease remover, deodorizer, disinfectant… It is impressive for making everything shine at home.

• **Its advantage.** It is used pure, diluted in water (50/50) to clean windows or toys, or combined with salt (to make copper shine)

☞ Did you know?

Marseille soap is the only cleaning product that has had the honor of having its production method standardized by Louis XIV. Indeed, in 1688, through the Edict of Colbert, the king introduced regulations regarding its production: cooking in large cauldrons and exclusive use of pure vegetable oils and forbidding the use of animal fats. Unfortunately, although the king passed a law on the manufacturing method, nothing was planned to protect its name or determine its composition. As a result, there are many counterfeits containing additives. It is necessary to pick an authentic one to obtain the same outcomes as a century ago. The soap should say "72% oil" and have the name of the soap factory that makes it. You can also recognize it thanks to its distinctive smell.

or baking soda (to unblock drains). It is used cold for cleaning moderately dirty floors and walls and greasy kitchen furniture and utensils; removing stains from clothes before washing; deodorizing toilets and drains; and softening fabrics. It is used hot or lukewarm for cleaning very dirty floors and blackened pans and for descaling kitchen utensils and unblocking a sink.

▶ Black soap

In solid, soft, or liquid form, black soap is made of lye and a fatty matter such as olive oil, flaxseed oil, walnut oil, corn oil, or even glycerin. It is natural, ecological, and easy on the environment, but it has one drawback: a distinctive smell that is not always popular.

• **Its strength.** It is a powerful cleaner, grease remover, bleaching agent, and insecticide. Black soap in liquid form or as a paste can be used to prepare dish soap, and it is unequaled when it comes to removing grease and stains.

• **Its advantage.** It overcomes everything: grease, ink, bloodstains . . . and is suitable for all surfaces, such as wood, linoleum, tiling, enamel. It is perfect for removing stains on laundry but is best combined with white vinegar, baking soda, or lemon when used to wash clothes, as it tends to turn it gray after a while.

❶ WARNING: Black soap is very concentrated and if it is not diluted enough, it will leave marks on the material. You should follow the recommended dosage.

▶ Baking soda

Baking soda is a white powder that either comes from natron, a mineral that forms at the surface of sodium-rich lakes, or, more commonly nowadays, is a blend of chalk and salt obtained from deposits in Africa or North America. It is also produced in labs.

• **Its strength.** It can be used for everything: removing grease, descaling, deodorizing, bleaching, reviving colors, cleaning, softening . . . and for removing stains. Thanks to its composition, baking soda dissolves the grease and proteins responsible for stains.

• **Its advantage.** It can be used in powder form, as a paste or diluted. Two or 3 tablespoons added to the wash enhances the cleaning action and bleach and softens laundry. Add 4 tablespoons of baking soda per quart (liter) of water for a prewash stain remover for shirt collars and sleeves, as well as for grease, blood, grass, red

TIP

Grate away

To dilute it more easily, grate it or make shavings.

wine, and red berry stains. Leave for at least 1 hour.

⓵ **WARNING:** Do not use on wool, silk, or aluminum.

BEING RESOURCEFUL WITH STAINS

Stains are sneaky and it's often when we are not at home that they tend to appear out of nowhere. Luckily, there are unexpected emergency solutions for when you are at a restaurant or at work.

▸Aspirin

The bloodstain on your pretty sweater will no longer be a headache thanks to aspirin. Moisten a tablet with water and gently rub the stain with it. Rinse lightly. Note for headache sufferers: Tylenol (acetaminophen) does not work; it is the specific chemical composition of aspirin that works.

▸Butter

When it comes to tar and motor oil, fight fire with fire. Butter and olive oil hold on to and remove grease, even on the skin! You just need to smother the stain with butter, leave for a few minutes, then wipe off with a paper towel. Butter must be washed off with soapy water.

▸Natural cork

• **A stain on wood?** Retrieve the natural cork from the wine bottle—but use a good bottle of wine, as modern corks are no longer natural. The clean side of a natural cork will erase white marks on wood, especially waxed wood.

• **If it's very dark wood,** burn the cork lightly before rubbing. It also works on copper stains (see also "Special Cases").

▸Cigarette ash

Does your silver bangle have a black stain? Rub the piece of jewelry delicately with a cloth sprinkled with cigarette ash. The black stains will disappear and it will shine bright again.

▶Metal key

For bloodstains, dampen the stain with cold water, place the fabric on a hard surface, and rub gently with a metal key ring.

▶Soda

The descaling effect of soda is well known, but it has another quality: It is extremely good at removing grease, blood, and ink stains on fabric.

Pour soda directly onto the stain. Leave for 1 to 2 hours, and then wash with soapy water.

▶Toothpaste

• **Stains on your white sports shoes?** Brush them with toothpaste for guaranteed immaculate whiteness.

• **Have your bottles and glasses** left marks on the wooden table? With a soft, dry sponge (no scouring pad) and a quarter-sized amount of toothpaste, scrub the surface lightly using circular motions. Then dry with a slightly damp cloth and leave it to dry. Wax if necessary.

• **A pencil mark on a wall?** Rub gently with a small, soft bristle brush, using circular movements in order to not spread it further. Leave for a few minutes before rinsing with a slightly damp sponge and then dry by dabbing with a nonfluffy cloth.

▶Sparkling water

It's a miracle product for removing stains from rugs, carpets, car seats, fabrics, suede, and leather. It gets rid of anything: red wine, blood, tomato sauce, and urine stains. Apply some sparkling water on the stained area and dab lightly with a paper towel. This doesn't leave white marks and will get rid of smells too. The sparkling water must not contain too much sodium or it could discolor, so pick water that is not too rich in minerals.

▶Flour

You are at a restaurant and, of course, you get sauce on your shirt. Don't hesitate to ask the waiter for a small bowl of flour and sprinkle your stain with it. After 10 minutes, dust it off; you will be impressed  with the result. Cornstarch is the most effective flour. This method also works for absorbing a grease stain on upholstery or on wood.

▶Oil

Is your marble covered in white marks? Cover the stains with a greasy substance, like salad oil, olive oil, or any other vegetable oil. Remove the excess with a paper towel. Stains and white marks will no longer show . . . as long as the marble is kept dry. If a liquid falls onto the marble, it's okay: Just cover the stain with oil again to recapture its beautiful appearance.

▸Milk

Pour hot milk onto a red wine stain, absorb it, and start again: The stain will be gone. As it is gentle, it is suitable for delicates like velvet, wool, or suede.

▸Onions

Are your knife blades showing rust stains? Scrub the problem areas with an onion cut in half.

▸Talcum powder

• **Like flour,** talcum powder works on any grease stain, thanks to its great absorbing

Milk for faded washing — TIP

Your white dress ended up in the color wash by mistake and now it's pink! Soak it in a bowl filled with milk overnight and it will recover its true color.

power. Sprinkle talc immediately onto a stain on a T-shirt, cotton dress, or wood. Leave it until absorbed, then rub delicately with a soft bristle brush, using circular movements to avoid spreading it.

• **If the stain is not fresh,** cover the talcum powder with a paper towel and iron with a cool iron.

Fake sugar for real stains — TIP

An artificial sweetener can also be used on grease stains. Leave it for 10 to 15 minutes and brush. It is advisable to machine wash it a bit later to get rid of any traces.

If there was a miracle recipe,
we would know about it!
Stain removing methods vary
according to the type of stain—
silk, marble, wood, and so on.

A SOLUTION
FOR EACH STAIN

THE ABCs OF STAINS

Most stains will disappear if treated quickly. Sometimes they prove to be stubborn and you need to show some creativity.

B like . . .

▸ Butter

Scrape most of the stain without spreading it further. Absorb the grease with talcum powder or cornstarch. Leave until the stain disappears, then dust off.

• **If that is not enough:** Cover the stain with a quarter-sized amount of black soap paste. Leave for 15 minutes or so (overnight if the stain is very old). Black soap will absorb the grease. Rinse with clean water, then machine wash the item.

▸ Beer

Cold water should be enough to remove a beer stain on almost any material. If it persists, use some white vinegar mixed with cool water (50/50).

• **For wool,** go straight to using vinegar.

• **For silk, satin, and velvet,** rub delicately with a piece of fabric dipped in 90 percent alcohol.

• **For synthetic fabrics and suede,** replace the 90 percent alcohol with denatured alcohol.

• **A beer stain on a stone floor** will need to be treated with a mixture of water and hydrogen peroxide (2 parts water for 1 part hydrogen peroxide).

• **Marble** may require additional cleaning if the stain persists after being cleaned with black soap. In that case, tap gently with ammonium hydroxide.

▸ Blood

Contrary to received wisdom, bloodstains disappear easily as long as you act quickly. Douse the blood with sparkling water, then wipe it off with paper towels. You can also dissolve the stain with saline solution.

• **If a bloodstain remains:** Soak the item in salty or vinegary water. Then rinse with clean water.

As a last resort

 TIP

If the bloodstain is really ingrained, scrub it with toothpaste. Leave for at least an hour, then machine wash.

• **For delicate fabrics:** Start by dabbing with cold water; if the stain persists, dab gently with hydrogen peroxide. Rinse with cold water. Velvet is best cleaned with 90 percent alcohol.

• **In case of a stubborn stain:** Use diluted ammonium hydroxide, then rinse with cold water.

• **Worth noting:** Aspirin is very effective against bloodstains. You just need to scrub the stain with cold water in which an aspirin tablet has dissolved.

C like . . .

▶**Champagne**

Good news, this sparkling nectar does not stain! A bit of water and there will be no trace left.

▶**Cherry**

Lemon juice is the most effective! Dab the stain with a nonfluffy cloth and leave for a

few minutes. Then rinse with clean water.

• **On wool and cotton,** a 50/50 mixture of water and 90 percent alcohol will eliminate cherry and blackberry stains. Dab the stains delicately. Be careful not to use 90 percent alcohol on synthetic and artificial fiber clothes.

• **Special case:** leather and marble. Neither will withstand the acidity of the lemon. On leather, use a blend of 1 part denatured alcohol for 9 parts water. Dab, then rinse with a lightly moistened cloth. Carry out a test before starting and stop if it is not conclusive. Just use Marseille soap or black soap on marble.

▶**Chewing gum**

You need to harden it by applying a bag filled with ice cubes for about 30 minutes.

Noir fiction

TIP

Remove mold from books by sprinkling the pages with talcum powder. Leave for 2 or 3 days before brushing off the excess with a soft brush.

Once it is hard, you can peel it off delicately with the flat blade of a knife. Repeat the operation if necessary.

• **Has the chewing gum left a colored stain,** despite all your efforts? Use a toothbrush to rub it with toothpaste. Is it a greasy stain? Clean it delicately with a cloth dipped in black soap. Lemon juice is best on synthetic fibers; apply glycerin or 90 percent alcohol on delicate fabrics and leave for 30 minutes. Whatever method you use, rinse carefully with lukewarm water. Always try on a hidden piece of fabric first.

❶ WARNING: Remove chewing gum before placing the item in the washing machine or it will become fixed permanently and could contaminate the rest of the clothing.

▸Chocolate

Generally, cold water is enough to get rid of a chocolate stain. If it is persistent, rub gently with a cloth dipped in soapy water (made of lukewarm water and black soap) and that should do the trick.

• **If the chocolate is too ingrained,** dab it with white vinegar or ammonium hydroxide water.

• **To remove a milk chocolate stain,** pour sparkling water on it, leave it to absorb, then wipe off with a paper towel. Dab delicately with 90 percent alcohol. Place a dime-sized amount of black soap paste on the stain, then machine wash.

▸Coffee

As a general rule, you just need to moisten a coffee stain lightly and then rub it with a bit of black soap or Marseille soap before washing. But there are special cases and appropriate measures:

• **Stain removal with 90 percent alcohol.** Mix half water, half 90 percent alcohol in a glass. Dab the stain with a cloth soaked in this solution. Dry with a dry cloth. This method is suitable for silk, satin, velvet, leather, carpet, terra-cotta tiles, and brick.

• **For suede,** use an egg yolk diluted in a bowl of water. Dab the stain with this mixture and rinse with clean, lukewarm water.

E like . . .

▸Earth

Leave the earth to dry, then brush it off.

• **If the stains have become wet** or if they have left marks: Wash them with a mixture made from 1 tablespoon of black soap, 1 tablespoon of white vinegar, and 1 quart (1 liter) of lukewarm water. Rub gently. Rinse with clean water or with a damp cloth.

• **If the stains are persistent:** Start again, using more vinegar. You don't have any vinegar? You can replace it with lemon juice.

• **The orange stains won't go away despite all your attempts:** Dab them with a cloth moistened with ammonium hydroxide. Don't forget to rinse.

F like . . .

▸Felt-tip pens

Dab the stain with a paper towel moistened with soapy water (mix of water and liquid black soap) or alcohol until the stain disappears.

• **For woolens,** do the same with the juice of one lemon. Rinse everything and machine wash it.

▸Fruit juice

Wash with soapy water, rub lightly with salt, and then rinse carefully.

• **Wool deserves a special treatment:** Beat a teaspoon of egg yolk with a teaspoon of glycerin. Leave it for a few minutes, then rinse with lukewarm water.

G like . . .

▸Glue

First, scrape off any excess with a spoon or spatula. Then dab the stain with a cloth dipped in denatured alcohol.

• **If the stain persists,** you will need to determine the type of glue. Heated up white vinegar will eliminate white, acrylic, or vinyl glue. Acetone will get rid of polyurethane glue and neoprene adhesive, and soapy water will get rid of epoxy glue.

▶ Grass

• **For nondelicate fabrics:** Scrub with very hot, soapy water and rinse. If the stain is stubborn, lemon juice will be perfectly suitable for fabrics that do not risk becoming discolored; otherwise slightly diluted white vinegar (1 part vinegar for 2 parts water) will do.

• **For delicates and colored fabrics:** Use denatured alcohol.

• **Satin, silk, velvet, wool, and fur:** Use ammonium hydroxide to erase these unsightly stains, lightly diluted: 1 part ammonium hydroxide for 3 parts water. Rinse with clean water.

• **For suede:** Use a few drops of ammonium hydroxide in a glass of water or denatured alcohol will be effective.

▶ Grease

Don't use water, as it will spread the stain. The rule is the same for all materials: Absorb the grease. Sprinkle with talcum powder or cornstarch and leave for as long as required: from 30 minutes to 12 hours. You then just need to dust it off and the stain should disappear. If the stain is old, that's another story:

• **Fragile fabrics:** Try turpentine. Pour a few drops of this essence on a clean, white cloth and dab the stain with it. Then wash or rinse according to the instructions on the garment. Ammonium hydroxide can also be used. Mix 1 part lukewarm water, 1 part laundry detergent, and 1 part ammonium hydroxide. Dab the stain with a cloth dipped in this solution.

• **White fabrics:** Mix 2 tablespoons of soda crystals in a bowl of water. Dampen the stain with this solution and leave for 5 minutes. Then wash.

• **Leather:** You need to heat the stain so that the grease comes out. A hairdryer is best. Be careful to remain at a distance of at least 4 inches to avoid burning the leather. Then use talcum powder or cornstarch as normal.

• **Rugs, carpets, or wood:** Place some paper towels on the stain and lightly place a cool iron on them. The paper towels will absorb the stain.

I like . . .

▸Ink

Absorb the ink as much as possible with paper towels, then dampen with milk. Vinegar and lemon water are also effective, except for wool, which prefers milk.

• **Leather cannot withstand the acidity of these products.** Cotton dipped in cleansing lotion with a drop of vinegar will be enough for getting rid of the stain.

L like . . .

▸Limescale

• **For chrome-plated items and chrome-plated steel,** use a cloth dipped in apple cider vinegar, as this gives good results.

• **For Plexiglas and plastic,** don't use vinegar, as it is too acidic. Marseille soap or black soap is perfect for removing unattractive stains.

• **For a crystal vase stained by limescale,** peel three potatoes and place the peels in the vase; make sure the peels are diced so that they come out easily. Fill the rest with water. Leave it to macerate for 4 days, then empty the vase. Before rinsing, clean the outside of the vase by rubbing it with a raw potato slice. Rinse with a large quantity of hot water. Dry with a soft, nonfluffy cloth.

M like . . .

▸Makeup

Avoid using water, which will set the stain. Use a greasy substance like butter to eat up the stain, then clean the grease with talcum powder or cornstarch.

Otherwise, dab the stain with a fabric dipped in ammonium hydroxide 28 percent. Then sprinkle the stain with talcum powder or cornstarch. Leave until it is fully absorbed and dust off.

• **If the stain is ingrained:** Sprinkle with talcum powder or cornstarch. Leave a paper towel on the covered stain. Place a cool iron on the paper towel in short bursts so that it absorbs the product with the heat.

• **On leather:** Proceed as above with talcum powder or cornstarch.

• **For a red lipstick stain:** Dab the stain with a cotton swab dipped in glycerin. You can also rub the stain with 90 percent alcohol or with a mixture of 2 parts water and 1 part white vinegar.

⚠ WARNING: Makeup remover eliminates red lipstick but is then difficult to get rid of.

▶Milk

Above all, do not use hot water, which will "cook" the stain. Wash with soapy water and rinse.

• **For stubborn stains:** Ammonium hydroxide 28 percent will do the trick, even on silk. Then rinse with clean water.

• **As a last resort:** For the most stubborn stains, use turpentine. Rinse well after rubbing.

▶Mold

Mix 2 quarter-sized amounts of toothpaste with some baking powder or baking soda: It transforms into an effective paste for eradicating traces of mold on all surfaces. Rub, rinse with clean water, and dry.

• **For mold on the walls or ceiling:** Scrub with a brush or the soft inside part of bread. Then wash with a mixture made from ¼ cup (60 milliliters) of baking soda and 1 cup (235 milliliters) of hot water. Dry.

• **Have black stains appeared on your sun loungers?** Mix 1 tablespoon of cornstarch, a quarter-sized amount of black soap paste, the juice of one lemon, and 1 teaspoon of salt. Apply to the stains and leave it to dry. Brush, rinse with vinegary water (2 tablespoons of vinegar for 6 cups [1.5 liters] of water) and leave it to dry outside.

• **Is your shower curtain dotted with black stains?** There is no need to throw it away. You can eliminate these mold stains by scrubbing them with the abrasive part of a sponge dipped in hot vinegar. Then you just need to put it in the washing machine on a cold cycle, adding 3 tablespoons of baking soda to the wash.

▶**Motor oil**

Remove as much as possible by scraping gently with a spatula or spoon. Soften the stain with a quarter-sized amount of butter. Leave for at least 1 hour, then wipe off with a paper towel. Scrape again. Then soap with black soap and rinse with clean water.

O like . . .

▶**Oil paint**

Use pure turpentine, then wash with black soap and rinse.

• **For ingrained stains,** make a mixture with 4 tablespoons of denatured alcohol, 3 tablespoons of liquid black soap, and 1 tablespoon of baking soda. Apply the mixture on the stain and leave for an hour. Wash with black soap or Marseille soap. Rinse.

▶**Orange**

Rub the stain with lukewarm water mixed with liquid black soap or dab it with lukewarm glycerin before rinsing with clean water.

▶**Oxidization**

Your jewelry and silverware can be blemished with these ugly black stains, so act now! Cigarette ash can help you. Mix it with the juice of a lemon and rub the stain with a cotton pad, rinse, and you're done! If you don't have any ash, grab a soft toothbrush covered in a dime-sized amount of toothpaste, then rub and rinse.

P like . . .

▶**Peach and apricot**

Apply glycerin on the stain and leave for at least 1 hour. Then wash with soapy water (a mixture of water and black soap), then rinse with clean water.

R like...

▶ Red berries

Get rid of most of the stain with cold clean water before applying lemon juice; the stain should disappear.

• **If the stain persists,** cover it with a dime-sized amount of black soap paste. Leave for a few minutes, then rinse. You can use hot milk instead of lemon juice. If the stain is ingrained, you will need to apply hydrogen peroxide (1 part hydrogen peroxide to 10 parts water) and rinse well.

• **On silk:** Dab with a piece of fabric dipped in 90 percent alcohol, then rub gently with a clean cloth.

▶ Red wine

First and foremost, dilute the stain with cold water, even better if it's sparkling mineral water. You can also sprinkle it with talcum powder or cornstarch. Leave for as long as possible, then brush off.

• **If the stain persists,** moisten it with hot milk and leave for at least 1 hour. Rinse and wash with soapy water. This milk solution is recommended for wool. White vinegar also gives good results with

suede. Leather should be cleaned with 90 percent alcohol.

▶ Rust

A rust stain disappears easily with lemon juice combined with table salt. Sprinkle half a lemon with salt, then scrub before rinsing with clean water.

• **For suede,** no need to add any products, as steam is enough. Gently scratch off the rust with a spoon, then remove the rest of the stain by spraying a bit of steam (from quite far away) with the iron. Rub with a soft brush.

• **If your knives have rust stains,** give them a second lease on life with the help of an onion. Take half an onion, dip it in a bowlful of granulated sugar, and rub the blade with it. In a few seconds, it will be immaculate again.

• **For marble,** dab the rust stain with a cloth or cotton swab dipped in hydrogen peroxide (diluted in 20 parts water). This method also works for ink stains.

• **Rust stains on tin** will disappear if you rub it with slices of raw potato covered in baking soda. Rinse, then polish gently with chamois leather.

S like . . .

▶Shoe polish

Greasy and colored, shoe polish stains are insidious because they come ingrained inside the fibers like a dye. So, unless the fabric is delicate, rub the stain with a toothbrush covered in black soap paste, then rinse with sparkling water. Machine wash afterward.

• **For delicate materials and fabrics** that cannot be washed, like suede, wood, fur or silk, remove as much polish as possible by scraping lightly, absorb the grease with paper towels, and then apply turpentine.

• **For leather,** apply a paper towel on the stain and place a cool iron on it to bring out the grease.

• **For wool,** dab with a cotton swab dipped in acetone.

▶Spinach

Spinach stains are stubborn. Good news: By rubbing with a slice of raw potato, the stain will disappear. Rinse once with warm, soapy water, then with clean water.

Getting rid of a white mark

You've succeeded in removing a stain from your shirt but a white mark remains. No problem. Heat up some water in a pan and place the fabric over the boiling water. The steam will make the mark disappear.

▶ **Sweat**

To get rid of those nasty white marks on your shirts, scrub them with a very lightly moistened bar of Marseille soap (with 2 or 3 drops of water) on the front and the back. Then leave to soak in cold water (hot water sets white marks). Rinse. If traces remain, repeat.

• **If the stains are ingrained:** Scrub them with a soft sponge dampened with a mixture of 4 tablespoons of salt and 1 quart (1 liter) of hot water. Rinse with clean water.

• **Other alternatives:** Pure white vinegar and diluted ammonium hydroxide.

I like . . .

▶ **Tea**

• **If the stain is still damp:** Clean it quickly with soapy water (1 tablespoon of black soap for 1 quart [1 liter] of lukewarm water). Rinse with vinegary water (1 part vinegar, 2 parts water).

• **If it's dry:** Dab it with a nonfluffy cloth dipped in a mixture of 1 part white vinegar and 1 part 90 percent alcohol.

• **For synthetic fabrics:** Apply warmed glycerin, leave it for a few minutes, and then rinse. To remove an ingrained stain, leave the clothing to soak for 5 to 10 minutes (as you see fit) in a mixture of lukewarm water and white vinegar, before scrubbing it with a quarter-sized amount of black soap. Rinse.

• **On wood:** Dab the stains with a cloth dipped in lemon juice. Don't forget to rinse.

Tannin in porcelain cups

To remove traces of tea in porcelain bowls, scrub delicately with a sponge dipped in a mixture of 1 part table salt and 1 part white vinegar.

▸Tomato

• **If the stains are recent:** Dab them delicately with a nonfluffy cloth dipped in milk. Wipe off the excess with paper towels, and rinse with clean water. Then clean with black soap and rinse again. You can replace the milk with lightly diluted denatured alcohol.

• **If the stains are old:** Scrub with a mixture of soapy water and a few drops of hydrogen peroxide. Rinse with clean water.

U like . . .

▸Urine

• **Has baby been up to no good?** No worries, the stain and odor will disappear quickly if you sprinkle talcum powder over it while it is still damp. Leave it to dry until it is fully absorbed, then brush off the excess.

Run out of black soap? 💡 TIP

Sprinkle with baking soda. Leave to absorb, then dab with a cloth moistened with white vinegar.

Antismell 💡 TIP

If the smell lingers, cover the stain area with baking soda. Leave overnight before brushing or vacuuming off.

• **Is it an older stain?** Prepare a mixture of water and ammonium hydroxide in equal parts, then dab it with a nonfluffy cloth dipped in this mixture.

V like . . .

▸Verdigris

It is the worst enemy of copper and brass. Strong methods are needed to remove these greenish stains. Remove the verdigris with a sponge, then polish with half a lemon sprinkled with salt, before rinsing with a large quantity of clean water and wiping it dry. You can also use white vinegar diluted with 1 tablespoon of salt. Rinse and wipe dry.

▸Vomit

To avoid the smell lingering for a long time, clean the stains carefully and in depth. Douse them in sparkling water. The vomit will come off the fibers with the bubbles. Leave on till the fizzing subsides then clean off with paper towels. Scrub with a brush dipped in vinegar or ammonium hydroxide. Rinse and then, if possible, machine wash with black soap.

W like . . .

▸Wax

There is no need to rush to remove wax immediately, as you would only make things worse by spreading it. Be patient

Being resourceful

TIP

You don't have any stain remover close at hand? Use toothpaste! Spread a dime-sized amount of toothpaste on the stain with your fingers. Leave for a few minutes, then rinse and wash.

☞ You don't know where the stain comes from?

Sometimes we discover a stain but we can't find out where it came from. You have to proceed in stages. First, try to remove it by dabbing with a cloth dipped in cold water. If the stain persists, wait for the fabric to dry, then rub delicately with a cloth dipped in turpentine, and rinse with clean water.

and leave it to dry. Once it has hardened, remove as much wax as possible with the blade of a knife. Place two or three paper towels on the area and iron the stain. The wax will be absorbed by the paper with the heat. Repeat the operation until there is no trace of grease on the sheets.

• **Has the wax gone but a greasy mark remains?** No problem. Sprinkle it with talcum powder or cornstarch. Wait until it becomes totally absorbed, then dust it off and repeat if necessary.

Every place in the house—walls, floors, bedding—attracts a certain type of stain and reacts in a specific way to stain removers. Products should be chosen carefully according to the material. At the risk of being repetitive, don't forget to always test on a hidden area.

STAIN REMOVAL: SPECIAL CASES

WOOD

Wood deserves to be treated with special care. Whether it is untreated, varnished, or waxed, it doesn't like water or heat and hates most chemicals. To complicate matters further, stain removers react differently according to the variety of tree. So, it's necessary to test on a hidden area first.

Whatever the stain removing method, the steps are the same: Use a nonfluffy cloth, ban the abrasive sponge, and always follow the grain.

▶ Grease stains

• **On untreated or waxed wood:** To remove a grease stain, sprinkle it with talcum powder or cornstarch, which will absorb it. Leave for at least 12 hours. To accelerate the process, cover the powder with several paper towels. Pat the paper delicately with a cool iron (not hot!). The paper will absorb the grease. Change the paper towels regularly and repeat as long as the stains are visible.

• **If it's an old stain,** add a few drops of turpentine to the talcum powder or corn-

starch. Apply this paste with a soft cloth and leave for at least 6 hours.

▶ Water or wine marks

• **On waxed wood:** Natural cork will eliminate water or wine marks. Make circular motions from the outside to the inside. If the wood is very dark, burn the cork lightly before rubbing. Then wax.

• **Alternatively:** Rub the mark gently with a paste made of table salt and water (2 teaspoons of salt for 1 teaspoon of water) and the help of a nonfluffy cloth. Rinse with a cloth moistened with pure water.

▶ Ink or pen stains

On waxed wood: You will eliminate them by dabbing them with a cloth dampened with milk or pure lemon juice. If they are ingrained, rub gently with a white eraser

Getting rid of a cigarette burn on wood

It is possible to tone down a burn on wood as long as it is not too pronounced. You need to make a paste by mixing 1 tablespoon of flaxseed oil with 2 drops of peppermint or tea tree essential oil (for light furniture) and a bit of cigarette ash. Rub the burn with this mixture. It will disappear after a few minutes.

or dab it with a cloth soaked in 70 percent alcohol. Rinse and dry.

▸ Candle stains

Remove the wax delicately with a spoon, then remove the grease stain with talcum powder or cornstarch following the method explained in the Plexiglas and

Plastic section of Chapter 6. If the grease persists, you can rub the stains with a sponge sprinkled with baking soda. Rinse with a sponge moistened with water. Dry as fast as possible with a cloth.

▸ Glue stains

Dab the stain with a cotton swab or a small cloth dampened in acetone. As this product could lighten the wood, act fast and rinse immediately with a clean damp cloth.

☞ Special cases

Painted wood furniture: Great care is required. Clean it with a cloth soaked in turpentine. If it is very dirty, clean it with a sponge soaked in lukewarm water mixed with some soda crystals. Wipe and polish.

Varnished wood: Be careful with stains. Do not scrub! Most stains just come off with lukewarm water. For white marks, dab the stain with a mixture made of 1 teaspoon of 90 percent alcohol and 1 teaspoon of olive oil.

Fly mementos

Little black spots on your furniture? These are fly excrement. To remove them from varnished wood furniture without damaging it, you just need to dab the stain with a clean cloth dipped in 1 tablespoon of white wine and remove the excrement gently.

▸Mold stains

Start by rubbing with a wet sponge. If this is not enough, dab the stains with a cloth dampened in ammonium hydroxide or hydrogen peroxide. Be careful, these two products can lighten the wood.

▸Blood or urine stains

Absorb as much liquid as possible with talcum powder or cornstarch. Then wash with a sponge dipped in hot water and Marseille soap. If this is not enough, remove the stain with a cloth dipped in lightly diluted ammonium hydroxide. Rinse as quickly as possible with a damp cloth.

▸Sauce stains

Sprinkle generously with flour. Leave for at least 1 hour. Dust off. Then clean with a sponge dipped in multipurpose clay cleaner or dab the stain with a cloth dipped in turpentine.

BEDDING

As a mattress is generally kept for 8 to 10 years, it is normal that the ravages of time will leave unappealing traces on it.

▸Cleaning and disinfecting

You need hydrogen peroxide for urine and bloodstains and many others. This natural disinfectant is remarkably effective. Spray a solution made of 2 parts water and 1 part hydrogen peroxide onto the mattress, then scrub with a cloth folded into a wad. Leave it to dry. Rinse with a sponge dampened with clean water. Leave it to dry for at least 8 hours. Use the hairdryer to accelerate the drying process.

▶ **Stubborn stains**

It's hard to avoid it: Ammonium hydroxide is the most suited. Open your windows wide, put on household gloves and a mask to protect you from the ammonium hydroxide fumes, and proceed with caution to avoid any splatters. Scrub your mattress with a washcloth or a sponge dampened with lightly diluted ammonium hydroxide (1 cup [235 milliliters] of ammonium hydroxide in a salad bowl of hot water), focusing particularly on the stains. Rinse with water, using a damp cloth.

⓵ WARNING: If you apply too much water, it could get into the mattress, which could also cause mold. After a few hours of drying, sprinkle the mattress with baking

To do every 2 weeks — TIP

In order to keep your mattress and pillows clean and germ-free, use baking soda. This 100 percent natural miracle product has the power to destroy dust mites, disinfect, clean, and deodorize. Sprinkle with a generous dose of baking soda. Leave for about 30 minutes then rub in the baking soda with a soft brush. Leave for a few minutes more. Finally vacuum the powder away.

soda for two reasons: accelerating the drying process and eliminating the smell of ammonia. Vacuum the baking soda away just before going to bed.

FLOORING

Floors attract all kinds of stains: mud, spilled wineglass, whatever the cat left behind. The quicker you respond, the less the damage.

▶ **Carpet**

• **To give it a deep clean:** Mix 2 parts sparkling water for 1 part white vinegar, then scrub with a heavy-duty scrub brush. Use white vinegar with stubborn stains.

• **If the stains persist:** Treat them with a cloth dampened with ammonium hydroxide.

• **90 percent alcohol** also gives good results.

• **For grease and organic stains** (blood, urine, etc.), talcum powder or cornstarch works very well.

▶Linoleum

Baking soda strikes again and attacks stains left by burns, coffee, candles, wax, and glue. You just need to sprinkle a handful and scrub with a damp sponge. Rinse and dry.

▶Wood

• **Is your varnished wood floor** dull and blackened in places? Dilute a capful of liquid black soap in a large quantity of hot water. Use a microfiber wipe or a mop lightly dampened with the mixture to clean your parquet floor. Rinse and polish. If this method of cleaning is not enough, add a few drops of white vinegar, rinse, and dry quickly. Above all, do not use an abrasive sponge, as it will scratch it. If the black marks are still there, there is only one solution: Sand and varnish again with a specific product.

• **The advantage of oiled wood flooring** is that it is protected from stains and dirt and requires little attention. A stain? Wipe immediately. If the stain is already dry, opt for a sponge lightly dampened with lukewarm water and 2 drops of black soap.

▶Seagrass rugs and carpets

Seagrass is susceptible to white marks and mold.

• **To avoid white marks:** Wipe off any drops of water immediately with paper towels

A magic eraser

TIP

You don't have the courage to clean traces of shoes and shoe polish? You can magic them away with an eraser!

and dry with hairdryer while making circular movements from the outside to the inside.

• **Too late?** Half a capful of ammonium hydroxide mixed with 1 teaspoon of black soap in 5 quarts (5 liters) of lukewarm water will eliminate any unfortunate stain. Scrub with a brush. Rinse and dry.

▸ Terra-cotta floor tiles

Lemon juice is unrivaled in its ability to combat stains on terra-cotta floor tiles. Scrub them with a mixture made of 2 tablespoons of lemon juice for 1 quart (1 liter) of water.

Grease stain? Sprinkle with talcum powder or flour and leave until it is fully absorbed.

• **Has your dog made a mess?** Bring to a simmer 3 parts flaxseed oil to 1 part turpentine. Brush this solution onto the stain with a large brush. Leave for 5 minutes, then rinse with clean water. Make sure to air the room properly.

▸ Polished concrete

It cannot withstand harsh products. Forget abrasive brushes and acidic products like bleach or other limescale removers, as they would "attack" and destroy the polish covering the concrete.

Marseille soap and talcum powder will be enough for grease stains. Rub the product in with circular movements. Then leave until completely absorbed. Repeat the operation if necessary.

WALLS

Every wall has its share of stains, be it in the bedroom of your budding artist who

mistakes the wall for a sheet of paper or in the kitchen, where fruit juice is spilled and oil splattered. They are not that easy to clean.

....

▸Wallpaper

All stains disappear with soapy water on washable and nonwoven vinyl wallpapers. On the other hand, you have to be resourceful when you can't use water to clean them.

• **Fingerprints will disappear** if you rub them gently with the soft inside part of a piece of bread or you can erase them with a white eraser.

• **Grease stains** are absorbed with talcum powder or cornstarch. Dab the stain with the powder so that it sticks and wait at least 10 hours before dusting off.

▸Cleaning a wall covered in textured paint

Textured paint is a magnet for dirt. To clean it, you need to brush it first, then run a sponge soaked in a mixture of white vinegar and salt over it. For stubborn stains, apply ammonium hydroxide with a cotton swab, then rinse.

▸Painted walls

White erasers get rid of almost all marks, whereas multipurpose clay cleaner deals with most stubborn stains.

• **Fingerprints and dust marks** disappear after being rubbed with the inside of a potato cut in two.

• **Ballpoint pen and ink stains** can be removed by dabbing them lightly with a cloth moistened with denatured alcohol or even more simply, by rubbing gently with a cloth covered with a dab of toothpaste. Grease stains will be absorbed by talcum powder or cornstarch.

TOILETS

Everything looks fine in the apartment you've just moved into, apart from the unappealing toilets. There is no need to invest in new materials, as natural products come to our rescue yet again.

▸**Yellow streaks**

Throw in a handful of soda crystals or a spoonful of baking soda and the deposit will disappear in 5 minutes. If it is stubborn, remove the water from the toilet bowl by pushing it over the U-bend with the toilet brush. Pour 1 quart (1 liter) of vinegar and leave it to stand overnight. The deposit will be gone by morning.

• **The hard way:** Pour into the toilet bowl 3 tablespoons of baking soda, 3 table-spoons of fine table salt, 8.5 fluid ounces (250 milliliters) of white vinegar, and some hot water. Leave for a few minutes, then scrub with the toilet brush.

▸**Black marks**

For black marks along where the water runs off, spray a bit of vinegar on the stains so that you can stick a few paper towels to the surface. Spray them with hot vinegar until they become soaked. Leave for at least 1 hour.

6

. Maintaining, renovating .

PROTECTING
FURNITURE AND OBJECTS

Wood · Glass · Metals
Leather · Tiling

MAINTAINING AND RENOVATING OBJECTS AND THE HOME NATURALLY

MAKE YOUR HOME SPARKLE AND SHINE!

If your rug is looking faded, your silverware tarnished, your furniture dull, and your sofa worse for the wear, there is no need to have a complete makeover. Roll up your sleeves, get ready, and be the one to make your home beautiful again.

There are many clever ways of bleaching, brightening colors, and giving a second life to worn objects. There is no need to spend a fortune on industrial products—many natural products work just as well, if not better.

▶ **Good habits**

• **To avoid renovating,** have a good clean. Our homes have to withstand damp, dust, heat, cold, as well as us handling and moving things around, going in and out of rooms, and using water constantly. A house will deteriorate quickly if we don't take care of it regularly. Here are the good habits to adopt to avoid serious deterioration and having to do extensive work:

• **By airing every day** for at least 15 minutes, in summer and winter, you decontaminate indoor air by getting rid of damp and of all the emissions from our devices and ourselves.

• **Cleaning regularly.** Dusting and removing grease are two essential steps to preventing the house from becoming mucky. You should vacuum at least three times a week, if not daily. Wash and remove grease once a week at minimum, especially in the kitchen and bathroom, to avoid the buildup of scale and mold. Clean your curtains, rugs, and carpets at least twice a year, and change your sheets every week if possible. Dust your objects at least once a week; use a slightly damp cloth or, even better, a microfiber cloth, which is very effective at limiting airborne dust.

• **Tidying.** Put clothes in closets, books on bookshelves, toys in their crates, as everything that is left lying around gathers dust and deteriorates.

Safety first

To avoid accidents, be it with natural products or not, respect safety rules:

• *Keep products in their original packaging to avoid any confusion. Baking soda can be mistaken for powdered sugar or salt.*

• *If you make your own laundry detergent or any other cleaning product, never store them in water or soda bottles or in food or candy boxes. If swallowed by mistake, these products could have serious consequences.*

• *Label homemade products carefully and legibly. List their components. If someone else uses it, they must know what they are using.*

• *Do not try to save time by mixing products. The result would be disappointing and, above all, could be dangerous; you might create a chemical reaction such as toxic fumes.*

• *Dangerous or not, always store household products out of the reach of children and pets. The ideal thing is to keep them in a cabinet up high.*

WOOD

It's all about the variety

Wood has many enemies: heat-induced cracks, discoloration due to the sun, swelling and warping caused by humidity, as well as stains, scratches, and even burns left by various objects. To brighten it up, it is best to proceed with caution, as solutions will vary according to the wood variety and the way it has been treated. To avoid unpleasant surprises, always carry out a test on a hidden area before attempting to renovate an entire area or removing a very visible stain.

▸ Restoring untreated timber

The most effective method is to apply a cloth dampened in soapy water, made by mixing a quarter-sized amount of black soap with lukewarm water or with a few drops of lemon lotion (see recipe, right). Wring out the cloth thoroughly. No drops of liquid should fall onto the wooden surface. Afterward, dry carefully with a clean, dry cloth. If stains remain, you can sand them lightly with very fine sandpaper. Always sand in the direction of the grain to avoid making additional scratches.

▸ A new lease of life for waxed wood

Waxing is good but with time, too much wax makes the wood dirty. To bring back its original shine, remove the wax once a year.

Turpentine is perfect for removing all these layers of wax that have accumulated. You just need to scrub the piece of furniture with a clean, nonfluffy cloth soaked with a few drops of this essence. Dry carefully, then apply a bit of lemon lotion. Wait an hour or two before applying beeswax once again to protect it.

The "lemon lotion" recipe

This is the miracle recipe for cleaning and protecting furniture. Mix 5 tablespoons of olive oil, 5 tablespoons of filtered lemon juice, and 15 drops of lemon essential oil (Citrus limonum) for its fragrance and its antimicrobial properties. This lotion can be prepared ahead of time and keeps in the refrigerator. Remember to label the product to avoid any risk of confusion.

• **Water stains on waxed wood** can be removed with a natural cork. Make circular movements from the outside to the inside.

• **You can eliminate an ink stain** on waxed wood by dabbing it with a cloth dampened with milk or pure lemon juice. If it is ingrained, you will need to scratch it gently with very fine sandpaper.

▸**Varnished wood prefers tea**

To clean it, brighten it, and even remove fine scratches, use a nonfluffy cloth to dust it first. Then clean it with tea. Leave three sachets of black tea to brew in 1 quart (1 liter) of boiled water. Allow to cool down, then soak another cloth in the liquid, rinse it out, and scrub the piece of furniture with it. Always follow the grain. Once it is dry, make it shine with a soft cloth.

❶ WARNING: Tea should only be used on varnished wood (furniture, flooring, paneling etc.); otherwise it could stain untreated or waxed wood.

• Is your varnished wood statuette dirty? Clean it carefully with a cloth dipped in a blend of turpentine and olive oil, in equal parts. Polish it to make it shine again.

Express wax removal

Don't have the courage to remove all those layers of wax by scrubbing? Use a hot hairdryer but be careful not to hold it too close to the wood. Always stay 2.5 to 4 inches (6 to 10 centimeters) away from the wood. Move it back and forth, with a regular motion; the wax will gently melt and all the impurities that have become ingrained will come off. Once it has softened, remove the wax with a nonfluffy cloth. Wait for the wood to cool down before applying another layer of wax.

▸**Furniture in painted wood needs to be handled with care**

Clean it with a cloth soaked in turpentine. Leave it to dry completely. To make it shine again, you can wax it with white wax, a natural beeswax that is completely colorless.

If it is very dirty, clean it with a sponge soaked in lukewarm water mixed with a few soda crystals. Wipe and polish it.

Water stains?

TIP

Do you have a water stain on your solid wood sideboard? Rub it gently with a paste made in equal parts toothpaste and baking soda. Make circular movements from the outside to the inside, making sure not to go over the edge of the stain.

▶ Reviving a dull piece of furniture

Egg white is excellent for adding shine to waxed, varnished, or lacquered furniture. You just need to rub it delicately with a mixture of 8.5 fluid ounces (250 milliliters) of water and 3.5 fluid ounces (100 milliliters) of egg whites, leave it to dry, and polish it with a soft cloth.

▶ Make it shine!

Is your recently waxed dresser not shiny? Sprinkle some cornstarch and rub with a soft cloth. The starch will absorb the excess wax and the piece of furniture will shine brightly!

▶ What about cracked wood?

If it has small cracks, choose wood filler. It comes in a tube and is ready to use; you just need to choose the hue that is most like your piece of furniture. With a small spatula, fill in the crack, then gently remove any excess. Leave it to dry properly. You just need to wax or polish it, according to what wood it is. If it is a large crack, it is best to ask for expert advice.

☞ *Did you know?*

To get rid of a scratch on walnut furniture, you just need to rub lightly with a walnut shell. Makes sense, doesn't it?

GLASS AND CRYSTAL

Beautifully clear

Glass and crystal really hate limescale. Luckily, there are many ways of getting rid of it. However, beware of the chemical reaction that occurs between the lead inside glass and crystal and some of the products used in the dishwasher: It whitens them irreversibly. So it is best to wash crystal glasses by hand and to leave the more everyday ones for the dishwasher.

▶ **Beautifully clear with white vinegar**

• **Your glasses will retain their shine** if you get into the habit of adding a bit of white vinegar to your dishwashing water. One or 2 tablespoons should be enough but it is up to you to adapt it according to the number of glasses. Then rinse dry.

• **Once every 2 to 3 months,** allow them to soak for 10 minutes or so in white vinegar. Rinse with a large quantity of clean water before drying them carefully.

• **If they are very dirty,** move on to the big clean. Leave them to soak in very hot water with soda crystals. Rinse with a large quantity of clean water, then dry them carefully to remove any trace.

⚠ WARNING: To avoid broken glass, lay out a dishcloth at the bottom at the sink.

▶ **Getting rid of residue at the bottom of a wine carafe**

Pour 2 cups (475 milliliters) of hot (but not boiling) white vinegar and ½ cup (120 milliliters) of uncooked rice into the carafe. Leave for 10 minutes, then shake vigorously. The residue will become attached to the rice and will come out. All you need to do is empty and rinse it. Is the residue clinging on? Fill the carafe with hot (not boiling) white vinegar and ground eggshells. Leave overnight. The next day, shake vigorously, then empty the mixture. Rinse with hot water and wipe dry.

▶ **A stained vase?**

Peel three potatoes and place the peels in the vase; make sure the peels are diced so that they come out easily. Fill the rest with water. Leave it to macerate for 4 days, then empty the vase. Before rinsing, clean the outside of the vase by rubbing it with a raw potato slice. Rinse with a large quantity of hot water. Dry with a soft, nonfluffy cloth.

▶ Super clean windows

Have you run out of window cleaning products? It is the easiest thing to make. Mix ¾ quart (¾ liter) of water with ¼ quart (¼ liter) of white vinegar. Pour into a spray bottle and clean away. Dry off with

How can I get rid of scratches on glass?

Although it is true that solutions do exist, unfortunately they are not always effective. It will all depend on how deep the scratch is. Be gentle and patient or you could make the scratch worse. Make small circular movements.

Rub the glass with a piece of linen, folded into a wad, lightly damp, and sprinkled with cigarette ash. What if you don't smoke? Use a quarter-sized amount of toothpaste on a dry cloth or even a dry sponge soaked with multipurpose clay cleaner.

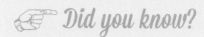
Did you know?

To release two glasses stuck together, there is no need to use force; instead, pour cold water or ice cubes in the top glass (that is stuck), then place the bottom one in hot water.

a clean, nonfluffy cloth and then with crumpled newspaper: Your windows will be sparkling.

METALS

Watch out for oxidization

Most metals hate the open air and blacken with time; others like stainless steel and brushed steel become dull and covered in stains. To avoid this, look after them regularly. As a general rule, you just need to rub them with a damp cloth sprinkled with baking soda, rinse them, and dry them with a dry cloth on a regular basis. If your metals are looking really unhappy, don't panic. Here is how you can solve it in each case.

▶ Dazzling copper and brass

If it is not too tarnished, scrub it with half a lemon sprinkled with coarse salt;

then rinse with clean water and make it shine by rubbing it energetically with newspaper.

• **If your pan is really too dirty,** put together a paste made from 1 part white vinegar (or lemon), 1 part flour, and ½ part salt. Apply generously with a cloth, making circular movements. Leave for several hours before rinsing and polishing with a polishing cloth. Do you have a vegetable patch? Use fresh sorrel leaves to scrub your pan.

▶Fighting verdigris

To remove the greenish stains ruining your beautiful copper tray, strong methods are needed. Remove the verdigris with a sponge; then polish with half a lemon sprinkled with salt, before rinsing with a large quantity of clean water and wiping it dry. You can also use white vinegar diluted with 1 tablespoon of salt. Rinse and wipe dry.

The right recipe for looking after metals

• You can clean copper, chromium, steel, stainless steel, gold, silver, and any other metal by making a paste with 3 tablespoons of baking soda and water. Apply, leave briefly, rinse with hot water, and then polish with a soft cloth.

• To add shine, remember to use newspaper (not glossy magazine paper): the ink cleans and makes metals shine.

❶ **WARNING:** Verdigris can cause burns and release toxins. In case of contact with the skin, rinse immediately with soapy water; then rinse with a large quantity of clean water.

▶Slowing down oxidization

Wax your copper items with a fine layer of colorless wax after cleaning them thoroughly. Leave them to dry, then polish with a soft cloth: This will save you from having to clean them too often.

▸ Adding shine

If you don't have any cabbage in your garden, buy some to scrub your copper items with their leaves.

BRONZE

A soft patina

Whether it's door handles, window fasteners, or your favorite little ornament, your bronze items deserve to be looked after regularly to avoid darkening and losing their shine. Mix 1 tablespoon of flour, 1 tablespoon of salt, and 1 tablespoon of vinegar until it turns to a paste, and then rub it on to the surface of the brass or copper. Leave it for a couple of minutes, and then wash it off with hot soapy water.

☞ *Did you know?*

Bronze is a blend of copper and tin. This is why, like brass, it is susceptible to verdigris.

▸ For bronze items that are really dirty and dull

Use a cloth dipped in a mixture of 1 part lemon juice and 2 parts denatured alcohol. You can choose a folk remedy: rubbing them with warm red wine!

▸ Fighting verdigris

The recipe is the same as with copper: hot vinegar (or lemon) with a generous serving of coarse salt. Rinse very carefully with water and dry thoroughly. Warning! Golden bronze items are fragile: Always carry out a test on a very small surface first.

TIN

Bringing back the shine

Tin items are often very decorative but they blacken with time.

▸**Restoring its shine:**

• **For polished tin:** Clean the object with a cloth dampened with warm beer. Allow it to dry and then polish with a soft cloth.

• **To restore its earlier patina:** Rub a natural cork making circular motions from the outside to the inside. No cork at home? Swap it for a peeled garlic clove.

▸**Rust stains?**
Rub the tin with slices of raw potatoes covered in baking soda. Rinse, then polish gently with chamois leather.

▸**Eliminate traces of corrosion**
Scrub the tin with extra-fine steel wool dipped in flaxseed oil, olive oil, or another vegetable oil, and then polish carefully.

CAST IRON

Black is black.

Cast iron recovers easily, be it in chimney grates, andirons, coat hooks, or door handles.

▸**Intensifying the color**
After scrubbing it with a steel brush to eliminate any rust and dust particles, you just apply basic black polish or, for a more nuanced effect, a mixture of brown, blue, red, and black polish, on the whole surface. Then polish it with a cloth. Cast iron is a porous material, so it absorbs the polish once applied and polished, and therefore will not stain hands.

• **What about cast iron pans?** This polish-based renovation is obviously not suited to objects used for food. For your casserole dishes, you just need to oil the inside and outside with vegetable oil. Polish and the cast iron will be gleaming and protected from rust.

STAINLESS STEEL

Same treatment for chromium and stainless steel

These two metals are everywhere in our homes—pans, domestic appliances, salad bowls, dish and pot racks, lamp bases, and so on—and they do require all our attention. Not only do they get scratched but they also show marks—fingerprints, limescale, splashes of water—so it is not easy to maintain them in their original state.

▶ Lemon juice to shine

• **To add shine to your surfaces,** you just need to clean them with lemon juice. Rinse with a large quantity of clean water before drying with a nonfluffy cloth.

For it to be even more effective, you can use some lemon lotion (see Wood section), as it cleans, adds shine, and above all protects from water and marks. Leave it to dry for a few minutes and then polish.

▶ Rust stains and scratches

• **If your knives have rust stains,** give them a second lease on life with the help of an onion. Take half an onion, dip it in a bowlful of granulated sugar, and rub the blade with it. In a few seconds, it will be immaculate again.

• **Scratched metal?** The solution is the same as with scratched glass (see Glass and Crystal section).

PRECIOUS METALS

Make it shine

Special care needs to be taken with our valuables in gold, silver, precious stones, ivory, and so on, if they are to shine without getting damaged.

▶ Silvery silver

To make all your silver items sparkle again, whip one or two egg whites to stiff peaks,

You can count on Coca-Cola

It is incredible but true: Coke eliminates the worst dirty marks and even rust on chrome and stainless steel. Pour the soda on the area, leave it to stand for 2 minutes, and rub it gently with a non-abrasive sponge. It works like magic.

Are your pliers completely rusty? Leave them to soak overnight in soda and it will be as good as new.

and then add a few drops of white vinegar. Apply this mixture to the jewelry with a paintbrush. Leave it to dry, and then polish with a cloth: They will be as good as new.

• **Stubborn black stains?** Cigarette ash can help you. Dip a cotton pad into a mixture of ash with a little lemon juice, and rub the stain with it. Rinse it and done! If you don't have any ash, grab a soft toothbrush covered in a dab of toothpaste, and then rub and rinse.

• **To avoid silver oxidizing too quickly:** Place your jewelry and cutlery in a dark flannel or in dark fine tissue paper.

▶ **Precious gold jewelry**
Gold jewelry is extremely fragile and cannot be cleaned with just any product. Bleach, for instance, should be banned, as it blackens it.

To avoid scratching it, use a soft cloth and a flexible toothbrush.

• **It looks like copper.** Onion is the most effective method. Boil an onion in water.

Instant bath

Place an aluminum sheet at the bottom of your sink. Arrange your silver items so that they don't touch each other. Cover with boiling water and add 3 handfuls of coarse salt. This whitens silver immediately; you just need to rinse carefully and dry with a soft cloth. No, it's not magic; rather, electrolysis happens and silver whitens, while aluminum blackens.

❶ WARNING: *Don't do this if you wear a ring containing precious stones.*

Once the water has cooled down, dunk the jewelry in it. Rinse, then polish it. They are as good as new! This method is not recommended for jewelry set with precious stones.

• **For removing traces and fine scratches**, toothpaste is amazing. You just need to spread it on the whole surface of the jewelry. Leave it to dry, and then rinse and polish.

• **Guaranteed shine.** Mix a pinch of cigarette ash to a few drops of lemon juice and rub the jewelry gently with it. Rinse with a large quantity of clean water. Alternatively, sprinkle it with baking soda and polish it with a soft cloth.

▸**Glittering stones**

Clean your diamond ring with a microfiber cloth dipped in water and one drop of 90 percent alcohol. Don't forget to clean the inside of the ring, as this is where the dirt becomes ingrained. Dry it with a clean and dry cloth.

🛈 WARNING: Don't use a brush, which could displace the stone from its mount, or baking soda, which could scratch it.

▸**Whitening ivory**

Has your Chinese statuette yellowed? Rub it with some lemon juice and a pinch of fine table salt, but don't leave it in contact with the ivory for too long. Wipe and then polish with a cloth dipped in oil. You can also soak ivory in milk or rub it with cotton wool dipped in hydrogen peroxide.

PLEXIGLAS AND PLASTIC

Transparency is a must.

It is so sad to see our see-through items—acrylic tables and chairs, salad bowls, plastic salad spinner—become dull and stained.

▸**Bringing back the transparency**

Solvents are banned unless you want to see your items become irreversibly opaque and stained. Marseille soap and black soap are perfect for degreasing.

Protective oil TIP

To protect them from water and to avoid marks, polish your Plexiglas or plastic items with vegetable oil or with some lemon lotion (see Wood section). Leave it to dry and then polish to a shine.

However, the most important step is the drying! To remove any traces of water, you need to polish with a soft cloth or a piece of thin felt, until you achieve the desired shine.

▸ Getting rid of scratches

You can't always guarantee that it will work, but it is worth trying. Using a slightly damp piece of felt sprinkled with cigarette ash, rub delicately in circular movements from the outside to the inside. Toothpaste always works well. As with all recipes, always test in a hidden area first.

❶ WARNING: Don't dust your Plexiglas dining table with a dry cloth! By being rubbed against the surface, the fine dust particles could create micro-scratches.

MARBLE

Beauty treatment

Whether it is on the mantelpiece, a bathroom sinktop, a table, or a floor, marble will die unless it is not looked after. But don't worry—everything can be saved.

Before attempting anything, you must do a thorough cleaning: Dust and remove grease from the surface with lukewarm water mixed with black soap, and then rinse.

▸ Salvaging dull and whitened marble

• **Dull marble:** If, despite all your efforts, the marble remains dull, you need to take drastic measures. It is time for exfoliation. Rub it gently by making circular motions from the outside to the inside with very fine sandpaper or extra-fine steel wool. This way it will shine again.

• **Is the marble not completely smooth?** You can rub it with a cuttlefish bone splashed with a bit of water: Its slightly abrasive action will make the surface soft as silk. This also works with granite.

▸ Day cream to protect

Colorless wax spread thinly with a cloth will protect it and make it shine. When it is dry, polish it with chamois leather.

▸ Removing grease stains

Sprinkle talcum powder onto it, as it will absorb the grease. Leave it to stand as long as necessary (at least 10 hours).

• **If the stain is ingrained:** Add a few drops of turpentine to the talcum powder.

• **Rust or ink stain:** Dab with a cloth or a cotton pad dipped in 1 part hydrogen peroxide to 20 parts water.

• **Other stains will come off** with a sponge dipped in black soap.

TIP

Oh no, a scratch!

Before taking drastic measures, try this: Rub it with a rolled damp cloth, sprinkled with cigarette ash or dipped in toothpaste.

▸ Filling in the cracks

Pour a bit of white wax (or candle) into the crack. Allow to harden. Remove the excess wax with a knife and then polish.

⚠ WARNING: Marble's worst enemy is acid in any shape or form. So avoid using lemon or vinegar, as they will only tarnish the surface.

That's it—our objects are as good as new.
But that was just the first step.
Now it is time to go around the rooms.
The rejuvenating treatment continues for
our wallpapers, tiles, yellowing kitchen
appliances, worn carpets in the living room,
and unappealing bedding in the bedroom.

ROOM BY ROOM
BEAUTY TREATMENT

THE KITCHEN

It is quick and easy to find solutions for tiles, appliances, stainless steel, chrome, countertops. In the kitchen, we need to use our eyes as well as our sense of smell to track down bad odors.

▸ **Countertops: Each material has its own treatment.**

Widely sold countertops have generally been treated to be protected from impacts and stains . . . almost. They do lose their shine if they are not well looked after. Then it is time to act. Except for scratches, techniques vary according to the material. For scratches, toothpaste remains the best solution. Add a pinch of baking soda for it to be even more effective.

• **Tiled countertop.** If the joints look grimy, just rub them gently with a toothbrush covered with baking soda.

• **Laminate countertops.** Stubborn stains? No need to scrub. Start by removing grease with dish soap or a blend of water and black soap (1 teaspoon of black soap in 1 quart [1 liter] of lukewarm water). Here is the tip: Go over it with a cloth dipped in lukewarm milk, and then polish it with a dry cloth; any stain will disappear for good.

• **Treated wood countertops.** The advantage of wood is that you can always salvage it. Clean it with a cloth dampened with a blend of hot water and 3 drops of black soap or with lemon lotion.

• **If the countertop is really damaged,** you just need to sand it completely in the direction of the grain, concentrating on the stains and scratches. Then, brush the surface with a mixture of 1 part flaxseed oil to 1 part turpentine to protect and harden it. It is best to do a test in a hidden area, as flaxseed oil tends to darken wood; if the wood appears to become darker, add more turpentine. Leave it to dry and polish.

• **If stainless steel, zinc, or resin countertops never look sparkling clean,** use a multipurpose clay cleaner or a blend of 1 part water, 1 part 70 percent alcohol. Never scrub or micro-scratches might appear. Leave it to dry and polish with a microfiber cloth, and your countertop will look brand-new. Avoid using corrosive cleaning products, especially bleach, as it could stain irrevocably.

• **Is your granite countertop stained?** Scrub it vigorously with a cloth dipped in a paste made from 5 tablespoons of water mixed with ½ cup (120 milliliters) of baking soda.

Apply a large quantity of flaxseed oil on a clean and dry surface to protect and waterproof it again. Allow the stone to absorb the oil and then remove any excess with paper towels. After half a day of drying, you just need to wipe it with a wet sponge to finish off.

▶ **Ceramic and induction cooktops**
If you can't remove black stains on the cooktop, turn to the multipurpose clay cleaner. Apply some with a damp sponge and leave for a few minutes before rubbing with the soft side of the sponge; the grease will come out gradually.

Rub the cooktop with half a lemon and rinse it with a sponge soaked in soapy and vinegary water, to recapture its original shine. Wipe and polish.

▶ **A gleaming gas range**
If gas burners go out unexpectedly, it is time to give them a good cleaning. To do

A broken tile

Oh no! A tile from your kitchen countertop has cracked. You just need to change it.

1. Using a small chisel, remove the joints surrounding the tile by tapping lightly on the handle with a hammer.
2. Remove the damaged tile.
3. Take off any tile glue left on the countertop to avoid any excess thickness when the new tile is applied.
4. Then apply a few dabs of tile adhesive on the new tile and put it in place.
5. Leave it to dry for a few minutes before sealing around the tile.
6. Remove any excess sealant with a damp sponge.

If most of the joints have become yellow, apply a liquid sealant on the whole countertop. This technique also works for wall tiling.

☞ Did you know?

Flaxseed oil is particularly hygienic because it contains polyphenols, a natural disinfectant.

this, allow them to soak in vinegar overnight and then rinse them in clean water. You need to dry them meticulously so that there is no trace of water left in the holes.

· **For ingrained burn stains around the burner,** do the same thing. The best thing is to layer paper towels around the burners and to douse them in pure white vinegar. Leave overnight and you will see how these deposits have disappeared by morning.

· **To make the gas range shine,** add a few drops of white vinegar on a sponge soaked in soapy water and wipe.

▸Bringing back the color to electrical appliances

Make a solution or liquid paste consisting of baking soda and water. Leave it on the smooth surfaces of your appliances. Leave it to dry a little before simply wiping with a very clean and nonfluffy cloth. Colors will be revived and shiny, and whites will become white again.

▸What about the range hood?

· **To know whether your range hood filters need to be changed,** switch on your hood fan and place a paper towel against it. If the paper towel falls, then the hood is no longer working as it should.

· **Your hood has metallic filters.** These can be washed by hand with water and dish soap, or you can put them in the dishwasher.

If it's a charcoal filter, you don't need to clean it. However, you do need to change it every 4 months.

Gleaming kitchen sinks

Both stoneware and porcelain sinks withstand scrubbing and wear and tear without any problems. You just need to rinse it thoroughly after applying scouring powder or dish detergent. On the other hand, for a stainless steel or resin sink, it is best to avoid using a scourer and all abrasives.

• **For resin kitchen sinks,** just use Marseille soap and then scrub with a cloth lightly dipped in turpentine or with a sponge soaked in a mixture of 1 part baking soda and 1 part water to remove grease stains. Tip: Another way to make it shine again is to use sparkling water.

• **For stubborn stains on stainless steel,** it will be necessary to clean with baking soda diluted in water (1 part water for 3 parts baking soda). It will be clean as it was originally if you sprinkle it with the equivalent of a large tablespoon of water. It will become glossy as you polish it with a soft cloth.

TIP

A chip in the ceramic kitchen sink?

Have you dropped something in the sink and scratched the enamel? Get an enamel repair kit to apply with a brush. These kits are very convenient and can be found in DIY stores.

• Sand the surface around the crack with a very fine grit sandpaper, and then clean and dry the area carefully.

• In a small dish, place a small quantity of coloring the same color as your sink.

• Cover the entire enamel crack with the freshly made filler.

• To finish off, sand very gently.

The result is satisfying but don't expect a miracle; the repair will not be completely invisible, as it is impossible to obtain the exact same color as the original enamel. Once it has been sanded and polished with very fine sandpaper, you can try to improve the color with a special touch-up paint for enamel surfaces (found in DIY stores).

▶Faucets

• **Thanks to its acidity,** lemon is particularly effective against limescale. Scrub your faucets with half a lemon, leave for 10 minutes, and then rinse and dry. If the limescale is stubborn, sprinkle the lemon with fine table salt before scrubbing.

• **Oh no, the faucet is leaking a bit.** Don't wait—change your washers. The amount of water seems small but in fact, 1 drop of water dripping every 2 seconds represents a little over 1 gallon per day. If it drips every second, then that is over 2 gallons of water wasted every day, or 422 gallons over a year, the equivalent of 100 showers!

☞ *Did you know?*

To find out how to unscrew the P-trap from the sink, you need to know that practically all daily objects unscrew counterclockwise, like a jar. As the P-trap points toward the bottom, you unscrew it like a jam jar held upside down.

▶Beware of bad smells if the drain becomes clogged up.

Little by little, garbage accumulates in the pipes and bad smells start to appear. To avoid this, a little exfoliating treatment is needed: You just need to mix 1 cup (235 milliliters) of soda crystals or baking soda, 1 cup (235 milliliters) of coarse salt, and 1 cup (235 milliliters) of vinegar. Pour the mixture down the drain, leave it for 1 hour at least, and rinse with boiling water.

• **The sink P-trap** needs to be cleaned each year. The role of this U-shaped pipe, found under the bathroom and kitchen sinks, is to hold water in the bend to block bad smells coming up from the pipes. Think about the environment and stop using chemical products to dissolve the dirt that collects there. All you need to do is to unscrew the P-trap from the sink (by placing a bowl underneath to collect any water it contains). After cleaning the P-trap, clean thread and washer with black soap, replace the washer on the

P-trap, and then screw it tightly back on, but not too much to avoid squashing the washer.

• **To be sure that the P-trap is not leaking,** place a paper towel underneath it and turn the tap on. If a drop lands on the paper towel, unscrew the P-trap again and check that the washer and screw thread are clean.

◆

THE LIVING ROOM AND DINING ROOM

As we eat, play, relax, and pile up our stuff there, it is not easy to keep this area clean. However, there are natural solutions to re-create a sparkling atmosphere.

▸A shiny glass coffee table

The main enemies of glass are limescale and scratches. All you need is a sponge dipped in a few drops of 70 percent alcohol and a microfiber cloth to make your table shine again in no time.

▸A chimney as good as new

Is the inside of your chimney black with soot and can you barely see the flames through the fireplace insert? There are super simple solutions without using any chemical products!

First, clean the inside of the chimney by removing all the ashes. Give it a good vacuum.

Then brush with a heavy-duty scrub brush dipped in a mixture made from 1 quart (1 liter) of hot water and 3 cups (700 milliliters) of white vinegar.

• Clean the fireplace insert window. Take out a bit of ash and remove the solid pieces. Crumple some newspaper into a ball, moisten it with lukewarm water, and press it into the ash that you have just removed from the fireplace. Rub the ball in small, circular movements against the fireplace insert window. Once the window is clean, clean the surface with a damp sponge. White vinegar

combined with a few grams of coarse salt also works very well. Rub the fireplace insert window with this mixture using a sponge. Rinse with clean water and dry with a nonfluffy cloth.

⚠ WARNING: Remember to sweep your chimney regularly to avoid any risk of fire.

▸ Glossy books

These are the pride and joy of our bookshelves but sadly time and repeated handling has made them lose their luster. As a result, our bookshelves look like a flea market booth. It is time to give them our attention.

• **Leather-bound books** will recover their original color with the help of flour! Dilute a tablespoon of flour in a bowl of cold water and rub your leather-bound books with a cloth moistened with this solution. Rinse and dry. Then, whatever cleaning method used, protect them by waxing them with uncolored wax (pure beeswax). Polish with pantyhose rolled up into a ball.

• **Dusty pages?** Vacuuming them with the dusting brush is a start but it is not enough. To remove their yellow or grayish tinge, hold the book very tightly and rub the edge of the pages with a flat nail file until they recover their whiteness.

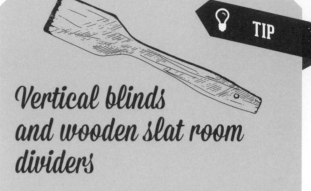

TIP

Vertical blinds and wooden slat room dividers

To recapture their original brightness, remove grease from wooden or plastic slats with a cloth dipped in 70 percent alcohol. Attach this cloth around a kitchen spatula with two elastic bands and it will slip easily between the slats!

• **Salvaging a wet book.** Sprinkle a bit of talcum powder on each page, and then prop it under a heavy object to avoid any loss of shape. Leave for 24 hours, and then shake the book gently over your sink to get rid of the talcum powder.

• **A musty smell.** Has your old book spent time in a cellar and do the pages smell musty now? Sprinkle the pages with baking soda. Leave overnight before dusting it over the sink.

• **Stain-free paper.** You will remove traces of mold with a cotton swab dipped in water and ammonium hydroxide (1 tablespoon of ammonium hydroxide for 5 tablespoons of water). Ink stains will disappear if you dab them with a cotton swab dipped in hydrogen peroxide (1 part peroxide to 12 parts water).

▶ Dull gold wood frames

Eggs are not only useful in the kitchen, but they can also revive gold paint. After dusting the frame thoroughly, apply a mixture of egg whites whipped to a stiff peak and a tablespoon of warm vinegar with a brush. Rinse as you go along with a damp cloth and dry.

⊘ WARNING: It is best to seek advice from a specialist in the case of old style gilding so that he or she can recommend a product specific for this kind of gilding.

▶ Dusty lampshades

Before starting, you need to dust. We don't realize it but dust accumulates on lampshades. Gently vacuum with the dusting brush and you will be surprised to find a lampshade that actually lets the light through! If the fabric has become yellow, just rub it with soft bread pellets.

• **Stained lampshade?** Give it a shower.

TIP

A luminous idea

Potato starch has surprising cleaning properties. So, there is nothing better than a potato cut in two for eliminating fingerprints on doors and window frames as well as light switches. You just need to rub the fingerprint with the potato half with small, circular movements and then dry with a dry cloth.

❶ WARNING: There is always a risk of shock with light switches, so turn off the electricity before starting.

What is important is to act quickly so that the glue does not have time to dissolve. Moisten with lukewarm water with a sink showerhead, soap delicately with a special wool detergent, and rinse off. Dry with a clean kitchen towel.

▶ Happy indoor plants

Are your house plants dying? There are many possible reasons—overwatering, not enough light—but have you thought about dust? As it accumulates on the leaves, dust slowly suffocates the plant.

☞ Did you know?

If you can, get into the habit of showering your plants in your bathtub or shower once a month, as it will spare you the tedium of having to clean each leaf.

Don't let this happen. This is when we start regretting having chosen a magnificent ficus tree with its splendid foliage because there are no two ways about it—you have to dust each leaf!

The leaves will shine brightly once wiped with a sponge dabbed in beer, vegetable oil, makeup remover, or a teaspoon of baking soda in 1 quart (1 liter) of water. Your fig tree is going to be happy!

❶ WARNING: Baking soda should not be used to water indoor plants.

THE BEDROOM

The main piece of furniture here remains the bed. It must be impeccably clean.

▸ Refreshing the bedding

As a mattress can be kept 8 to 10 years, it is normal that the ravages of time will leave unappealing traces on it. Take drastic measures and make the most of a Sunday morning to do a deep clean.

❶ WARNING: If you use too much water, it could get into the mattress, which could

TIP

Baby's soft toys

If they don't fit in the washing machine, seal them in a plastic bag with 1¼ cups (300 milliliters) of baking soda. Shake and leave for 1 hour. Take the soft toys out and brush them.

TIP

A pleasant-smelling disinfecting cleaner

For the monthly cleaning of your mattresses, now all nice and spotless, here is a very simple solution that you can make in advance:

In a spray bottle, mix 2 tablespoons of baking soda and 6 big spoonfuls of hot water. Every week, before making a clean bed, spray this solution onto the mattress and let it dry for at least an hour. You can add 8 drops of tea tree or true lavender essential oil for their fragrance as well as their great disinfectant power.

also cause mold! After a few hours of drying, sprinkle the mattress with baking soda for two reasons: to accelerate the drying process and to eliminate the smell of ammonia. Vacuum the baking soda away just before going to bed.

▶ Deodorizing a cabinet

What a disaster! You've come back from a month of vacation and you left a damp sheet in your closet. Result: a bad smell and mold on the walls. But don't panic, everything will be okay.

Start by airing your closet and checking that there are no moldy items inside. Clean thoroughly with a blend of 10 fluid ounces (300 milliliters) of white vinegar, 7 fluid ounces (210 milliliters) of water, and, for its disinfectant and purifying properties, 5 drops of tea tree essential oil. Pay particular attention to the mold, then dry carefully. Leave the door open for several days to let the air circulate.

• **To get rid of the bad smell,** place some pieces of charcoal in a small linen bag. They will absorb the smells in a day or two. If you don't have any charcoal, you can replace it with a small bowl filled with baking soda, as that is also a great way to absorb odors.

❶ WARNING: Don't use tea tree essential oil next to children, pets, or a pregnant or breastfeeding woman.

THE BATHROOM

The bathroom is a symbol of hygiene but it can quickly appear to be the opposite when tiles look dull, sealants become black, panes turn cloudy, and black marks have appeared in the bathtub. With a bit of effort, everything will become clean and inviting again.

▶ Making an enamel or ceramic bathtub come back to life

A bathtub becomes dull as time goes by. To make it shine again, it's really easy: Wipe the whole surface with a cloth soaked in hot white vinegar. If the result is not yet perfect, then rub it with half a lemon covered in salt. Make sure you ventilate the room while doing this.

• **Brown stains around the drain?** Make a paste from baking soda. Mix 2 parts baking soda for 1 part hydrogen peroxide and stir well. Apply the paste onto the stains and leave it for 30 to 60 minutes. Then scrub the stains with a soft sponge.

• **Chips on the surface.** They can be repaired but it will never look perfect. Use the same method as you did with a ceramic sink (see the Kitchen section).

• **Only a specialist should deal with a resin bathtub.** The repair is carried out while the resin is hot, using a material identical to the original in terms of composition and color. You should allow $100 to $200.

• **Gaps in the enamel, hole in the bathtub?** You have used a product that is too harsh and now the bathtub feels rough because the enamel has been stripped down. It is possible to re-enamel but it is tricky, so best to call in a professional. It is the same if there is a hole. Given the additional risk of a minute leak, the specialist may recommend fixing it with fiberglass or investing in a new bathtub.

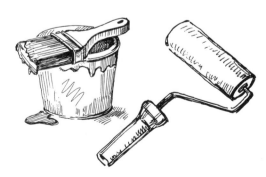

Replacing joints every year

WHEN SEALANTS ARE BLACK, DAMAGED, OR FADED,
THEY IMMEDIATELY MAKE THE WHOLE ROOM LOOK UNCLEAN.
IN ADDITION, THEY GRADUALLY BECOME POROUS AND RISK CAUSING INFILTRATIONS.
CLEANING THEM REGULARLY CAN PROLONG THEIR LIFE
BUT EVENTUALLY THEY WILL NEED TO BE REPLACED.

1. Start by removing the old sealant: Take out the damaged section and pull so that all the sealant comes out. Remove any residue with a plastic scraper. This will allow maximum adhesion for the new bath sealant.

2. Prepare the surface by removing any grime with a sponge dipped in 70 percent alcohol, and then dry carefully. You can use masking tape to obtain a smooth joint with no smudges. This adhesive should be stuck on in a straight line along the wall and on the enamel.

3. You just need to apply the new joint with a sealant gun in a straight line all along between the enamel surface and the wall or tiling.

4. As soon as the sealant is applied, dip your finger in soapy water and gently run your finger along the joint to even and smooth it.

5. Remove the masking tape. New bathtub sealant dries in 20 minutes, but allow 24 hours before it is completely dry.

Clean it with Marseille soap, rinse well, and leave it to dry. Apply a first layer of lacquer paint with a suitable paint roller. Once the paint is dry, apply a second layer and leave it to dry for at least 4 days. As with any lacquer work, it is tricky and rarely looks perfect.

▶**Wall tiles and shower door**
Have your tiles lost their sheen and your shower door become cloudy? It's because of this darn limescale. There are many solutions, so it's up to you to find the one that's best suited to your needs.

Black soap removes grease and traces of limescale if they are ingrained. But be careful with the dosage: 1 drop of black soap in a bowl of hot water is enough; otherwise it could leave streaks. Black

soap has another benefit: It leaves a thin film on the surface, which prevents limescale from forming. A damp sponge sprinkled with baking soda also yields good results. White vinegar is stronger and will get rid of the most stubborn stains.

It is best to use it cold with colored tiles. With encrusted limescale, you can also try out rubbing the whole surface and sealant with lemon sprinkled with coarse salt.

All these products need to be rinsed off with water and the surface wiped off, as the secret with all wet surfaces is to dry them well, preferably with a microfiber cloth.

• **Nice and white joints.** Toothpaste whitens them. You just need to apply a pea-sized amount of toothpaste on a toothbrush and brush the joints, then rinse off. For joints that have really turned black, mix 4 tablespoons of baking soda with 3.5 fluid ounces (100 milliliters) of white vinegar in a spray and spray this onto the joints. Leave for 24 hours, rub, and then rinse.

TIP

A bath for hairbrushes and combs

Hair doesn't like dust and becomes dull when it comes into contact with it, so it is important to use brushes and combs that are clean. Remove any hair that has become attached (comb your brush!), and then give them a bath. Pour a mixture of 1 part water for 1 part white vinegar in a bowl. Leave the brushes and combs to soak in it overnight. You can also add a few drops of true lavender essential oil, which keeps head lice away. The following day, rinse with a large quantity of lukewarm water.

Is your hairbrush handle made of precious wood? Use a gentle shampoo instead of vinegar. Leave your brush to soak in your sink full of hot water and a dose of shampoo. Rub very gently and then rinse thoroughly.

Descaling your showerhead easily

You just need to give it a bath. Fill a plastic freezer bag with white vinegar and place the showerhead inside, affixing the bag to the hose with an elastic band. Leave it for an hour.

▶ **Pampered toilets**

Everything looks fine in the apartment you've just moved into, apart from . . . the unappealing toilets, with their black streaks and yellowish deposits at the bottom. There is no need to invest in new materials, as natural products come to our rescue yet again.

Better for your toilets than for your health?

Has your soda gone flat? Pour it into the toilet. It's a fantastic limescale remover.

• **Yellow streaks.** Throw in a handful of soda crystals or a spoonful of baking soda and the deposit will disappear in 5 minutes. If it is stubborn, remove the water from the toilet bowl by pushing it over the U-bend with the toilet brush. Pour 1 quart (1 liter) of vinegar and leave it to stand overnight. The deposit will be gone by morning.

• **The hard way:** Pour into the toilet bowl 3 tablespoons of baking soda, 3 tablespoons of fine table salt, 8.5 fluid ounces (250 milliliters) of white vinegar, and some hot water. Leave for a few minutes and then scrub with the toilet brush.

• **For black marks along where the water runs off,** spray a bit of pure vinegar where the stains are so that you can attach a few paper towels. Spray them with hot vinegar so they become soaked. Leave for at least an hour.

• **To avoid having to do it all over again,** place two clean oyster shells at the bottom of the toilet cistern, and they will absorb all the limescale that it

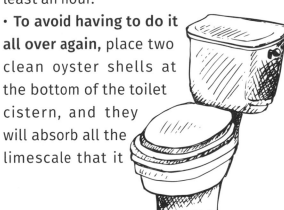

contains. A good reason to treat yourself with a delicious seafood platter!

---◆---

THE FLOORS

We stomp over them, stain them, and scratch them, so it is quite normal after a while for them to look a bit messy. Promise, they will look nice and welcoming again with a few well-chosen steps and products.

▸**A smooth linoleum**

New plastic or PVC floor coverings look great—wooden floor, concrete, stone, or tile imitation—as long as they don't become stained or faded. The first thing to do to renovate this surface is to remove grease from it with water mixed with white vinegar and Marseille soap.

⚠ WARNING: These floor coverings will not tolerate abrasive products, bleach, acetone, or even black soap, which is too potent and will become sticky.

• **Removing stains.** Baking soda strikes again and attacks stains left by burns, coffee, candles, wax, glue . . . You just need to sprinkle a handful and scrub with a damp sponge. Rinse and dry.

• **Protecting.** Flaxseed oil is one of the main components of linoleum. It is therefore ideal for protecting your flooring. Pour a small dose of flaxseed oil directly onto your flooring by making concentric circles with a cloth. Wait a few minutes and then polish with a soft cloth.

This is effective in two ways: Flaxseed oil repairs cracks while nourishing the flooring. Even better, if the linoleum swells in one area, leave a heavy object on it after applying the oil, and the linoleum will recover its original shape after about 12 hours.

• **Making it shine.** Whisk two egg yolks together and then mix them with 1 quart (1 liter) of water. For a guaranteed shine, apply this lotion evenly onto the flooring and leave it to dry without rinsing.

• **A scratch?** You will need an ink eraser, the one that is pink on one side and blue on the other. Use the blue part to erase the scratch until it disappears.

🔆 *Fan of essential oils*

Some essential oils destroy dust mites. You can make an anti–dust mite solution by mixing into a spray 1½ quarts (1.5 liters) of water, the juice of two lemons, and 2 teaspoons of lavender or mint essential oil. Spray onto the carpet, mattress, pillows, and any other place where they might hide, and leave it to dry naturally.

❶ WARNING: *No child, pregnant woman, or pet should be allowed into the room for 2 hours.*

▶A healthy carpet

If you have coughing fits, it may be because of the carpet. Dust mites are at home on this floor covering and they cause respiratory allergies. So, do not hesitate, stock up on baking soda! It is famed for being a potent killer of dust mites and it also deodorizes and revives colors. You just need to scatter the baking soda onto your carpet and leave it to stand for at least an hour before vacuuming it away.

• **Stained carpet?** To give it a deep clean, mix 2 parts sparkling water with 1 part white vinegar and brush with a heavy-duty scrub brush. If the stains are ingrained, use pure vinegar.

• **If the legs of a piece of furniture have left a mark**, leave a damp cloth and then place a hot iron on it. Iron against the grain and the marks will disappear.

▶Untreated, varnished, or polished wooden floors

Solid parquet floors have a unique smell and patina, but they are so fragile! The smallest drop of water or hot object leaves an ugly gray or black mark. Polishing it again and again makes no difference; in fact, it makes it look duller. You have to start all over again.

• **Step 1:** stripping down. Oak, like sweet chestnut, cannot stand large quantities of water, as it turns black. There is only one way to get rid of the layers of wax—elbow grease! Put on mask and gloves, get onto your knees, and scrub with steel wool for hardwood floors, always in the direction of the grain. Once the surface is clean, dust carefully with the vacuum cleaner. With very large surface areas, you can also remove the wax with turpentine.

• **Step 2:** repairing. Any hole or crack needs to be filled. Fill the holes with wood filler,

Make your own wood filler

TIP

You just need to retrieve the wood dust from the sanding of your parquet floor and mix it with wood glue. Use this filler the same day, as it dries very quickly.

using a scraper. Leave it to dry for several hours, as indicated in the wood filler instructions, and then sand and vacuum.

• **Step 3:** just polish. Choose hard wax that you will melt in a double boiler. The secret of cabinetmakers is to apply two thin layers of wax rather than one thick layer. As you apply it, wipe the wax layer with a clean and lint-free cloth. Leave it to dry for 24 hours. Then apply a second layer of wax to obtain a perfect finish. Proceed as with the first layer and wait for another 24 hours. Finally, polish the parquet floor with a woolen cloth or a sheepskin, making circular movements. Ideally you should not walk on it for 48 hours.

⚠ WARNING: Start with the section of the room that is opposite to the door so that you can leave without walking on the wax.

▶ Varnished parquet flooring

Is your varnished parquet floor dull and blackened in places? Dilute a capful of liquid black soap in a large quantity of hot water. Use a microfiber wipe or a mop lightly dampened with the mixture to clean your parquet floor. Rinse and polish. If this method of cleaning is not enough, add a few drops of white vinegar, rinse, and dry quickly. Above all, do not use an abrasive sponge, as it will scratch it. If the black marks are still there, there is only one solution: Sand and varnish again with a specific product.

▶ Oiled parquet flooring

The advantage of oiled parquet flooring is that it is protected from stains and dirt and requires little attention. Be careful: Water

TIP

Help, my wooden floor squeaks!

To put an end to it, insert talcum powder or melted paraffin between the wooden slats. Some cabinetmakers use Marseille soap flakes.

should be banned, as it can darken an oiled parquet floor. It should simply be dusted regularly with a lightly dampened mop.

• **If your oiled parquet floor is not looking good,** it is because it may be time to apply a new oil layer. Indeed, a parquet floor should be oiled every 6 months to a year, depending on the oil and how much the parquet floor is used.

• **Oh no, a stain!** Wipe it immediately. If the stain is already dry, choose a sponge moistened with lukewarm water, to which you will add 2 drops of black soap.

▸**Luminous tiles**

Do your tiles look dull? Take drastic measures and give them a shock treatment by applying a paste made from 1 part water and 1 part baking soda. Leave for an hour and then rinse with clean water. If you have boiled potatoes for dinner, take advantage of it: Their cooking water is an excellent cleaner for tiles. Pour it very hot onto your tiled floor, making sure not to burn yourself. Scrub with a heavy-duty scrub brush, wait 10 minutes for the starch to absorb the grease, rinse with a mop, and dry.

• **Rust stains?** None can withstand the combination of lemon and salt. Cover the stain with lemon juice and then sprinkle with fine table salt. Wait for at least an hour. You just need to scrub and rinse.

———————◆———————

THE WALLS

Whether wallpaper or paint, the wall coverings of a house require constant attention. Despite this, accidents happen so fast. Quick, we need solutions!

▸**Wallpaper—watch out, it's fragile**

There are several types of wallpaper: washable, nonwashable, vinyl, nonwoven vinyl.

• **For washable and nonwoven vinyl types,** refurbishing them (almost) is easy: Soap your wall with lukewarm water mixed with Marseille soap. Be careful not to use too much water: Dampen your sponge and use it to wipe without scrubbing. Then rinse with clean water.

A scratch on brand-new wallpaper

**YIKES, A PIECE OF BRAND-NEW WALLPAPER HAS BEEN TORN OFF!
THERE IS ONLY ONE SOLUTION: CHANGE THE PANEL.
RELIEF! THIS TYPE OF WALLPAPER IS STILL IN STOCK AND YOU WERE ABLE TO BUY A NEW ROLL.**

1. Start with the tricky part: peeling off the panel without tearing off the surrounding panels. First wet the paper; even if it is not washable, it doesn't matter, as we're changing it! Dilute 2 or 2 tablespoons of soda crystals in a bucket of hot water. Dampen your wallpaper by dabbing it with a sponge dipped in that liquid. Be careful not to touch the neighboring panels. Be patient; continue to dab until the paper starts coming off. Peel it off the wall gently. Once the panel has come off, rinse the bare wall and dry.

2. Prepare the wallpaper glue, cut your panel to the right size, and then apply the glue onto the panel, with particular attention to the sides. Apply it carefully, making sure that it lines up with the existing panels.

3. Smooth it from the center to the sides and then run your finger, without pressing, on the sides to make them adhere.

• **The other types** of wallpaper can't take water. You just need to dust them with a microfiber cloth.

• **Getting rid of stains.** All stains on washable wallpaper disappear with soapy water. On the other hand, you have to be resourceful when dry cleaning must be used. Fingerprints will disappear if you rub them gently with the soft part of a piece of bread (not the crust) or you can erase them with a white eraser.

• **Grease stains** will be absorbed by talcum powder or cornstarch. Dab the stain with powder until it sticks and wait at least 10 hours before dusting it off.

▶ **Stain-resistant paint**

We need to take action when the little one pretended to be an artist and mistook the wall for a sheet of paper, or when we want to change a picture on the wall and it has left a visible mark. Most mat and satin paints can be cleaned safely, provided you don't soak the wall or scrub too much.

• **Acting on stains.** White erasers get rid of almost all marks, potato pulp eliminates fingerprints and dust, and a grill-cleaning block does away with most stubborn stains. Ballpoint pen or ink stains can be removed by dabbing them lightly with cloth moistened with denatured alcohol or even more simply, by rubbing gently with a cloth covered with a dab of toothpaste.

❶ WARNING: If it is a large stain, the cleaning may leave a mark. There is then only one alternative: Wash the whole wall! Mix 3 tablespoons of soda crystals in 1 quart (1 liter) of hot water. Clean the walls with a large sponge. Start with the bottom of the wall to avoid dirty streaks on clean wall. Rinse with clean water.

THE PATIO FURNITURE

Our garden furniture is attacked day after day by the sun, the rain, the salty air. After a while, it shows but there are really simple solutions for brightening it up in such a way that will make your terrace proud.

▶**Teak furniture**
Rub the furniture with a brush dipped in pure black soap paste to restore its original color. Rinse with clean water and leave it to dry naturally. Then oil it with teak or flaxseed oil. This will nourish and protect it.

▶**A PVC set of patio furniture**
Dust your PVC outdoor furniture with a dry microfiber cloth as regular maintenance. Remove sunscreen or food stains

TIP

Eggs for shining

With a large brush, apply a thin layer of egg whites whisked to a stiff peak on the piece of furniture. Leave it to dry. Polish with a soft cloth. It will shine as if it has just come out of the store!

Has mold appeared on the fabric?

Mix a tablespoon of cornstarch, a quarter-sized amount of black soap paste, the juice of one lemon, and a teaspoon of salt. Apply to the stains and leave it to dry. Brush, rinse with vinegary water (2 tablespoons of vinegar per 6 cups [1.5 liters] of water), and leave it to dry outside.

with a damp sponge and liquid black soap. Is there a stubborn stain? Scrub it with a brush and black soap in paste form, as it is more concentrated.

• **If your white PVC furniture is turning gray,** brush it with water mixed with a few drops of hydrogen peroxide; then rinse with a large quantity of water.

▶Rattan furniture

If the rattan furniture has become yellow, start by cleaning it with soapy water. Pour hot water into a salad bowl and add 2 to 3 drops of black soap. Then scrub it with a heavy-duty scrub brush and very salty water to whiten it.

Don't forget to rinse well to get rid of the salt. Leave it to dry and wipe with a soft cloth.

▶A wooden patio

Grab your push broom, dip it in a bucket filled with 5 quarts (5 liters) of lukewarm water mixed with a capful of liquid black soap, and scrub. You will easily get rid of mold and other stains with black soap, which is known for its antiseptic, degreasing, and stain-removing properties. Make sure you rinse with clean water and dry with a mop, as puddled water is very bad for wood.

❶ WARNING: Avoid using a high-pressure jet, which damages the surface of the wood over time.

▸ Spot-free sun loungers

Two tablespoons of liquid black soap in a bucket of hot water and a soft bristle brush, and you are ready to scrub the fabric of your sun loungers. Rinse with clean water and leave it to dry.

▸ Gorgeous wrought-iron

Is your beautiful old wrought-iron gate really starting to feel the ravages of time? You can clean it with a sponge dipped in black soap (2 tablespoons per bucket of water), rinse, and, above all, dry to prevent rust. If the gate is exposed to the elements, it is advisable to coat it with a layer of varnish.

• **Is your vintage wrought-iron patio set really dirty?** Wash the table and chairs with soapy water mixed with ammonium hydroxide (1 tablespoon per quart [liter] of water). Once cleaned, protect them by polishing them with white wax.

7

· More ·

HOMEMADE
PRODUCTS

Scouring · Disinfecting · Perfuming

HOW DO I BEGIN?

It's best to begin by making a simple recipe, such as a multipurpose cleaner or a washing detergent. Once you have the knack for it, you'll be able to think big and make a range of products on a monthly basis.

▶ Get organized

Making your household products requires a minimum amount of organization. It's a bit like preparing a good meal—first and foremost, you have to plan the recipe and collect the ingredients, containers, and utensils.

▶ Get properly equipped

Search for suitable containers for your products. Make sure you recycle, and in particular seek out old laundry detergent and dishwashing liquid containers, old spray bottles, and airtight plastic or glass jars. To avoid any risk of confusion, don't use food containers, such as jelly jars. All these containers must be scrupulously cleaned and, ideally, sterilized.

• **To sterilize plastic materials and all spray bottles,** you can use alcohol (minimum 60 percent by volume). Soak a clean cloth or paper towel with alcohol and rub the inside of the container with it. If this isn't possible, pour the alcohol inside the container, seal it with a stopper, and shake it several times so that it reaches all the surfaces.

• **To sterilize spray pumps,** pump some alcohol so that you fill the circuit completely. Then pump the bottle until it's empty to flush it out completely and dry it.

❶ CAUTION: Wear protective gloves because alcohol is harmful to the skin.

• **For other materials** like glass and aluminum: Sterilize in boiling water. Half fill a large saucepan with water and completely immerse the container. Bring to a boil, and continue to boil for at least 5 minutes. Remove the container cautiously with the aid of a clean utensil (such as ice tongs, salad tongs, or any other heat-resistant utensil) and a paper towel. Transfer the container to a clean cloth and allow to dry.

❗ CAUTION: Be careful not to burn yourself. Using a pressure cooker or a baby's bottle sterilizer will make the job easier and limit the risk of burns.

• **Prepare the materials you need** for your recipes as well: wooden or plastic spoons, measuring cups, scales, sponge, and so on. You should sterilize them as well. Make sure you have some cloths. Don't bother with cleaning wipes, because they're wasteful and thus not eco-friendly. Use your prewashed old sheets or T-shirts instead.

▸**Labeling**

Labeling is essential. No two products have a more similar appearance than a liquid laundry detergent and a dishwashing liquid. Be very careful not to confuse them: If you put laundry detergent into the dishwasher, it'll be overrun with foam. Be careful to write the name of the product, a list of its ingredients (also useful if you want to repeat or improve the recipe), what it's used for, the directions for use, and the date it was made on a label and attach it to the container.

❗ CAUTION: Don't make labels colorful or pretty. Household products must always be kept out of the reach of children, as a mishap can happen so quickly. Children must not have the opportunity to mistake a product for snacks. Labels must be very plain. Feel free to draw a skull and crossbones to avoid any accidents.

◆

THE PRODUCTS

Here's a review of the some of the products we've discussed earlier in the book and a few new ones. Most of these products are available in the supermarket

Suitable materials for successful cleaning

Having the right products for cleaning is all well and good. But you should also equip yourself with the right tools.

You will need:

- *clean, lint-free or microfiber cloths;*
- *an all-purpose sponge for large areas;*
- *a soft toothbrush (there's nothing better for getting into the gaps);*
- *a scrubbing brush (plastic ones are less effective, because the bristles quickly start to bend under pressure) for rubbing without scratching;*
- *a clean floorcloth;*
- *soft sponges for every surface;*
- *a scraper for glass;*
- *and a broom;*
- *a bucket or bowl;*
- *a shovel;*
- *a vacuum cleaner;*
- *and protective gloves.*

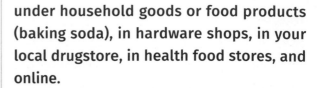

under household goods or food products (baking soda), in hardware shops, in your local drugstore, in health food stores, and online.

. . . .

Don't be fooled by pretty packaging or scented or improved versions. Manufacturers are starting to get on this bandwagon and are bringing out products that are advertised as natural but that still contain undesirable ingredients. Choose products that are eco-labeled.

▸ Black soap (savon noir)

Extremely popular in France, savon noir ("black soap") has been used for centuries.

In tablet form, paste, or liquid, black soap is made of potash and fat, which can be olive oil, flaxseed oil, walnut oil, corn oil, or even glycerine. Although natural, eco-friendly, and environment-friendly, it has one drawback: a distinct odor that is not always appreciated. Black soap is a powerful cleaning agent, grease remover, whitener, and insecticide. Dilute it in water—approximately 1 cup (235 milliliters) (liquid soap) or 2 to 3 tablespoons (paste) per 1 quart (1 liter) of water. Black soap is one of the essential ingredients in making dishwashing liquid, a multipurpose cleaning agent, or a cleaning agent for floors. It can tackle anything (grease, ink, and bloodstains) and is gentle enough for any surface (wood, linoleum, floor tiles, enamel).

⚠ CAUTION: While it's ideal for laundry stains, it's better to combine it with white vinegar, baking soda, or lemon for the washing detergent because it tends to turn the laundry gray in the long run.

▶ White vinegar

White vinegar is industrially produced by the acidification of beet or corn alcohol. Although industrially produced, white vinegar is a 100 percent natural, eco-friendly product because it degrades rapidly and doesn't leave any trace in the environment. It cleans and sanitizes and is an anti-limescale agent, a descaler, a fabric conditioner, a color enhancer, a grease remover, a deodorizing agent, and a disinfectant. It's amazing for giving everything around the house a shine. It's one of the key ingredients of homemade household products.

It can also be used undiluted or diluted in water (50/50) to clean windows or children's toys or can even be combined with salt (to polish copper) or with baking soda (for unblocking). It can be used cold on floors and walls that are not too soiled; on clothes to soften them or remove stains before washing them; on furniture and greasy kitchen utensils; and on toilets and in pipework to deodorize them. It can be used hot or tepid for very dirty floors and blackened saucepans or to descale cooking utensils or unblock a sink.

☞ *Did you know?*

Do not use black soap on granite—it whitens it. It should also be avoided for cleaning cat litter boxes, as they can't abide the odor, unlike bleach, which they adore.

① CAUTION: When handling hot white vinegar, it's better to wear protective gloves and open the windows, because it emits fumes that can be irritating. Never combine white vinegar with other chemical products such as bleach; if you do, a volatile mix will be triggered or toxic fumes will be released.

▶**Lemon**

Lemon juice contains citric acid and is an effective substitute for bleach. It whitens, removes rust, eradicates limescale, disinfects, polishes copper, deodorizes, and so on. You can also use citric acid instead of lemon, making sure that you follow the instructions for use.

① CAUTION: Some materials don't tolerate acids. Never use it on marble and stone. Also make sure that you don't use it with baking soda or soda crystals; if you do, a volatile mix on contact with water will be triggered.

▶**Essential oils**

Although strictly speaking essential oils don't remove grease and are not cleaning agents, they have, for the most part, disinfecting, deodorizing, fungicidal (antifungal and antimold), and purifying properties that are invaluable for our interiors. Essential oils can be seen as the wild cards that are needed to keep a house clean and fresh.

They can be used either undiluted or diluted, but you can also combine them with natural cleaning products such as baking soda, black soap, Marseille soap, or even white vinegar. You just need to add a few drops to the products. However, it's not recommended to incorporate them into a commercial household cleaning agent, as chemical reactions could result in toxic fumes.

Generally, you add 30 to 50 drops per quart (liter) of mixture to perfume household products and 1 to 2 tablespoons per quart for a disinfectant.

⚠ CAUTION: Essential oils must be handled with caution. Follow the directions for use: Wear protective gloves, avoid direct contact with the skin, and follow the recommended dosages; otherwise they can very quickly become toxic and harmful. Above all, never use them near people with allergies, pregnant women, children, and pets.

▸ Hydrolate, a perfumed water

Hydrolat is composed of a minute amount of essential oils and 99 percent water, so it's safe for everyday use. However, once opened, it doesn't keep as long as essential oils: 6 months if kept away from direct heat and light. It's a perfect solution for perfuming the laundry and it can be used undiluted as a pillow mist.

▸ Beeswax

The production of beeswax is one of the many talents of our wonderful bees, and it's widely used in cosmetics and even in food. Wax and wood are natural allies, as the beeswax nourishes, protects, and gives it a shine. While beeswax is the key ingredient of polish—a preparation used to nourish and protect wood—it's also invaluable for protecting stone, plaster, and terra-cotta. To make a good household wax, mix beeswax with oil of turpentine, cover, and leave for 24 hours.

Then continue to dilute this mixture with oil of turpentine.

Different types of waxes vary in quality, depending on usage. It's better to choose very pure white wax for protecting and polishing. However, a word of warning: If the product is naturally sourced, the manufacturer may very well have resorted to chemical products to whiten it. Go for

💡 TIP

Laundry with a fresh, clean scent

You can use hydrolat (flower water) instead of water in the reservoir of your steam iron. Hydrolat and orange flower water are best for this purpose.

multipurpose beeswax flakes that are 100 percent guaranteed to be free of pesticide residues and nontoxic for the environment. You can also use wax instead of paraffin to make beautiful candles. If you add a few drops of essential oil, you'll produce nonpolluting scented candles. You can use white wax, but yellow wax is also suitable. Finally, white wax is used to make a particularly nourishing and protective shoe cream. Just add some flaxseed oil to the wax.

▶ Multipurpose baking soda

Baking soda is edible, biodegradable, nontoxic, free of preservatives, water soluble, odorless, an antacid, anti-limescale, a mild abrasive—this fine white powder has numerous advantages.

For the most part, baking soda is used on its own or mixed with water. But it is possible to increase its effectiveness by combining it with other products that are equally natural. Baking soda can be combined with lemon, coarse salt, and white vinegar. Baking soda is a white, biodegradable powder derived either from natron (a mineral that is formed on the surface of lakes rich in sodium) or from a mixture of chalk and rock salt, drawn from deposits in Africa or North America (currently the most commonly used). It is also produced in laboratories.

Baking soda is used in powder form, as a paste, or diluted. Adding 2 to 3 tablespoons to the laundry detergent enhances the washing performance and whitens and conditions the laundry. If you add 4 tablespoons of baking soda per quart (liter) of water, you'll have a prewash, stain-removing solution for tackling shirt collars and sleeves, grease, blood, grass, red wine, and red berry stains.

• **Baking soda is also the key ingredient** of cleaning products and disinfectants suitable for bathroom fittings and the kitchen, and it eradicates dust mites and other unwelcome visitors. What's more, its effectiveness at neutralizing and absorbing odors makes it an outstanding deodorizing agent. Versatile and harmless, baking soda is also very cost-effective. It can be found in supermarkets, drugstores, and health food stores.

❶ CAUTION: Never use baking soda on wool, silk, or aluminum.

• **Mixing white vinegar with baking soda** triggers a chemical reaction. The mixture becomes frothy and swells because of the release of carbon dioxide. It isn't harmful, but to avoid any irritation to the nose and eyes, open the windows or dilute it.

▸**Marseille soap or oil soap**
Marseille soap has been produced in France for the last 600 years. It is a staple in French culture and it's beginning to gain popularity in the United States. While it still may be difficult to find at your local supermarket, it is readily available at many natural health stores and online. Biodegradable, genuine Marseille soap is composed of 72 percent vegetable oil (olive oil, coconut oil, palm oil) and soda ash. It's free of perfumes, colorants, and artificial additives and is handmade. The green soap is made from olive oil and from coconut oil and/or palm oil; it is particularly recommended for beauty care. The white soap is made from palm oil (extracted from the fruit of the palm tree), peanut oil, or coconut oil and is used for laundry care and household chores.

• **Marseille soap is an excellent fabric stain remover** and an effective grease remover. If used in dry form, it can tackle most greasy stains by absorbing them.
• **In liquid form,** it can tackle stubborn stains such as fruit, fat, makeup, and drinks, and is an amazing grease remover. Mild and gentle, it's suitable for most

materials: exclusively water-soluble materials because you need to rinse the soap out.

• **To use Marseille soap flakes for laundry,** dissolve them into 3½ tablespoons per quart (liter) of hot water. In liquid form, the dosage will depend on the item to be cleaned. In tablet form, you rub it on the item, undiluted.

▸Flaxseed oil

Flaxseed oil is extracted from the flax plant using the cold-pressed method for culinary use. Then, using the hot-pressed method or with the aid of solvents, the rest of the oil contained in the seeds is extracted. Due to its water-repellent and anti-dust properties, it's highly valued for household chores, particularly for protecting wood, stone, floor tiles, and cork. Flaxseed oil is found in black soap, in nourishing creams for leather, and in vegetable-based inks.

You'll find it in grocery stores for culinary use and in drugstores, health food stores, supermarkets, and hardware stores for household chores.

☞ Did you know?

Marseille soap had its method of production codified by Louis XIV. In 1688, the king laid down, by means of the Edict of Colbert, the rules that institutionalized the manufacture of Marseille soap:

- *Soap must be heated in great cauldrons*
- *Compulsory use of pure vegetable oils*
- *All animal fats prohibited*

Unfortunately, while the king regulated the method of production, there was no provision made for protecting its name or determining its composition. Therefore, there are numerous imitations containing additives or other substances. You should make sure that you choose a "genuine" soap. It can also be recognized by its very distinctive scent.

▸Soda crystals

Soda crystals (or sodium carbonate) are obtained from sea salt and chalk and are available in the form of small, odorless, white granules. They're biodegradable and, like baking soda (they have certain similarities), are harmless to the environment; however, soda crystals can sometimes irritate the skin, so it's better to wear protective gloves when handling it. Soda crystals are more powerful than baking soda and are used for softening water (their pH is milder than that of baking soda), cleaning, disinfecting, and so on. You can find soda crystals in some supermarkets, natural food stores, and online.

Soda crystals possess some impressive natural properties that are the basis of powerful multipurpose cleaning products. They are fungicides, antibacterial agents, and neutralizing agents.

• **To disinfect:** Put 1 teaspoon of soda crystals in 1 quart (1 liter) of very hot water and you're done. This is an ideal recipe for floors, kitchen countertops, or bathrooms and will eradicate the smallest bacterium without leaving behind the unpleasant odor of bleach.

• **To remove grease:** Combine it with a few flakes of Marseille soap mixed in a little water. Perfect for your kitchen.

• **To soften:** A distinctive feature of soda crystals is that they can soften water, which improves the performance of some cleaning agents such as laundry detergent, with the result that you can use less of it. To unblock pipework, pour a handful of soda crystals to the bottom of the sink and add 1 cup (235 milliliters) of white vinegar. Leave to act for 30 minutes before rinsing in boiling water. If the pipework is really blocked, use a plunger in addition to this recipe.

⚠ CAUTION: Soda crystals must be handled with great care. While their corrosive properties make them very effective, they're as formidable on grime as they are on the skin! To avoid any skin irritations, make sure that you wear protective gloves each time you use them.

And like any household product, keep it out of the reach of children. In addition, exercise caution, because soda crystals are not suitable for all surfaces, namely wood floors, polished furniture, or aluminum, as they could damage them.

▶ Sodium percarbonate

Sodium percarbonate is a granulated powder that, when combined with water, releases "active oxygen" (hydrogen

peroxide), with its whitening properties and powerful disinfectants. It has the same grease-removal properties as soda crystals. It's useful for whitening and removing stains from fabric; for cleaning and disinfecting floors, patios, enamel bathtubs, and bathroom tiles; and for removing mold and moss. In the United States it is most often sold as the product OxiClean.

• **Directions for use:** Just mix 1 to 3 tablespoons per quart (liter) of water.

🛈 CAUTION: Use with care and avoid all contact with the skin and eyes. Make sure that you wear protective gloves each time you use it.

▸ **Soap bark**

Soap bark (Quillaja saponaria) is boiled down to make completely natural detergents, such as a multipurpose cleaner; the base for your household products; or a homemade dishwashing liquid. Extracting the essence is very simple: Boil the bark in water on a low heat for 10 to 15 minutes. It can also be used as a laundry detergent (avoid using it on white

clothes). Allow approximately 1 to 2 tablespoons of powdered dried bark per wash, or 10 percent as a liquid extract.

🛈 CAUTION: Panama powdered dried bark can irritate the respiratory tract. Do not inhale from the packet, and preferably wear a dust mask when handling it.

▸ **Turpentine oil**

Turpentine oil is a colorless essential oil with an aroma of pine. It's not water-soluble and is used as a solvent for thinning grease, paint, polishes, household products, and perfumes. It removes stains from every material, even delicate fabrics, such as silk. Turpentine oil removes mold from leather. It's also effective in cleaning the screens of electronic devices, such as touch screens.

• **Turpentine oil** is invaluable to cabinet-makers: It's combined with beeswax to nourish and protect wood and to remove scratches from furniture. Combined with denatured alcohol or olive oil, it acts on wood stains. Mixed with flaxseed oil, it eradicates perspiration stains. The dosage varies according to use: undiluted for stains; 1 part oil of turpentine to 1 part flaxseed oil for wood; and dilute with water for bathroom fittings.

❶ CAUTION: Oil of turpentine is a dangerous product that must be used and stored carefully. Keep it out of the reach of children and pets and in a ventilated room. Avoid contact with the eyes. It can also cause irritation on contact with the skin. Wash your hands with soap and water after each use. It can be fatal to a child if ingested.

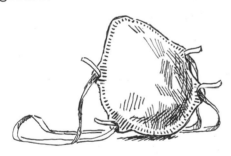

TIP

Your grocery list

Depending on the size of your house and needs, the products you make will vary. Here is a list of essential products to put in your cupboard:
• A multipurpose product for grease removal
• A laundry detergent and a fabric conditioner
• A dishwashing liquid
• A dishwashing powder
• A liquid rinse
• A glass-cleaning product
• A product suitable for all floor surfaces
• A product for descaling the bathroom fittings
• A product for cleaning, disinfecting, and polishing bathroom fittings

You should also have products handy for:
• cleaning wood, silverware, copper, and leather;
• freshening the air in your home;
• deodorizing;
• perfuming your home.

ESSENTIAL MULTIPURPOSE PRODUCTS

If time is short, make these products a priority. They are multipurpose and suitable for most surfaces. Although essential oils are optional, they are valued for their perfume, as well as for their disinfecting and antifungal (antimold) properties and as an insect repellent.

▶The multipurpose cleaning agent

This cleans with its antibacterial properties, and it removes grease from every surface. This product will keep safely for more than 2 months, if stored away from direct light and heat. It can also be used as a spray.

To make a 2 quarts (2 liters) container, you will need:

- Optional: 25 drops antibacterial essential oils (singly or combined), such as tea tree, eucalyptus, true lavender, lemon, peppermint, or cinnamon.

- 2 tablespoons black soap for removing grease
- 1 quart (1 liter) water
- ½ quart (½ liter) white vinegar

Mix the black soap with the essential oils. Add the white vinegar. Pour the solution into a 2-quart (2-liter) bottle and then add water. Shake vigorously. It's

TIP

A perfumed vinegar

If you're unable to use essential oils and can't tolerate the odor of white vinegar, perfume it.

You will need:
- **peel of 5 oranges and 1 lemon (or vice versa)**
- **½ quart (½ liter) white vinegar**

Put the peel in a large, airtight glass jar. Cover the peel with white vinegar. Seal and leave to soak for approximately 10 days away from direct light. Strain the mixture through a coffee filter to remove all the impurities and peel.

ready. Take a sponge to apply it, leave to act for a few minutes, and then rinse in clean water.

▸ The dust remover

Oh, dust. No matter how many times you remove it, it comes back 5 minutes later. Dust is responsible for respiratory allergies, because it's composed of very fine fibers and debris, many and varied germs, dust mites, polluting components, and airborne pollen and fungal spores: All the more reason to get rid of it as quickly as possible.

You will need:

- **1 clean 500 ml spray bottle**
- **1 tablespoon black liquid soap**
- **½ quart (½ liter) demineralized water**
- **15 drops purifying essential oil (lemon, tea tree, or eucalyptus)**
- **1 sponge or 1 microfiber cloth**

Pour the 1 tablespoon of black soap into the spray bottle. Add the water and then the essential oil. Shake vigorously to blend these ingredients thoroughly. Spray onto the surfaces to be dusted. Avoid getting delicate surfaces, such as wood, too wet. Wipe immediately with a clean microfiber cloth. This product keeps for 2 months if stored away from direct light. Keep out of the reach of children.

Did you know?

HISTORY OF EQUIVALENCE
Some powders and liquids have different weights according to their density. Ideally, make your own equivalence table by weighing the products, once and for all.

For example, 15 grams of liquid are equivalent to:
- *1 tablespoon*
- *3 teaspoons*

- *A breakfast cup or a medium-sized glass are equivalent to:*
- *7 fluid ounces (210 milliliters) liquid*
- *12 tablespoons (180 milliliters)*
- *½ cup (120 milliliters) powder, baking soda, or similar*

A coffee cup or a wineglass is equivalent to:
- *3.5 fluid ounces (100 milliliters)*
- *6 tablespoons*

Suitable essential oils

ALTHOUGH THEY'RE OPTIONAL, THESE ESSENTIAL OILS ENHANCE THE EFFECTIVENESS OF YOUR RECIPES AND, AS AN ADDED BONUS, PERFUME THEM EXQUISITELY. YOU CAN COMBINE THREE OR FOUR OF THEM.

▶ Tea tree (*Melaleuca alternifolia*): A disinfectant, an antiviral, a parasite repellent, a dust mite repellent, and antifungal. It's the key ally of fresh, clean homes.

▶ Mandarin, grapefruit, lemon: Antiseptic, antibacterial, and antiviral. These essential oils also help to remove limescale and give a shine to enamel. Their citrusy fragrance is ideal for bathrooms.

▶ True lavender (*Lavandula angustifolia*): Antiseptic, antibacterial, antiviral, a moth repellent, and a flea repellent, with a soothing perfume.

▶ Black peppermint oil (*Eucalyptus radiata*): An antibacterial essential oil and an average parasite repellent. An excellent odor neutralizer.

▶ Lavender aspic (*Lavandula spica*): Has average antibacterial properties and very effective antifungal properties (mold).

▶ Palmarosa (*Cymbopogon martinii*): An important, broad-spectrum, antibacterial agent. The palmarosa essential oil neutralizes most bacteria. Its antifungal properties destroy most fungi caused by fungal infections. An insecticide and insect repellent, its perfume is similar to that of the rose, and therefore ideal for disinfecting the ambient air and repelling mosquitoes and other insects.

▶ Rose-scented geranium (*rose geranium; Pelargonium x asperum*): A repellent that also wards off insects. Its light perfume is very similar to that of the rose and is a treat for the living room.

▶ Scots pine (*Pinus sylvestris L*): Antibacterial, antiviral, antifungal, and antiseptic for the respiratory tract. Its fresh and resinous odor is very pleasant. It has considerable antiseptic properties.

▶ Atlas cedar (*Cedrus atlantica*): A mosquito and moth repellent.

▶ Citronella (*Cymbopogon nardus*): It's renowned for its ability to repel all insects. But it also has antiseptic and antifungal properties, particularly when citronella permeates the room. It's also a very good deodorizing agent and combats the odor of stale cigarette smoke effectively.

SPECIFIC PRODUCTS

While multipurpose products are used for just about everything, you can have fun making an entire range for the perfect household. From the kitchen to the toilets, the recipes are made from the same ingredients but in different proportions. There's nothing stopping you from creating your own recipes; you just need to carry out an initial test on an inconspicuous part of the object to be cleaned (as long as it hasn't stained before) to make sure that it tolerates this treatment. And above all, exercise caution: The products are natural, but chemical reactions can be triggered, causing adverse changes in the compounds or generating fumes that should not be inhaled.

The kitchen

Full of grease, germs, and odors, the kitchen is the most frequently cleaned room. Luckily, there are some super-effective natural products.

▶ **A scouring cream**

If you use this for your ceramic burners and saucepans, the grease deposits will disappear. Never use it on aluminum.

You will need:

- **1 glass jar**
- **6½ tablespoons baking soda**
- **7 fluid ounces (210 milliliters) white vinegar**
- **5 drops essential oil (lemon or tea tree)**

Pour the baking soda into a salad bowl and then add the white vinegar. Add the essential oil or essential oils. Take a sponge and remove some of the cream straight from the jar, and then rub the burners and saucepans. Rinse in clean water and wipe dry.

Bathroom fittings

Limescale is one of the home's sworn enemies. It seeks out any place in contact with water and deposits its scale, mold, and dull film. Also, it shortens the life of many of our household appliances. Descalers must be used regularly to combat it.

TIP

A nice and clean refrigerator

Use this lotion to eliminate odors and the risk of bacteria. The baking soda will neutralize the odors and the lemon will disinfect.

You will need:

- **2 tablespoons baking soda**
- **juice of ½ lemon**
- **5 drops lemon essential oil**

Pour some tepid water into a bowl until it's half full, add the baking soda and dissolve it. Add the lemon juice and the essential oil, and mix.

Take a microfiber cloth and spread this lotion over all the internal surfaces of the refrigerator and even the seals. Dry thoroughly with a microfiber cloth.

▸Scouring, descaling, and disinfecting

Your tiles, bathtub, shower, and sink quickly become gray and stained because of this wretched limescale. Baking soda gets them looking pristine again. It cleans, disinfects, and scours without scratching. Lemon "devours" limescale and whitens and polish these surfaces. Don't make vast quantities, as this cream quickly deteriorates. Keep for no more than 1 month.

You will need:
- **1 airtight jar**
- **20 tablespoons baking soda**
- **10 tablespoons lemon juice**
- **15 drops lemon essential oil**

Mix the baking soda and the lemon juice in a bowl. It's quite normal for it to froth. Add the essential oil and then mix again. To clean the surfaces, take a damp

sponge and remove some of the cream straight from the jar, and then scrub. Rinse in clean water and wipe dry.

▸Shiny, clean tile joints

If tile joints in your shower are black, it's because of limescale. Toothpaste whitens them. Just put a dab of toothpaste onto an old toothbrush, scrub the tile joints, and then rinse. If they're heavily stained with black deposits, here's a recipe that's 100 percent effective, as long as you're not afraid to use a bit of elbow grease.

You will need:
- **1 spray bottle**
- **8 tablespoons baking soda**
- **7 fluid ounces (210 milliliters) white vinegar**

Mix the baking soda and the white vinegar in a large bowl. Be careful because this triggers a chemical reaction: It will froth, which is normal. Then pour the mixture into a spray bottle. Spray onto the tile joints and leave on for 12 hours. Scrub and then rinse.

Spotless toilets

To descale the toilets, generally you just need to pour ½ quart (½ liter) of boiling white vinegar into the toilet bowl and leave in for 1 or 2 hours. Put on protective gloves, of course, and then scrub the surfaces with a moderately abrasive sponge and flush the toilet. Be mindful of the white vinegar fumes that can be an irritant; open the windows or ventilate the room. If there are substantial stains, a bit of elbow grease is required.

▶ A powdered descaler for toilets
You will need:
- **2 tablespoons finely grated Marseille soap**
- **½ cup (120 milliliters) citric acid**
- **½ cup (120 milliliters) baking soda**
- **3 tablespoons soda crystals**
- **30 drops essential oil (lemon, tea tree, eucalyptus)**

Mix the soap, citric acid, baking soda, and soda crystals in a salad bowl (use a wooden spoon or wear protective gloves). Pour the mixture into an airtight jar. Add the essential oils, while taking care to shake them thoroughly to dissolve them.

Flush the toilets to wet the toilet bowl surfaces. Then spread 6 tablespoons of the powder over the whole toilet bowl. Try to do this in the evening so that it can act overnight. The next day, put on a pair of protective gloves and scrub with a sponge soaked in hot water. Flush the toilet to rinse.

Clothing and bed linen

Making your own laundry detergent is incredibly cost efficient. Plus, preparing a homemade washing detergent using natural, organic products prevents many allergies and preserves the environment.

▶ A traditional laundry detergent
For 2 quarts (2 liters) of laundry detergent, you will need:
- **6½ tablespoons Marseille soap flakes**
- **2 quarts (2 liters) of water**
- **3 tablespoons soda crystals**
- **10 drops of true lavender essential oil to disinfect and perfume (optional)**

Odorless pipework

White vinegar and essential oil ice cubes are a good solution for deodorizing your pipework, while preventing fungal growth and unpleasant odors. The ice cubes melt gradually and run slowly along the pipework, thus giving the white vinegar and essential oils the time to act. Mix some white vinegar, 5 drops of tea tree essential oil, and 5 drops of true lavender essential oil in a bowl for their disinfecting and antifungal properties. Pour this mixture into an ice cube mold and put in the freezer. One evening a week, place an ice cube at the entrance of each drain (the sink, washbasin, shower, bathtub).

Heat 1 quart (1 liter) of water in a large saucepan. Once it simmers, add the Marseille soap flakes and the soda crystals. Mix these ingredients until they've dissolved and leave to cool for at least 1 hour. Combine the mixture with a blender. Then pour the mixture into a jerrican and add 1 quart (1 liter) of tepid water and the essential oil. Shake it all thoroughly and leave to stand overnight. The next day, if the washing detergent is too thick, add 1 quart (1 liter) of water. Shake the jerrican vigorously before each use so that the ingredients blend thoroughly. Pour some of the laundry detergent into a mustard jar until it's half full, and deposit the mixture straight into the drum of the machine. This amount will be sufficient for one wash.

• **For a whiter than white wash**

Add 3 tablespoons of soda percarbonate to the washing detergent compartment of the machine.

• **For intense colors**

Add 3 tablespoons of baking soda to the laundry detergent compartment of the machine.

▶ **A fabric softener**

Fabric softeners soften the fibers of materials that have taken a pounding because of hard water. It also gives your laundry a fresh, clean scent.

The most effective and most eco-friendly product is white vinegar. Just add some white vinegar into the fabric conditioner compartment of the washing machine and your laundry will be soft and smooth again. White vinegar removes laundry detergent residues, and its anti-limescale properties get your colored laundry and whites looking pristine again. The unpleasant odor of white vinegar disappears very quickly, but you can also perfume your vinegar by adding 10 drops of your favorite essential oil to the bottle and shaking it thoroughly.

If the water is very hard in your area, you can add some baking soda to soften it to regulate the pH of the water.

You will need:

- **20 drops essential oil of your choice (optional)**
- **17 fluid ounces (500 milliliters) water**

- **10 fluid ounces (300 milliliters) white vinegar**
- **1 bottle with a capacity of 1½ quarts (1½ liters) (a water bottle or similar)**
- **2 tablespoons baking soda**

Choose a large, tall container for this mixture, because the combination of baking soda and white vinegar will froth, and there's a risk of it brimming over. It's not dangerous, but avoid inhaling the fumes.

Pour the baking soda into hot water (not boiling). Gradually add the white vinegar (be careful, as it will froth). Stir gently until the baking soda has dissolved. Add the essential oils (optional). Pour into the bottle. Shake the bottle vigorously before use to blend the ingredients thoroughly.

❶ CAUTION: Delicate fabrics such as silk and wool do not tolerate baking soda. Use Marseille soap only, and use white vinegar as a fabric conditioner.

▸A laundry detergent for babies

Make the basic laundry detergent recipe, but this time without the soda crystals and the essential oils. Essential oils are not recommended for children, but you can use an orange flower or lavender hydrolat instead, adding 3 to 4 tablespoons in the fabric conditioner compartment. Preferably, choose lavender hydrolat, because it's a suitable louse and dust mite repellent, or use orange flower water to soothe your little one.

❶ CAUTION: Aromatic flower waters deteriorate rapidly. Use them within 6 months

of opening. To store them properly, keep them away from direct light, make sure that they're airtight, and don't expose them to variations in temperature.

▸A cleaner/disinfectant to repel dust mites

Here's a very simple recipe to make in advance for the monthly cleaning of your mattresses. Baking soda cleans, disinfects, and neutralizes odors. In addition, it can destroy dust mites. Essential oils have the same insecticidal, insect-repellent, and disinfecting properties as baking soda. Mixing these two products makes them all the more effective. It keeps for at least 2 months. Shake well before use.

   You will need:
- **1 spray bottle with a capacity of 250 ml**
- **2 tablespoons baking soda**
- **6 large tablespoons hot water**

The damp cloth effect

If your laundry is very creased, moisten it by spraying perfumed water directly onto it before ironing. This will make ironing easier.

- **8 drops tea tree or true lavender essential oil**

Mix the baking soda and hot water in a spray bottle. Add 8 drops of tea tree or true lavender essential oil. Every week, before making your bed with clean sheets, spray this solution onto the mattress. Rub with a sponge and allow to dry for a good hour. Then vacuum thoroughly.

▸A perfumed water for your ironing

An aromatic hydrolat is the water collected after the distillation of a plant during the manufacture of an essential oil. Flower water is the "steeping" of flower petals in water. Unlike essential oils, hydrolats and flower waters have a low concentration of active ingredients and can be used instead of water in the reservoir of your steam iron, without the need for any special precautions. Lavender or orange flower hydrolats will be the most suitable to give a fresh scent to your laundry.

Hand-washing dishes

Dishwashing liquid is used daily and it can end up getting very expensive. Use natural products instead.

▸A washing-up product

You will need:

- **1 plastic bottle for the mixture, well rinsed in advance**
- **1 tablespoon baking soda**
- **½ mustard jar liquid black soap or 20 fluid ounces (590 milliliters) liquid Marseille soap (your choice)**
- **15 drops essential oil (tea tree, true lavender, or citrus)**
- **½ quart (½ liter) hot water**

Mix the baking soda, soap, and essential oil in a bowl with a plastic spoon. Then pour the mixture into the bottle and add the hot water. Shake well, and it's ready.

▶ An organic dishwasher liquid

You will need:

- **6 untreated lemons**
- **½ cup (120 milliliters) coarse salt**
- **7 fluid ounces (210 milliliters) white vinegar**
- **13.5 fluid ounces (400 milliliters) water**
- **1 large glass jar with lid, with a capacity of 1 quart (1 liter)**

Wash the lemons and cut them into small pieces. Set aside the peel, but discard the seeds. Put the pieces into the bowl of a food processor. Gradually add the salt. Pour this mixture into a saucepan. Add the white vinegar and water, and heat gently for 20 minutes, while stirring regularly. Leave to cool. Pour this thick cream into a bowl and mix again; there must not be any pieces left as they risk clogging the dishwasher. Finally pour the mixture into the jar.

You can use this cream to good effect, instead of industrial dishwashing liquid. The dosage is 1 large tablespoon.

▶ A dishwasher powder

For about thirty washes, you will need:

- **1 airtight jar with a capacity of approximately 7 ounces (200 grams)**
- **3½ tablespoons citric acid**
- **3½ tablespoons soda crystals**
- **3½ tablespoons sodium coco-sulfate (a cleaning agent available in health food stores, drugstores, hardware stores, or online)**
- **1½ tablespoons percarbonate of soda**
- **(Optional) 20 drops lemon essential oil (antiseptic, anti-limescale)**

Pour all the ingredients into the jar. Seal it and shake vigorously to blend thoroughly.

Put 1 to 2 tablespoons of this powder into the dishwasher detergent compartment and it's done.

▶ Homemade dishwasher tablets

You can make dishwashing tablets with this powder. Take some of the dishwashing powder that you've just made. Spray it with water so that it forms into a mass.

Economical liquid rinse

TIP

You can quite simply use white vinegar instead of a rinsing liquid.

Pour this mixture into ice cube molds. Leave to solidify overnight and then remove from the molds.

The floor

▸**A stain remover for floors**

This recipe is equally suitable for cleaning floor tiles, terra-cotta tiles, and wood flooring as well as laminated floors. It keeps well.

You will need:

- **1 plastic jerrican with a capacity of 2 quarts (2 liters)**
- **25 fluid ounces (740 milliliters) liquid black soap for grease removal and cleaning**
- **17 fluid ounces (500 milliliters) flaxseed oil for nourishing and polishing**
- **17 fluid ounces (500 milliliters) water**
- **30 drops essential oil**

Pour everything into the jerrican. Shake it before each use. Just mix a small amount of this solution with 2 quarts (2 liters) of water for clean, disinfected, and gleaming floors.

Windows and mirrors

▸**A window and mirror cleaner**

This is very simple to make with guaranteed results: clean and free of smears. It keeps well. You will need:

- **13.5 fluid ounces (400 milliliters) white vinegar**
- **3.5 fluid ounces (100 milliliters) water**
- **(Optional) 5 drops essential oil, preferably one that repels insects, such as palmarosa, rose geranium, or lavender**

Mix the white vinegar, water, and essential oil of your choice in a spray bottle. Spray onto the windowpanes or mirrors and clean from top to bottom, with the aid of a sponge. Then wipe with a microfiber cloth.

Wood

As wood is delicate, it needs to be nourished and requires special attention, otherwise you'll see white marks appearing. You should always use liquid solutions sparingly and dry immediately.

▸ **The lemon lotion**
Made with olive oil and lemon, this little recipe cleans, nourishes, and protects furniture, and is recommended by cabinet-makers. While olive oil nourishes the wood, lemon essential oil perfumes it and is also an antiparasite agent. Prepare this lotion in advance. It can be kept in the refrigerator for approximately 6 months. Label the product to avoid any risk of confusion.

You will need:
- **5 tablespoons olive oil**
- **5 tablespoons filtered lemon juice**
- **15 drops lemon essential oil (*Citrus limonum*)**
- **1 spray bottle**

Mix the olive oil with the filtered lemon juice and the essential oil. Pour this mixture into a spray bottle and shake vigorously. Just lightly spray this product onto the furniture and wipe with a clean, dry, soft cloth.

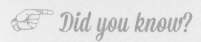

⚠ CAUTION: Each piece of furniture reacts differently to products. It's always wise to perform a test on an inconspicuous area of the furniture before starting.

▸ A homemade wax for solid wood furniture and solid wood flooring

Solid wood needs to be nourished. For this purpose, there's nothing better than a natural wax. Beeswax nourishes and protects and gives the wood a lovely sheen. By incorporating a few drops of citronella essential oil, Atlas cedar essential oil, or even lavender essential oil, the wood will also be shielded from unwelcome insect or parasite attacks.

You will need:

- 25 drops essential oil (optional)
- 1 glass jar with a wide opening, and lid
- 2½ fluid ounces (75 milliliters) flaxseed oil
- 5 tablespoons beeswax flakes
- 2½ fluid ounces (75 milliliters) oil of turpentine

Put the beeswax in a double boiler (see tip) to melt it. Carefully and gradually add the oil of turpentine and then the flaxseed oil. Be very careful—this mixture is highly flammable. Stir gently with the aid of a wooden spoon until a smooth mixture is obtained. Add 20 drops of Atlas cedar essential oil, citronella essential oil, or lavender essential oil (you can blend these three oils a little). Continue to stir with the wooden spoon, which you will have to discard afterward. Pour the mixture into the glass jar with the lid and leave to cool for several hours before sealing it. Your wax is now ready.

Dust and clean the furniture and then apply the wax with the aid of a paintbrush (thus avoiding making your hands dirty and applying too much wax) or a cloth. Make sure that the room is well ventilated. Allow to dry and then polish with a soft cloth.

Shoes

▶ A shoe polish

Did you know you could make your own shoe polish? The ingredients are the same as for wood. It's easy to make and the results are impressive: the leather will be nourished and shiny.

You will need:
- **6½ tablespoons beeswax**
- **20 fluid ounces (590 milliliters) oil of turpentine**
- **20 fluid ounces (590 milliliters) boiling water**
- **1½ tablespoons Marseille soap flakes**
- **1 tablespoon essential oil (optional)**

Melt the beeswax in a double boiler. Pour the oil of turpentine into another saucepan. When the wax has melted, remove from heat and pour it gently onto the oil of turpentine and blend until a smooth mixture is obtained. In another saucepan, melt the Marseille soap flakes in the boiling water and stir until it has been completely dissolved. Incorporate

How to use a double boiler
TIP

The function of a double boiler is to melt a product gently. In this case use a large saucepan with a little water (approximately the equivalent of two mustard jars). Put the product into a second, smaller saucepan. Put this container into the large saucepan so that the bottom of the second saucepan stands in the water. Warm up on a low heat. In this way, the product is not in direct contact with the heat, enabling the temperature to rise gently through the water in the large saucepan.

this soapy mixture into the wax and turpentine mixture while stirring rapidly to obtain an emulsion. Add the essential oil and blend thoroughly. Leave to cool. Then pour the mixture into an airtight jar and leave to stand for several days. Take an old woolen sock and rub your shoes with this product.

☞ Did you know?

Beeswax is a yellowish substance, produced by bees to make their honeycomb. It hydrates, protects, and cleanses.

8

· Natural ·

FRAGRANCES
FOR YOUR HOME

Getting rid of unpleasant odors
Choosing and diffusing scents

NATURAL FRAGRANCES FOR YOUR HOME

FRESH SCENT

The fresh scent of lavender, an appetizing smell of vanilla, exotic spices . . . A fragrance calms us down, energizes us or, like the smell of home baking, takes us back to our childhood. We like to wrap ourselves in these comforting scents.

Playing around with aromas and finding the right scents for your home can become a creative way to show your personality. Home décor stores, perfume stores, and even megastores have offered a wide range of home fragrances for years. Apple blossom, fig tree, forest rain, marshmallow fluff—we love these poetic names even though many of these products are anything but poetic because they are made from synthetic products and are not always good for your health. By diffusing their fragrance, they spread volatile organic compounds (VOCs), small invisible particles that are easily inhaled and that can irritate and cause allergies.

▸What if you had a go?

Creating a natural fragrance for your home is quite simple. Learn to play around with scents like a conductor directing an orchestra: With a candle here and a potpourri there, you can turn your house into a cozy home and let your imagination go wild.

But if you can trust your sense of smell regarding the choice of scents, you should still respect a few rules to obtain the right results. Each room should have its own fragrance: warm and welcoming in the hallway, invigorating and serene in the living room, hardworking in the office, and so on.

There is a whole range of natural products to help you create the right atmosphere. And there is nothing to stop you from creating your own fragrances. The result will match your expectations: a freshly scented and healthy home that reflects your personality.

❶ CAREFUL WITH ESSENTIAL OILS

These enchanting and convenient oils must be handled with care. You should follow instructions (wearing gloves, avoiding contact with skin, using the right dosage); otherwise they can quickly become toxic and harmful. You must also avoid using them near people with allergies, children, and pets.

INCENSE

To perfume the whole house

This is the method that lasts the longest because its light smoke infuses all the rooms in the house and becomes ingrained in absorbent material like fabric and books. Incense releases powerful scents and is best used alone. It loses its benefits when used with other fragrances and can even become nauseating.

It comes in the form of sticks, spirals, or small combustible cones. Good incense is made from crushed resin mixed with a combustible material (very fine wood shavings, ground charcoal, or even dried and ground herbs). Unfortunately, incense made with 100 percent natural products is increasingly rare. Many of the products sold as "incense" are in fact bamboo sticks coated in solvents and synthetic fragrances. Be careful, as these products are not actual incense and are potentially dangerous for your health.

▶ To be used sparingly

Health professionals are questioning the use of incense at home. According to them, the odors could be harmful, although no serious study backs this up. However, you should take some precautions to avoid any risks:

• Read the instructions carefully on the packaging and only choose incense that is 100 percent natural.

• Use incense occasionally and for a short amount of time.

• After each use, air the room properly to get rid of any smoke. The incense smell will remain because it becomes ingrained.

☞ *Did you know?*

Originally incense was only made from the resin of Boswellia sacra, a bush from the Burseraceae family that grows in the south of the Arabic peninsula (Yemen, Oman) and in Somalia. It used to be burnt slowly on burning coals. With time, the term incense was given to other resins such as frankincense (from the oliban, a tree growing in Somalia), myrrh, or benzoin. These kinds of incense were used for religious and spiritual rituals.

• Avoid using it in bedrooms before sleeping.

▶ **User manual**

To avoid any risk of fire (a spark can always fly out), place the cones in a small bowl. Sticks are usually sold in boxes with an incense holder. If not, place them in a small bowl filled with compacted sand.

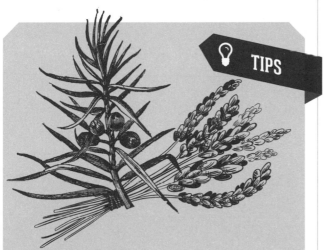

TIPS

Treasures in your garden

Is a juniper growing in your garden? Make the most of it—its bark is aromatic and burns very slowly like incense.

Dried lavender sprigs also burn quite slowly while diffusing their sweet smell. You just need to stick them (only the sprigs, not the flower) in a small bowl filled with sand.

The sand will hold them up and also put out any sparks. Spirals should be placed on high up on stands.

Whatever the type of incense you use, always place it far from any flammable objects, especially curtains. There is no point in lighting up several sticks at once. When incense burns, there should not be a flame, just a smoldering tip. To put out a stick or spiral, dip the smoldering tip in water; for cones, pour a bit of water into the bowl.

◆

SCENTED CANDLES

An unrivaled ambiance

When it comes to creating a festive mood, a positive mind-set, warm coziness in the living room, or an intimate atmosphere in the bedroom, there is nothing like a scented candle.

But flames do produce substances that can be irritants or bad for your health. So, once again, use them sparingly. In no way should you let a candle burn all day.

Convenient, pretty, and trendy, candles are taking over display stands. Unfortunately, not all are natural. The industrial ones can be polluting due to their synthetic fragrance, their wax (especially if it is of poor quality), and their synthetic wicks, which can melt or explode. To perfume your home, it is best to avoid tea lights sold in large packs, which are often of a low quality.

▶ Choosing well

Three criteria determine whether a candle is high quality: the wax, the wick, and the fragrance. A good candle burns slowly and evenly (its surface doesn't form a crater), the wick does not smoke, and the fragrance is diffused until the end.

• **Natural wax or paraffin:** Most candles sold are made from paraffin, a by-product of the petroleum industry that lets out polluting fumes when burning. Pick

Did you know?

To make 6½ tablespoons of wax, bees must travel around 25,000 miles (40,000 kilometers) and visit more than 500,000 flowers! This explains the high cost of pure beeswax candles.

natural wax, which does not emit as many VOCs. You can choose between a vegetable wax like soy wax, the most high-performing of vegetable waxes, or an animal wax like beeswax. No need to add a fragrance, as it has a natural scent and has a very plea-sant natural honey smell when it melts. Pick one that is 100 percent pure. It will be more expensive but it lasts longer and your health is priceless.

❶ BEWARE OF SCAMS!

Make sure your soy wax candle says 100 percent GMO-free pure soy. As it is a quality candle, it is often more expensive than the rest, so why don't you make it yourself?

▸About wicks

The wick is essential: Choosing the right one will mean that the candle will burn properly without smoking and will not burn or die out too fast.

Lead wicks are to be avoided at all cost (in fact, they have been banned on the U.S. market since 2003). Wicks must be 100 percent cotton.

To check whether the metal tab that holds the wick at the bottom of the jar is well centered, choose a transparent glass. It is a quality guarantee, as it ensures that the candle will burn consistently and until the end.

The wick must not be longer than 1 cm or it risks letting out noxious fumes. Cut the wick regularly (wait until the candle is cold) and, if necessary, place it back in the center while the wax is liquid.

▸Snuffing out a candle

Do not blow it out! Again, this will cause many particles to be dispersed into the air, as well as black smoke and an unpleasant smell. The tip of a knife will do. Fold the wick into the wax to put it out, and then hold it up again straightaway. It should go out immediately, without any smoke. Another advantage is that the wick will remain firm as it hardens. You can also use a candle snuffer (a kind of small pipe), which will trap the air and extinguish the candle.

REED DIFFUSERS

A long-lasting fragrance

Reed diffusers are the most ecological and simplest way to perfume your home over a length of time. They are decorative and can easily fit into any room, on a small round table or on a mantelpiece.

Reed diffusers are long (12 inches/30 centimeters) and fine rattan stems. Partly soaked in a scented liquid, they absorb

the fragrance by capillary action. The fragrance is diffused gently and naturally for weeks, without any burning.

To make the fragrance more or less intense, all you need is to take out or add a few stems.

POTPOURRI

The most attractive

Easy to make, potpourri is ideal to add a discreet fragrance to small rooms like the hallway, the bathroom, the toilets, and the office.

Take advantage of your walks to make your own. Everything is possible to create this bouquet of fragrances: from pebbles to shells collected on the beach, from the pine cone to the rosemary sprig, from the wild rose to the jasmine flower, citrus zests, and cloves.

Some elements have a scent while others are there to absorb it and diffuse it, so remember to add porous objects such as sand, limestone, clay disks, and so on, to your potpourri. All you need to do to refresh the fragrance is pour 5 drops

Don't have a reed diffuser?

There are other mediums that work by the same capillary action: clay or plaster disks and pebbles collected on the beach, as long as they are porous. To check their quality, place them in water and, if bubbles come to the surface, they are perfect—they are covered in small holes ready to store the drops of essential oil or perfume that you are going to pour over them.

of essential oil of your choice over it. Then seal the mixture into an airtight plastic bag for 24 hours to allow the scent to become absorbed. Place your potpourri in a pretty pot or bowl and you are done.

⚠ WARNING: Always ask an expert with regard to the choice of essential oil. Some oils, like cinnamon, cause skin irritation. Use gloves when handling essential oils. If a drop falls onto your skin, clean it with vegetable oil and then rinse with soap and water.

PILLOW MISTS

For sweet dreams

There is nothing better than slipping into scented sheets to drift off to sleep. These fragrances come as sprays and are lightly dosed to avoid being too overpowering.

Spray a little mist (press two or three times only) in the morning on a made-up bed, and then add a little spray once more onto the pillow in the evening before going to bed. You can also add fragrance to your bedroom curtains, your bed-spreads, and your towels.

❶ BE CAREFUL: Do not choose scents that are too powerful and too complex. The most effective scents to achieve perfect sleep are lavender and orange blossom.

• **Don't overdo it!** If you use scented washing powder or fabric conditioner for your sheets, don't add any more.

ESSENTIAL OILS

An essential tool

Trendy and natural, essential oils have been taking over the home for several years now. A drop here, there, and everywhere, they are said to have countless benefits. In fact, they have many therapeutic properties as a result of their manufacturing process. They are unmatched as hyper concentrates.

Nevertheless, they need to be used with care. You should follow instructions (i.e., wearing gloves, avoiding contact with skin, using the right dosage); otherwise they can quickly become toxic and harmful. You must also avoid using them near people with allergies, pregnant women, children, and pets.

It's a matter of taste when it comes to scent—sweet orange, lavender, and so on. Trust your sense of smell but bear in mind the type of atmosphere you want to create in each room of the house. Different essential oils are used in the living room and in the bedroom. You must also take into consideration their effects on our mood and our environment.

☞ *Did you know?*

Out of the hundreds of thousands of plant species across our planet, only 4,000 produce aromatic essences. But barely 400 produce enough for oil to be extracted.

Essential oil is the aromatic quintessence obtained by distilling with water vapor. To make 1 quart (1 liter), you need, for example, 22 pounds (10 kilograms) of cloves or 88 pounds (40 kilograms) of lavender flowers, and 220 pounds (100 kilograms) of rose petals for a 25 ml bottle! This high concentration explains the potency of its properties—and its price.

▶ Diffusing them well

To preserve all their therapeutic properties, the best thing is to use an atomizer/nebulizer diffuser. This specific device (available in organic stores) releases the pure oils without heating them for a better diffusion in the air.

❶ WARNING: Follow instructions carefully. These oils should not be diffused all day. The device should be switched on for 10 to 15 minutes, a maximum of twice a day, and with no one around.

• **To perfume your room** without having to leave it and to limit undesirable effects (irritations, overpowering smell), diffusion by ionization is probably the best alternative. Using ultrasound, the diffuser transforms water, mixed with a few drops of oil poured inside, into a cool mist that rapidly spreads across the room. Although it is true that it has fewer therapeutic properties compared to a nebulizer diffuser, it is an excellent way to add fragrance to a room, purify the air, and aid relaxation.

• **For a more short-lived effect,** you can use an oil warmer. Made of a small bowl under which a candle is placed, it allows essential oils to release their fragrances (but they will lose their therapeutic properties). Always cover them with water because if you burn them pure, they will release polluting vapors.

• **Clay disks are perfect for just diffusing** discreetly scented notes here and there.

• **For an immediate effect,** you can use a vaporizing spray.

▶**Follow the instructions carefully**

To limit the risk of allergies, be careful with your choice and your use of oils. It's also the best way to make the most of their benefits and their fragrances.

• **Choose 100 percent** natural essential oils that are unadulterated, undiluted, and free from terpenes. Pure 100 percent organic oils, certified by USDA Organic, are botanically and biochemically defined and chemotyped.

💡 **TIP**

Checking the purity of an essential oil

Contrary to what their name suggests, essential oils contain no fatty substance, unlike vegetable oils. To check their purity, leave a drop of essential oil on a piece of paper; once it has evaporated, it should leave no trace.

• **Read the contraindications carefully.** They can cause irritation and even become toxic for the respiratory mucous membranes when used pure or over a prolonged period of time.

• **Avoid diffusing** them in the presence of children aged 3 and under, pregnant or breastfeeding women, people with asthma or allergies, and pets (some can be lethal for cats).

• **Do not diffuse them** more than twice a day; otherwise, the air will become saturated.

• **Never diffuse them** while someone is sleeping, by day or by night.

• **Remember that some oils,** like citrus, are photosensitizing. So avoid applying them on the skin before going out in the sun, or you will end up with indelible marks. Others, like cinnamon, eucalyptus, and peppermint cause skin irritation. A drop on your skin can cause a burn, so make sure you always respect instructions and wear gloves to handle them.

• **They can be kept** between 12 to 18 months, away from sunlight.

• **To ensure that you get healthy oils** and to obtain professional advice, buy them in natural product stores and in pharmacies specializing in aromatherapy.

HYDROLATE

A delicate perfume

Also known as floral water, hydrolate is made of a miniscule amount of essential oils and 99 percent water, which makes it possible to use it daily without any concerns. However, once opened, it does not keep as long as the oils—6 months, away from sunlight and heat.

Added to perfume sprays and atomizers, hydrolate is perfect for perfuming linen or can be used pure as pillow mist.

Sweet-smelling linen

 TIP

You can use hydrolate instead of water in your iron. The best ones are lavender and orange blossom.

SPRAYS

Ease of use

No manipulation or emanations. The spray is the most effective and quickest way to add a touch of scent in a few seconds. They should be used in the center of the room, on curtains and fabrics, as well as on pebbles or on charms.

The only drawback is that the fragrance does not last long. However, this short duration is perfect for those who like to keep changing the fragrances around them.

You should of course avoid aerosols with synthetic components, which cause more harm than good. Make sure you choose vaporizers made with natural ingredients and without preservatives. Choose the ones labeled "USDA-approved organic." This label is the guarantee that the vaporizer is made from sustainably sourced compo- nents; is obtained through methods respectful of the environment; is free from syn- thetic components, solvents, artificial colorings or preser-

vatives; and contains at least 10 percent organic ingredients.

---◆---

5 RULES FOR HEALTHY AIR

....

Home fragrances are designed to add a delicate touch to clean and fresh air, rather than mask unpleasant odors. So before perfuming the air, purify it by adopting good habits.

....

The only drawback is that the fragrance does not last long. However, this short duration is perfect for those who like to keep changing the fragrances around them.

You should of course avoid aerosols with synthetic components, which cause more harm than good. Make sure you choose vaporizers made with natural ingredients and without preservatives. Choose the ones labeled "USDA-approved organic." This label is the guarantee that the vaporizer is made from sustainably sourced components; is obtained through methods respectful of the environment; is free from synthetic components, solvents, artificial colorings or preservatives; and contains at least 10 percent organic ingredients.

RULE #1:

....

Airing every day

....

Open doors and windows for at least 20 minutes in summer and winter.

In the summer, it's best to air in the morning when the presence of ozone—the main pollutant in the atmosphere—is at its lowest point. In the winter it's best to air in the evening, at nightfall, when the most common pollutants at that time of year (sulfur dioxide and nitrogen) are at their lowest point.

RULE #2:

....

Cleaning regularly

....

Don't let germs and grease settle in. Clean your kitchen, bathroom, furniture, and floors often. To get rid of dirt properly, it is best to do a deep clean once a week rather than do a superficial clean every day. For a natural clean, use miracle home remedies like soft soap, baking soda, or white vinegar, also known for their disinfecting, cleaning, and descaling properties.

RULE #3:

Dusting

Dust everything at least once a week. Use a slightly damp cloth or, even better, a microfiber cleaning cloth, which works very well on limiting airborne dust. Don't use a feather duster, which scatters dust mites.

RULE #4:

Washing

The big spring clean is not only for spring! Clean your curtains, rugs, and carpets at least twice a year. High-pressure steam eliminates nearly everything: bacteria, germs, fat particles, and dust mites. So, choose a steam cleaner. It uses water and does not need any detergent. Its dry heat works particularly well on all surfaces.

Change your sheets regularly, every week if possible. Wash them in hot water, which will kill all dust mites. Place a small piece of fabric, like a handkerchief, covered with 10 drops of real lavender essential oil in your linen for a guaranteed fresh smell.

Inspired vacuuming

TIP

Transform your vacuum cleaner into an excellent fragrance diffuser. Pour a dozen drops of essential oil (eucalyptus, thyme, or lavender) on the filter. The released air will be naturally perfumed and purified.

Do you have mint growing in your garden? Make the most of it: Scatter some on the floor and vacuum away.

RULE #5:

Tidying

Put everything away—clothes in cabinets, books on bookshelves, toys in their crates. If they are lying around, they will gather dust. As the Chinese science of feng shui recommends, you must let the energy (the qi) circulate around the home to avoid bad energies accumulating in cluttered corners.

An invigorating mood for the hallway, a warm one for the living room, a relaxing one for bedrooms, an appetizing one for the kitchen. The challenge is to add discreet and pleasant scent to each room, while making sure that the different fragrances do not clash.

A DIFFERENT MOOD FOR EACH ROOM

THE HALLWAY

Welcome!

Your hallway is like a business card and its fragrance is a bit like your smile. So, no burst of laughter! When we come through the door, a delicate waft should tickle our sense of smell, rather than assault it. It's all about nuance.

▸ Discreet scents

• **Are you fond of heady and floral fragrances?** Keep them for your linen drawers, as they could bother some people. Select scents that are more masculine and reassuring like cedar, myrrh, or sandalwood; acid and stimulating like citrus; or fresh and relaxing like lavender, mint, basil, thyme, and rosemary.

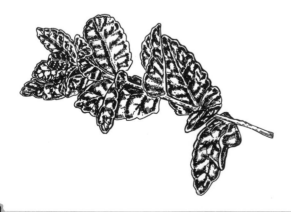

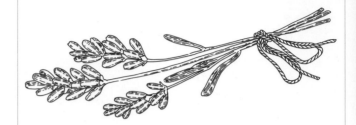

• **If your hallway opens directly onto the living room,** stick to one theme and use the same scent in both rooms.

▸ A suitable method of diffusion

The hallway is a place of transit, so candles and other flames should be avoided as a precaution. The slow and lasting diffusion of potpourri and reed diffusers is perfect for this space.

• **Is your hallway tiny** with no piece of furniture to place a reed diffuser? If you have one, perfume the door curtain. To avoid bothering your four-legged pets, spray the fragrance at shoulder-height and preferably on the inside to avoid possible staining.

• **Is your door curtain too precious** to even risk a minute stain on the inside? Pour a few drops of essential oil on a small piece of fabric and pin it to the top of the lining.

• **Creative tip:** Attach ceramic/clay diffuser pendants on the wall. You will only need to pour a few drops of essential oil on them regularly.

Homemade air freshener

Mix 1 teaspoon of baking soda, 2 cups (475 milliliters) of hot water, and 1 teaspoon of lemon juice in a spray bottle. Shake well before each use, and then spray. It will not stain when used in the air and even on fabrics. However, avoid spraying droplets onto wooden furniture, where it could leave marks.

▸**Do not forget the doorstep**

• **Pamper your doormat:** Dust it and apply some homemade air freshener (see recipe above) to produce a welcoming note.

You can also create a feng shui atmosphere in the corner of your doorstep. All you need to find are three attractive white pebbles and arrange them nicely in the inside corner (to avoid tripping over them) and pour the essential oils used in the hallway over them.

• **Don't forget:** It must smell clean when you come in, so it is really necessary to dust and clean. If you own an essential oil diffuser, it's time to use it. To purify the air and get rid of germs, pour in 3 drops of tea tree essential oil for its immuno-stimulant properties and 3 drops of eucalyptus essential oil for fighting respiratory complaints (and for its nice fresh smell). Plug it in 10 minutes a day, preferably in the morning.

While it is on (and for the next half hour), send your kids and pets to play in another room. Essential oils are potent, and children, people with asthma, and pets are very sensitive to them.

THE LIVING ROOM AND DINING ROOM

Ways and means

The fragrance must be warm, energizing, and relaxing all at once, like an invitation to stay.

▸**Liven things up!**

• **For a Zen atmosphere,** use lavender, orange, mandarin, rosewood, ylang-ylang, or pine. You can also mix bourbon geranium, with its floral notes of rose, with grapefruit essence, which has a heavenly scent and relaxing properties. The blend of mandarin and litsea citrata, with its splendid fragrance, also creates a joyful and relaxing atmosphere.

• **For an invigorating atmosphere,** opt for petitgrain, lemon, bergamot, rosemary, juniper, eucalyptus, coriander, lavender, or peppermint.

• **The blend** of lemon essence and broadleaved paper bark essential oil will produce fresh, invigorating notes and will be very effective at cleaning the air.

• **Lemon with lavandin** purifies and invigorates, just like the blend of lemon/grapefruit and lemon/scots pine, which has an uplifting smell and enhances breathing capacity.

• **For a dreamy atmosphere,** the diffusion of bergamot essential oil, with its refined tones, will allow you to wind down gently.

You can also combine a few drops of Yunnan verbena essential oil, which facilitates conversation, and of bourbon geranium essential oil, for its fabulous scent of rose.

▶ Guaranteed discretion

Lightness and discretion are a must in the living room. An overpowering smell could give you a headache or even disturb some of your guests. Achieve a pleasant, scented atmosphere by pouring 5 drops of essential oil into your radiators' humidifier or directly onto them (for cast iron radiators), spraying fragrance onto the inside of curtains, or having a bouquet of fresh-smelling flowers like freesias. You can also rub the non-visible part of a piece of furniture (to avoid any risk of stains) with a cloth infused with 5 drops of essential oil. In the winter, make the most of citrus fruit. Simply place the zest on a hot radiator (apart from electric radiators) or throw them into the chimney.

Deodorizing fabrics

Fabrics often retain bad smells. To do away with them, sprinkle furniture with baking soda and leave it for a night before vacuuming away.

▸ Get decorative

A bowl filled with rose petals is just the prettiest thing on the middle of the dining table or on a coffee table. It is perfect to diffuse a sweet smell and is so easy to make: All you need are petals. Plus, you can reuse them. When the petals are dry, you can create a potpourri by adding small white porous pebbles, a few cinnamon sticks, and whatever else takes your

fancy. To revive the fragrance, all you need to do is add a few drops of damask rose essential oil every now and again.

You can also make little aromatic pendants or pom-poms that you attach to door handles and windows. With a drop of perfume poured onto them regularly, they will release a sweet scent each time they are opened and closed.

▸ Fragrance and light

The living room is the kingdom of candles. Make the most of them for their festive spirit and warming glow. But not all day long, as candles release toxic fumes after a while. Choose five small ones over a large one so that the atmosphere is even more welcoming.

▸ Express fragrance

Are your guests coming and you haven't had time to air and perfume the living room? Burn a sugar cube soaked in water, in a bowl, to achieve an immediate smell of caramel.

THE STUDY

A studious atmosphere

When we settle down to work, fragrances must be chosen accordingly. Forget original or exotic perfumes; this is not the time to escape to faraway places. Do not opt for floral scents, like lily or jasmine, which are too overpowering and can give headaches.

▸ Restraint and finesse

Restraint is called for in the study. So, choose cedar, which facilitates concentration and reflection and clears your mind; sandalwood, which appeases the mind and keeps it focused; scots, pine which stimulates the intellect; or lemon, grapefruit, lemon verbena, patchouli, and pine, which are very good at keeping the mind alert. You can also choose among the essential oils that instill calm, comfort, and relaxation and stimulate the mind, such as verbena, orange blossom, lavender, or rosemary. To stimulate your creative side, use neroli, whose expansive/exuberant smell liberates creative energy.

It is best to aim for finesse when it comes to diffusion. Reed diffusers are well suited to the office, as they are slow and steady. Especially as you can add or remove reeds to adapt the potency of the diffusion. Discreet and pleasant, pebbles and ceramic pendants on the desk add the right fragrant touch and can also serve as paperweights. You just need to infuse them with one or two drops of fragrant essence. You could also light a candle, which, come evening, will create a warm atmosphere, provided that it is one with fresh, light, or spicy tones.

A USB stick as diffuser

TIP

Did you know you could buy a USB essential oil diffuser to plug into a computer or keyboard port? All you need is a drop or two of essential oil to obtain a slow and subtle diffusion.

▸ Farewell smoke rings

To get rid of the smell of tobacco, diffuse or vaporize a blend of 10 drops of fragrant verbena oil, bourbon geranium, or fine lavender and 5 drops of Atlas cedar.

THE BEDROOM

Conducive to sleep and . . . to love

The bedroom must be a place of rest and relaxation, so it's all about scents that are soothing and conducive to sleep

▸ Fragrances for sleeping

The best option for sleeping is to diffuse some lavender 15 minutes before going to bed. Relaxation is guaranteed when blended with wafts of sweet orange or mandarin. At night, grapefruit is useful for preventing obsessive thoughts and not worrying about the day's problems. Additionally petitgrain is a relaxant and mild sedative.

Floral fragrances are also welcome, as long as they are delicate like rosewood, bourbon geranium, jasmine, chamomile, or orange blossom. Steer clear of heady scents.

▸ Time for love

The scent should only become heavy and intoxicating when the bedroom becomes the place for love. In that case, go all out:

spiced candles and, for a passionate atmosphere, place 3 drops of ylang-ylang, jasmine, and bergamot on a plaster or clay disk, left on your bedside table or used as an essential oil heater.

However, avoid the constant diffusion of reed diffusers and potpourri in the bedroom. A gentle waft of perfume is good for going to sleep, but then our senses need to rest. The atmosphere at night should be neutral.

▸ **Scented bed linen**

The best thing in the bedroom is a nice clean smell and your sheets are your best allies. Wash them with a few drops of lavender essential oil or iron them with orange blossom for a good night's sleep. Or leave a drop of lavender on your pillow 10 minutes before going to bed for guaranteed sweet dreams. Pillow mists are also perfect for

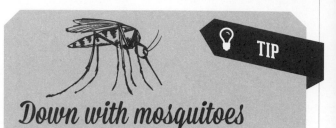

Down with mosquitoes

TIP

To ensure that all your efforts are not in vain due to a maddening little mosquito, adopt this home remedy: A simple pot of geraniums on the window will make them go away, as they hate the smell. Otherwise, pour 2 drops of bourbon geranium, clove, lemongrass, basil, or cedar essential oil on a handkerchief next to the bed or directly onto the sheets.

creating an atmosphere of calm and serenity. Easy to use, they are sprayed onto the pillow and on sheets, as well as on the inside of your curtains.

THE KITCHEN

An enticing smell

There is no need to add too much scent to the kitchen—it could spoil the taste of food. It is better to try and get rid of strong cooking smells.

▶A garden of fragrances

To obtain the most beautiful and pleasant bouquet of scents, put in a window box filled with aromatic herbs like basil, mint, and thyme. Moreover, these plants get rid of most undesirable insects. You should not perfume cabinets, as the smell could permeate food. You can, however, use a small bag (use organza-style jewelry bags) filled with laurel leaves, cloves, and peppermint to get rid of pantry moths.

Oh no, the toast is burnt!

To immediately get rid of this smell permeating the whole house almost instantly, open the windows wide and walk around all the rooms while shaking a dishtowel soaked in white vinegar.

▶Getting rid of bad smells quickly

• **To get rid of cooking smells** from fish, fries, and so on, boil a quart (liter) of water, the juice and rind of two lemons, five cloves, and a cinnamon stick. As it comes out of the pan, the vapor will neutralize bad smells and give off a delightful one. If the smell is persistent, use white vinegar instead of water. Make sure you air the room well, as it can be irritating. Don't leave the pan unattended, as the water evaporates in minutes.

• **To deodorize an oven** while neutralizing bad kitchen smells, you can cook 3 tablespoons of ground coffee and the rind of one orange. Place them in a small dish in a hot oven. As soon as the coffee starts to roast (5 minutes), switch off the oven and open the door to let the smells out. Leave the dish in the oven.

▶A spotless bin

To neutralize smells, pour a tablespoon or teaspoon (according to the size of the bin) of baking soda directly into the trash can.

Repeat this regularly, as the baking soda absorbs bad odors. At the bottom of the trash can, place a clean cloth infused with one drop of tea tree essential oil and one drop of lavender, which neutralizes smells and disinfects.

THE BATHROOM

Fresh and invigorating

It's up to you to select the scent according to what you want and need. Be careful, however, not to overdo it with disastrous blends. Think of matching the atmosphere with the fragrance of your shower products.

▶ According to your mood

To get off to a good start, there is nothing more energizing than a citrus smell. Do you prefer a breath of fresh air from the sea? Choose salty scents to tingle your nostrils. For a gentle start, play with the scent of red berries, peach, or vanilla.

Because of humidity, fragrances disappear quickly in the bathroom. The easiest way to refresh the fragrance is to pour a few drops of the essential oil of your choice on pebbles placed next to your sink or between your towels.

Little perfumed candles around the bathtub are pure bliss! But be careful—never let them burn unattended.

▶ The eternal problem of the restroom

The current trend is to perfume this room excessively to hide certain smells. That is a mistake—diffusing too much is sickening. The best deodorizer is the reed diffuser, thanks to its slow diffusion, as long as you adapt the number of reeds to the size of the room. Three reeds are enough for 32 square feet. It's up to you to find the right amount. You can also make a mini potpourri with a few porous pebbles, some pinecones, a bit of sand, and even some cinnamon sticks. Pour 3 to 5 drops of essential oil on it on a regular basis.

❶ BE CAREFUL: Toilet bowl deodorizer blocks have artificial smells that are heavy and sickening. If you insist on them, go for "neutral" blocks, which will allow you to choose a scent for your restroom more freely.

Minty or forest scents, like mint, eucalyptus, scots pine, or pine tree, are often preferred in the restroom because they bring a note of freshness and have cleansing properties. If you favor gentler smells, opt for citrus scents like orange or grapefruit.

TIP

No shelf on which to place a diffuser?

Leave a few drops of vanilla extract in the inside of the toilet roll. The paper will absorb the scent, which will be diffused every time you unroll it.

CABINETS AND STORAGE UNITS

A good, clean smell

Little sachets of lavender slipped in the linen are essential to perfume your cabinets. In fact, they are the stars of cabinets and closets, as they get rid of moths. Do you feel like changing the fragrance? Try thyme or marjoram, which have the same properties.

▸**Pamper your linen**

• **If lavender is the star,** cedar is king. A moth and mosquito repellent, it diffuses a delicate scent that goes famously with fabrics. In addition, it is popular among both men and women.

• **No cedar wood at home or at your local supplier?** No problem—just make it yourself. Get some small cubes of softwood (1 x 1 inch/3 x 3 centimeters); otherwise it won't absorb the oil. With a brush, coat them with Atlas cedarwood essential oil on both sides.

Seal them in an airtight plastic bag overnight so that the wood absorbs the

Odorless shoes racks

TIP

Go for a neutral smell. Fragrances will only highlight odors that are not always pleasant. Pick a combination that will absorb them. A few tablespoons of baking soda stuffed tightly into a stocking or a small dish will do. Remember to change it every 2 weeks.

fragrance fully. You can also use pieces of small vegetable crates or pour two drops of cedar essential oil on terra-cotta disc diffusers in your closets or on small clay pebbles suspended on coat hangers.

• **If you are not a fan of cedar** and if you are tired of lavender, pick vanilla, a sensual perfume ideal for sweaters and lingerie. Pour a few drops of vanilla extract on cotton balls.

▸ Don't forget your drawers

Now is the time to use heady and floral scents, as it's great for lingerie. The best thing is to infuse a handkerchief with the fragrance of your choice and place it at the back of your drawer. It will diffuse its fragrance over time.

PET'S CORNER

Spare their sense of smell

Pets have a very developed sense of smell and really don't like perfumes. So avoid spraying fragrances on their cushions, baskets, and so on. Do not use any essential oils, as they can be dangerous, even lethal for cats.

It is best to neutralize odors by sprinkling a bit of baking soda as an underlay in the cat's or hamster's litter box every 2 weeks. And for a light, clean smell, mix in a bit of talcum powder with the cat's litter, as the talc's freshness will cancel out the unpleasant smell.

Making your own candles, potpourri, lavender sachets, and other scented treasures gives you the satisfaction of creating, letting your imagination run wild, and saving money. And if your first attempts were not as good as you hoped, don't fret, practice makes perfect!

NATURAL HOMEMADE SCENTS

CANDLES

Let's go!

Do you want to make your own candles? Easy as ABC. To make natural ones, make sure you use the right ingredients.

▶The basic recipe

For a 2-inch (5-centimeter) diameter candle, you need:

- **½ cup (120 milliliter) non-GMO soy wax flakes**
- **An unwaxed round braided wick (3 millimeters in diameter)**
- **A wick tab**
- **30 drops essential oil**
- **1 small glass jar**

Melt the wax in a double boiler on a low heat. Remove as soon as it becomes a smooth "paste" with no lumps.

Remove the air trapped in the wick by soaking it in the warm molten wax for 2 minutes.

Remove the wick from the wax and place it on a sheet of aluminum foil. It must be completely straight. Leave it as is in the freezer for 5 minutes. Meanwhile, pour the drops of essential oil into the warm wax. Mix with a whisk.

Take the wick out of the freezer. Before removing it from the aluminum foil, check that it is completely straight and rigid. Otherwise, leave it to harden for a few more minutes.

Attach the tab to the base of the wick.

Place the wick in the jar, making sure that the tab is right in the center. To stabilize it, attach it with a bit of molten wax and wrap the opposite end of the wick around a pencil resting on the jar. Pour the molten wax into the jar with great care, making sure not to move the wick.

Allow to harden at least 12 hours before lighting.

▶A different wick for each candle

- Only use round cotton wicks (the flat ones are for paraffin).

CANDLE DIAMETER	WICK SIZE	
< .05 inch (1.25 centimeters)	R0	Round wick no. 3
< 1 inch (2.5 centimeters)	R1	Round wick no. 5
< 1.75 inches (4.5 centimeters)	R2	Round wick no. 7
< 2.5 inches (6.25 centimeters)	R3	Round wick no. 9
< 2.5 inches (6.25 centimeters)	R4	Round wick no. 11

When an appropriate wick is used, the candle burns normally. If it is too thick, it burns too quickly, the flame flickers, and black smoke comes out. If the wick is too thin, the candle does not burn well and the excess wax smothers the flame.

• Select the size of the wick according to the size of your mold.
• Find out the diameter by measuring the top of the jar, if it is cylindrical. If it is flared, calculate an average of the base and the top.
• Try wooden wicks: They crackle like a mini wood fire when they are burning.

▸ Which fragrance?

Carefully read the instructions for the perfumed oil and check its flash point systematically. It must be higher than 149°F (65°C) to avoid the whole surface of your candle catching fire. This flash point is specified on the packaging of essential oils and cosmetic fragrances.

▸ The main essential oils and fragrances that can be used safely (flash point > 149°F [65°C]) are the following:

• Amyris
• Aniseed
• Atlas cedar
• Bergamot mint
• Blue cypress
• Bourbon geranium
• Cade
• Camphor
• Ceylon cinnamon leaf
• Cinnamon bark
• Clove bud
• Cloves
• Copaiba
• Cornmint
• French lavender
• Gaultheria
• Geranium Egyptian
• German chamomile
• Inula
• Kaffir lime
• Lavandin grosso
• Lavandin super
• Lavender Bulgarian
• Lavender spike
• Lemon balm
• Lemon eucalyptus
• Lemongrass
• Lemon myrtle

- Lemon tea tree
- Lignum vitae
- Litsea citrata
- Lovage
- Mānuka
- Myrrh
- Oregano
- Palmarosa
- Patchouli
- Peppermint
- Petitgrain
- Pikenard
- Red cedar
- Rosalina
- Rosewood
- Sandalwood
- Tarragon
- Tropical basil
- Vetiver
- Ylang-ylang
- Zanthoxylum

◆

POTPOURRI

It's an art

Quick and easy to make, potpourri can be adapted in many ways. You can liven it up, depending on your mood and taste.

▶ With rose petals

- You need a big handful of scented flower petals (rose, lilac, honeysuckle, jasmine, geranium, peony, etc.).

Items of your choice:
- A few aromatic herb leaves (thyme, rosemary, mint, basil, sage, or laurel)
- The rind of an orange, lemon, or grapefruit (you can mix them up)
- A few sprigs of lavender
- One or two cinnamon sticks
- One or two vanilla pods, some star anise seeds, cloves, etc.

Lay out the petals on a baking sheet covered with parchment paper. Allow them to dry for 1 hour in an oven heated to 212°F (100°C). Place them in a salad bowl. Then it's up to you to choose among various possibilities. Treat yourself but don't use too many scents, as they would cancel each other out. Balance out strong smells, like cloves, with gentle ones, like vanilla.

Play around with scents, as well as with shapes and textures. Beauty is as important as fragrance in a potpourri.

Place everything in well-sealed plastic bag (it must be airtight). Leave it to sit overnight so that the scents can blend together.

Lay out your mixture in a bowl. Add a few porous stones, pebbles, or ceramic/clay diffuser pendants. This way, all you will need is to pour a few drops of essential oil to refresh the perfume when it fades.

You can also place your mixture in pretty organza bags.

▶With citrus

You need:

- **The rind of an orange or a lemon or both**
- **A few tea leaves**
- **Bergamot rind**
- **One or two cinnamon sticks**
- **A dozen cloves**

Peel the fruit, making sure to leave out as much pith as possible.

Place the rind on a drip pan covered with parchment paper.

Pop it into a preheated oven, set to 212°F (100°C). Allow to dry for 1 hour. When it comes out of the oven, the rind should break easily.

Allow it to cool; then place it with the other ingredients in a pretty pot.

You can refresh the scent by adding a few drops of essential oil now and again.

Potpourri does not last forever and with time it can become a dust magnet. Keep it for a year and then, if you have a chimney, throw it into the fire for a guaranteed lovely smell.

REED DIFFUSERS

Homemade

Reed diffusers are perfect to create a long-lasting fragrant atmosphere. Why don't you create your own blend?

▶A relaxed perfume

For a relaxed atmosphere, you need:

- **10 drops of petitgrain essential oil (*Citrus aurantium*)**
- **10 drops of ylang-ylang essential oil (*Totum Cananga odorata genuina*)**

- 10 drops of sweet orange essential oil (*Citrus sinensis*)
- 10 drops of true lavender essential oil (*Lavandula angustifola*)
- 13.5 fluid ounces (400 milliliters) of cold water

Mix everything together, and then pour into your reed diffuser. The rattan reeds will become infused with it. You can regulate the intensity by adding or removing reeds.

PILLOW MIST

Your own

Pillow mists are unrivaled for bringing a gentle scent to the bedroom. Spray them lightly on sheets, pillows, throws, and curtains. No need to spend a fortune, as they are very simple to make.

▶ **Cassiopeia mist**
With this recipe, your nights will be more beautiful than your days.

You need:
- 30 drops of true lavender essential oil (*Lavandula angustifola*)
- 20 drops of mandarin essential oil (*Citrus reticulata*)
- 10 drops of sweet marjoram essential oil (*Origanum majorana*)
- 1.5 fluid ounces (45 milliliters) of 70 percent alcohol (or odorless vodka)

Mix well and refrigerate the mixture for at least 24 hours; then pour into a vaporizer.

These mists should not be used by children, pregnant women, people with epilepsy or respiratory problems. Never spray onto the skin or eyes.

LAVENDER

Queen of creativity

Fresh or dry, lavender is the winner when it comes to perfuming all the rooms in the house, as well as linen, clothes, and closets. And there are many creative possibilities.

▶ Lavender moth repellent

Enjoy the fragrance of the fresh flower but don't throw it away when it is dry; instead, use it to get rid of moths in your closets.

• Remove the buds from the stems.

• Make gauze bags. You just need to cut 12 x 12-inch (30 x 30 centimeters) pieces of gauze, place a handful of dried flowers in the center, and close up each square with a ribbon, making sure not to leave any openings.

• Otherwise, you can use knee-high stockings. They are less attractive but just as effective at holding in the buds and making sure they don't fall out.

• Leave these in closets, drawers, and so on.

• When the flowers lose their scent, empty them into a bowl, pour in two drops of lavandin essential oil, and leave them in a sealed plastic bag overnight. They will give off a delightful smell again by the next day.

▶ Lavender incense

Have you used up all the flowers for scented bags? Now turn to the stems. If you plant them in a dish filled with sand, they will burn like incense sticks. Do not burn them all at once; burn them one by one, like traditional incense.

▶ The fusette, a very decorative object

In the south of France, it is a tradition to come together to make these pretty scented objects, which are then placed in closets, drawers, or grouped together in a bouquet in a basket. To refresh their scent, you just need to pour one or two drops of lavender essential oil on them.

To make one fusette, you need:

• **41 sprigs lavender, about 11 inches (28 centimeters) long**

• **2.73 yards satin ribbon, 0.25 to 0.30 inches (.65 to .75 centimeter) wide**

Remove the leaves carefully, making sure not to break the stems—leave the buds. Remove just enough to make the stems smooth. Group the stems together in a bouquet.

Tie them at the base of the flowers with one end of the ribbon.

Gently fold the stems over the flowers to cover them up.

Pull the ribbon out between two stems.

Begin to braid the ribbon by slipping it over a sprig and under the next one.

Carry on while tightening the ribbon firmly until the flowers are completely encased.

Once you've come to the base of the fusette, tie a knot and then braid the rest of the ribbon along the stems and finish off with a pretty rosette.

Now start again with a different color ribbon.

CITRUS SCENTS

Sparkling deodorizers

Citrus smells clean and offers a refreshing and energizing atmosphere. Plus they can be decorative.

▶ Pomander

Previous generations used to hang this orange covered in cloves with a pretty ribbon in the closet, but be innovative—place it on a pedestal table or on a bookshelf, as it is so decorative. Moreover, the combination of heady spice and citric sparkle make an absolute delight of fragrance, and it is the magic bullet against moths!

It's so easy to make; you need:

- **1 nice orange or lemon**
- **60 to 70 cloves**

Stick the cloves into the whole fruit. It is prettier to cover it completely but you can also create your own motifs.

Place the pomander in a small bowl or tie a pretty ribbon around it to hang it. It will keep for 2 months minimum, which is the time for it to dry.

❶ WATCH OUT, IT STINGS! Use gloves or a thick dish towel to avoid hurting your fingers while pushing the cloves in.

▶ Express deodorizer: the lemon-vanilla infusion

No diffuser nearby? Never mind, you can make an effective deodorizer in a few minutes with a cooking pot.

You need:

- **1 cooking pot**
- **1 nice lemon**

- **1 sprig rosemary**
- **1 to 2 spoonfuls vanilla extract**

Fill a small cooking pot two-thirds of the way with water. Add a lemon (washed and sliced), the sprig of rosemary, and the vanilla extract. Leave it to simmer on medium heat for as long as possible, adding water if needed. The air will smell lovely.

▶ Zero effort deodorizer

Quick, easy, and effective? You just need to leave orange, grapefruit, or lemon peel directly on a hot radiator (except for electric radiators) or throw them into the chimney. Place the zest in a low oven for 10 minutes to accelerate the diffusion. Open the oven door and a smell of sunshine will invade the house.

▶ Fresh air in a spray

Are you a fresh orange juice addict in the morning? Instead of throwing away the skin, use it to make a spray, which perfumes as well as purifies, cleans, and disinfects!

You need:

- **The zest of 3 oranges and 1 lemon (or the other way around)**
- **8.5 fluid ounces (250 milliliters) of white vinegar**
- **An empty spray bottle**

Place the zest in a large glass jar that can be hermetically sealed. Cover it with vinegar. Seal and leave to steep about 10 days away from sunlight. Then sieve the mixture through a coffee filter to get rid of all the impurities and zest. Pour into a spray bottle labeled with the name of the mixture.

You can spray this solution in every room and even use to clean surfaces because white vinegar and lemon purify and disinfect. The orange cancels out the strong smell of vinegar and gives a tangy touch. It can be kept as long as an industrial product.

INDEX